Art in Story

Art

Marianne Saccardi

in Story

Teaching Art History to Elementary School Children

Linnet Professional Publications
1997

FRANKLIN PIERCE
COLLEGE LIBRARY
RINDGE, N.H. 03461

© 1997 Marianne Saccardi. All rights reserved.
First published 1997 as a Linnet Professional Publication,
an imprint of The Shoe String Press, Inc.,
North Haven, Connecticut 06473.

Library of Congress Cataloging-in-Publication Data
Saccardi, Marianne.
    Art in story : teaching art history to elementary
school children / Marianne Saccardi.
       p.   cm.
    Includes bibliographical references and indexes.
    ISBN 0-208-02431-X (pbk. : alk. paper)
    1. Art—History—Study and teaching (Elementary)   2. Activity
programs in education.   I. Title.
N350.S23   1997
372.5'044—dc21   96-53494
                              CIP

The paper in this publication meets the minimum requirements
of American National Standard for Information Sciences—
Permanence of Paper for Printed Library Materials,
ANSI Z39.48-1984. ⊗

Designed by Abigail Johnston
Printed in the United States of America

CURR
N
350
.S23
1997

To Mom and Dad with love,

and

to the many children who over the years

have taught me how to see

Contents

Acknowledgments

There are many people who have helped me write this book, and I would like to thank them here.

First, always, my wonderful family:
My husband Thomas, who has always believed in this book and my ability to write it;
My son Christopher, who continues to be my computer mentor;
My son Daniel, who cheerfully helped to carry up and down stairs the hundreds of books used in writing this volume;

Pat Schaefer, who graciously granted me permission to use the story of Noma which appears in "Prehistoric Art" chapter 1;

Diantha Thorpe, my editor, who saved me from more mistakes than I care to count;

Marilyn Jody, who cheered and encouraged from the sidelines;

Marylyn Rosenblum, who suggested many years ago that I write a book about my experiences teaching art history;

The many librarians at the Greenwich Public Library, the Perrot Memorial Library, the Byram-Shubert Library, and the Upper School Library at Greenwich Country Day School, all in Greenwich, Connecticut, for their help, advice, and cheerful goodwill throughout the writing of this book;

My friends in Storytelling Anon who through the years have convinced me of the power of storytelling and have awed me with their talents;

Bob Jackson, who rescued me from a malfunctioning computer and printer and helped to bring order out of chaos.

Introduction

Sometimes I can't remember what I had for breakfast,
but I remember every story I ever heard.
—JAMES SANDY, town planner,
in the *Greenwich Time* (Connecticut), July 5, 1995

One of the delightful benefits of teaching is that one gains as much knowledge as one imparts. During my twenty years as an elementary school teacher, my best teachers have been the children themselves. And one of the most important lessons they taught me was their infinite capacity to take in the world, to notice even the smallest details, to look long and hard without tiring. The children helped me notice tiny plants and bugs I would have missed on my own. They helped me discover colors and shapes and patterns both inside the classroom and in the wider world outside. They were naturally drawn to beauty and found it in all the most unexpected places. Through their eyes I learned to see anew.

It was natural, then, when I began to reevaluate my curriculum after several years of teaching, that I pondered the value of introducing art history into the classroom. Certainly, art had already been an integral part of our classwork. We often expressed our social studies learning through art projects. We drew the insects, animals, and plants we studied in science. We drew storybook characters and scenes. And every Friday afternoon we rolled up our sleeves, donned our oversized shirts, and gave ourselves over to extended art activities involving a variety of media. But we had never studied the great artists of the world or viewed their work. It seemed foolish to defer this study to their high school or college years when the young children I taught were so ripe for such an exploration into beauty. And so I began to develop an art history curriculum for primary school-age children—a curriculum that was to expand over the years to include drama, writing, poetry, and children's literature.

Components of the Art History Lessons

I taught art history once a week. Each lesson took about an hour and was divided into several components to hold the children's attention:

Story

> When children enter into story, they are transported to other worlds, joining in the adventure and the excitement, freed of their own time and place—and somehow changed by the experience. They learn about the lives of others and in doing so develop a better understanding of their own lives (Barton and Booth, 1990, p. 14).

Children love stories. They are great storytellers themselves, and my classrooms have always been abuzz with stories of weekend trips, after-school activities, family happenings, and the latest in the sagas of various friendships. My approach to art history, then, was through story as a way to children's hearts and minds. When I told stories I could make direct eye contact with my young listeners and capture their interest. Each week I searched through books for facts about the artist or period I wished to introduce to my students, and then wove these facts into stories. I didn't worry excessively about whether the facts I used were one hundred percent verifiable or merely apocryphal. I simply wanted the children to connect emotionally with an artist. At the start of the lesson, I gathered the children in a circle and told them a story about the artist or time period we were going to study. The children loved these stories and remembered them years later. I fondly recall a sixth-grader coming back to visit the class in which he had been a "little kid" and reminding me of the time I told the story of Benjamin West, who made a paintbrush out of his cat's tail. I had told him that story four years before!

Viewing the Art

After our story, we viewed art works of the period or artist. Here I let the children take over, encouraging them to talk about the things they noticed, liked best, or wondered about. They often remarked on the content of an artist's painting and how the artist's subjects sprang from his or her life or time. I used the excellent reproductions available in many large art books written for adults and children. In addition, our public school had mounted traveling art prints that I borrowed often throughout the year. Videos, slides, and films were also an important part of our classes. Extensive lists of books and audiovisual materials appear at the end of each chapter for your convenience. Although older out-of-print books have been kept to a minimum, some do appear either because their reproductions are too valuable to ignore or because there would not be enough material on the subject without them. This part of the lesson can be as simple or as complex as you wish, depending on the age of the children.

Journal Writing

> When people write about something they learn it better. That, in a nutshell, is the idea behind asking students to keep journals . . . .[Journals] provide a place in which to write informally yet systematically in order to seek, discover, speculate, and figure things out. (Fulwiler, ed., 1987, p. 9)

The children kept a learning journal in which they wrote their questions, the most important facts and ideas they learned, what they liked best about an artist's work, etc. I began each year by giving many demonstrations of how to keep such a journal. For several weeks, we composed a learning journal together, and I wrote the children's ideas on a chart. After a while, even first-graders were able to keep their own journals. Some started their entries with drawings, but as the year wore

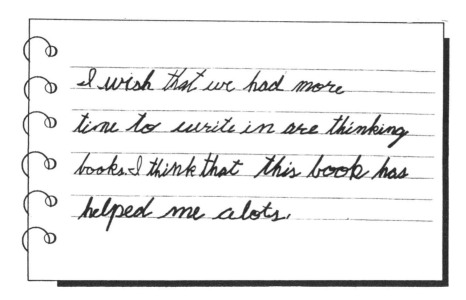

on, they began to write and to manage longer and longer entries. I responded to these journals each week, and it became a great deal of fun to carry on this dialogue about art with my students. I also began to value the journals as a way to discover what worked with the children and what didn't, and where their confusions lay. One second-grader wrote, "It was rely hard for Michelangelo wen he panted the 16 chpl." The children, too, began to look forward to this opportunity to reflect on their learning, and they took their journals home with great pride at the end of the year.

In this book I offer suggestions for journal writing for each lesson. These are only meant as suggestions and are, perhaps, most useful for those students who are not sure where to begin. You may want to offer your own prompts in response to class reaction to the lesson, or leave the children completely free to write what they wish.

Art/Drama Activity

Each lesson culminated with an art or drama activity. Sometimes these activities were so involved that they were carried over into the following week. Sometimes the children would role-play something they heard in the story I told. Often they would choose a poem that seemed to fit a particular artist's life or work from the many poetry books in the classroom. Almost always, we engaged in an art activity that required the use of media or technique we had just viewed in the artist's work. For example, after talking about Egyptian art, we assumed the role of palace artists and designed a tomb for the pharaoh. After studying the work of Winslow Homer, we painted pictures using watercolors.

Whenever we engaged in a drama activity, I made certain that the children were truly in character. In other words, if they were making cave drawings for good luck in a hunting expedition, for the duration of the drama they had to really believe they were prehistoric people whose lives depended upon the animals they killed. If there were signs that some of the children were not in character, I stopped the activity and began again. Creative drama, along with the stories, helped children remember artists long after we had ceased talking about them. It was commonplace for children to bring in their parents' art books to show the class the work of an artist we had studied weeks before.

A Culminating Activity

In the spring, I always gave the children the opportunity to put on a play about some of the artists we had studied during the year. The choice was completely theirs. Sometimes they chose Renaissance artists, sometimes American artists or Impressionists. One year they even chose to do picture-book illustrators. The children themselves worked in groups to write the script (which meant they blocked out scenes—first we'll do this, then this, etc.), make props and scenery, and devise costumes. They volunteered for the various acting parts and named their own director and stage crew. Everyone did something. We kept these plays simple, and much of the action and dialogue was improvised, but the children and their parents loved them. The plays became such a high point that new classes would often ask at the first art history session, "Are we going to do a play like your class did last year?"

How to Use This Book

I began teaching art history armed with only a college survey course. I made no attempt to give the children an in-depth study of art. I simply wanted to build on their natural affinity for beauty and their attention to detail, and to spark their enthusiasm for great works of art. I hoped that what we did together would be the beginning of an interest that would deepen with the years.

This book is the culmination of thirteen years of studying art history with children. It is not a scholarly treatise but rather a practical guide to help teachers introduce world-renowned artists to their students. It is meant to make teachers' busy lives easier by eliminating the need for time-consuming research. It is also meant to inspire confidence in teachers who do not have any training in art studies.

The book is organized in a way that makes teaching art history easy and fun. You will find within each chapter background information on the period or artist to be studied, a story to tell the children, suggestions for art and drama activities, ways to integrate art history into other areas of the curriculum, and lists of books and audiovisual materials. In the back of the book there is an index to the works of art by title in each chapter, and a resource directory of companies and institutions that provide audiovisual materials, sometimes free of charge.

I worked with young children, but the lessons here may be adapted for older elementary and middle school-age children as well. In fact, some of the suggested curriculum activities apply to older students. Because children (and adults) of all ages love stories, the beginning part of the lessons will hold for all grades. It may only be necessary to tell the stories in more sophisticated language. You may wish to use some of the information in the background section to elaborate on the story or to create additional stories of your own. You can also add depth for older students by going into greater detail regarding the artists' styles and works, and by choosing more complex works to view. You can give more scope to the elements of art such as line, form, and color.

The children themselves will naturally perform the art and drama activities with greater expertise and complexity. The books suggested cover a wide range of abilities, from picture books for young children to adult art books, and they may be used in a variety of ways. The adult books are a wonderful source of art prints for all children, even though the text may be beyond them. You may wish to read some of the children's books aloud, or to make them available for the children to read independently. Groups of children can use some of the books for research while preparing plays. If the narration in some of the suggested films is too difficult for your students, turn the sound off and let them enjoy the artwork depicted.

Of course, it is best to see the actual artwork itself, for no reproduction can capture in full the beauty of an artist's creation. If at all possible, try to arrange at least one museum visit during the year. I have found that these visits work best for small groups rather than for a whole class. I usually briefed one or two parents on the exhibits I particularly wanted the children to see and on what we had studied in class, and sent them off with a group of four students. The children prepared for the trips, too, by writing in their journals about the things they hoped to see and learn in the museum. Over a period of several weeks, everyone had a chance to go to the museum, and the trips were truly ventures into the world of art rather than social outings. In today's world of parents and caregivers working outside the home, this may be harder and harder to achieve. It is certainly an ideal to strive for.

As you view the table of contents of this book, you may wonder at some of the choices. Why include Donatello among the Renaissance artists and leave out Titian? Where is Renoir among the Impressionists? Why are some countries not represented at all? Two factors dictated the content of this book. First and foremost was the children themselves. The artists and periods included here are those the children have especially loved over the years. The second consideration was space. Many artists and periods I taught successfully had to be omitted here to keep this book within manageable proportions. These artists may appear some day in another volume.

Because children, especially the younger ones, have a fuzzy sense of time at best, there is no need to use this book in order. Children will not really have a sense of when the Renaissance took place—only that it was long ago. Simply teach those artists and time periods you feel your own students would enjoy in whatever order you feel comfortable. Perhaps the accessibility of materials or museum exhibits in your area will dictate the artists to be studied. Or the children themselves will suggest some names. Once you have used some of the lessons in the book and feel comfortable with the format, you may wish to devise your own lessons about artists you know your students would enjoy.

It is appropriate here to talk briefly about showing prints of nudes to the children. While I would never use blatantly erotic prints, I felt I could not keep such wonderful works as Michelangelo's *David* from the children because they revealed the human body. So I addressed this issue in the very first class each year when we discussed the *Venus of Willendorf* in prehistoric art. We first talked about the wonder of the human body and all the marvelous things it can do and about the fact that there is nothing evil or silly or unlovely about our bodies. I told the children I would from time to time be showing them works of art that celebrate the human body and that we were going to view them as just that—works of art and not "dirty" or forbidden pictures. I made it clear that I would not tolerate snickering, laughing, or jokes. Anyone who did so would have to leave the lesson. In all my years of teaching, I never had to ask a child to withdraw. You, of course, must make your own decisions about the art work you discuss with your students and the way you approach parents and school administrators. Only you know them and the community in which you teach.

Because much Western art up to and including the Renaissance was motivated by belief, it is inescapable that the early chapters of this book present a good deal of religious art. I always told my students that we were not studying a particular work of art because we necessarily shared the belief of the creator, but for the beauty of the artwork itself. The drama activities based on this art, too, often involve religious rituals. There are shamans and enactments of myths involving various gods. These exercises are not meant to capture the belief of a specific people, but are rather a blend of traditional stories and folklore passed down through the ages. If you or your community are not comfortable with any of the activities, simply eliminate them.

Over the years, I've had many moving instances of just how successful teaching art history to young children can be. Parents have talked about being pressed by their children to take them to museums, and of being amazed by how much the children were able to say about the various art works they viewed there. A high school student who had just returned from a trip to Italy came back to visit. "You know the stuff you told us about the art in Florence?" he said. "Man, you were right. It's awesome!"

So plunge in wherever the water feels fine. You'll love the results.

References

Barton, Bob, and David Booth. *Stories in the Classroom*. Portsmouth, NH: Heinemann, 1990. Presents the value of and need for storytelling and addresses some of the ways to make stories come to life in the classroom.

Fulwiler, Toby, ed. *The Journal Book*. Portsmouth, NH: Boynton/Cook, 1987. Contains invaluable information on the purpose and characteristics of journals and on how to use them in all subject areas in the classroom.

Part I
Art of the
Ancient World

1 Prehistoric Art

"Toros, toros! Bulls, bulls! Father, come and look at the bulls!"
—MARIA DE SAUTUOLO

Background Information

The art of the cave dwellers is among the most marvelous art in the world. During the Upper Paleolithic period, which lasted from about 40,000 to 10,000 B.C., early humans formed fertility statues of women from bone, ivory, and stone; carved figures of animals on their tools; and painted majestic creatures on their cave walls. While cave art has been found all over the world, these art works have been found primarily in the caves of Ventimiglia, Italy; Dordogne, France; and Altamira, Spain. Rock paintings done in the Middle Stone Age from 10,000 to 3,500 B.C. have been found in North Africa. In the 1960s cave paintings were discovered in Mexico.

The painters and carvers of whom we speak in this lesson were Cro-Magnons, tall people with high foreheads and larger brains than the Neanderthals. The ice was gradually receding, but Cro-Magnon's European home was quite a bit colder than Europe is today. Although we know very little about these people's lives, we can gather some information from the things they left behind: tools of bone, ivory, and stone with which Cro-Magnons hunted wild animals, many of which no longer exist, for food; needles of bone and ivory with which they probably sewed together the skins of those animals for clothing; and their incredible works of art in the form of figurines, decorated tools, and cave paintings. Since there is no evidence of farming tools, and because the climate was still quite cold for crops, we believe the people did not know how to farm but probably gathered nuts, roots, and berries.

The paintings Cro-Magnons did on cave walls are highly sophisticated. These early artists were incredibly successful at rendering three-dimensional objects on a two-dimensional surface. There are bulls that appear to be pawing the ground, ready to charge. One can almost see the steam coming from their nostrils. The colors are vivid, and gradations of shading are given. Amazing, too, is how

10

the artists use the cave walls themselves in the formation of their pictures. For example, the swollen mound of an animal's belly is placed in just the right position to take advantage of a bulge in the rock.

When we consider Cro-Magnon art, many questions arise. How did the people learn to paint and carve statues? Did they see bear-claw marks on cave walls and then try to carve forms on the walls with stone? How did they come to color in their paintings? The ocher found in the caves themselves gave them yellow, brown, and red colors. Black came from charcoal and lampblack from burning animal fat. White came from rare white marl (Ruskin, 1971). Did the people paint their bodies with these colors for religious ceremonies, accidentally smear some color on a cave wall, and like the effect? Why do figures of animals far outnumber figures of people on the cave walls? Why are the animals most often shown in side view rather than head-on? Why are so many of the "Venus" figurines similar—with exaggerated breasts and stomachs?

Life for Cro-Magnons was harsh and dangerous. The people spent much of their time hunting fierce animals and making clothing to protect themselves from the bitter cold. Why, then, did they take the time to create paintings on cave walls or carve figurines? Why, when they probably didn't live in caves anymore but in homes made of animal skins or wood, did they make their paintings in caves? And why did they place them in the darkest recesses of the caves rather than at the entrance where they would be easily seen and enjoyed? The stories that begin the lesson on prehistoric art are an attempt to answer some of these questions.

LESSON 1: Carved Figurines

❑ The Story

(Tell this story in a very quiet voice and with great drama. Act out sitting alone, picking up a rock, and beginning to carve. If you have drums in the classroom, have a few children beat them softly while you speak.)

It was a time long, long ago in a land we now call Austria that there appeared on the earth the first movable, beautiful thing we now call art. It was a precious thing, which looked like rock and could fit in a man's hand. Yet it was formed by the fingers of a woman and it was, in fact, the shape of a woman.

Over 20,000 years ago, early people had a hard life. They lived close to the elements of cold, fire, water, and earth. They ate berries and bark and the animals they could hunt. They treasured children, for their children frequently died before they had a chance to grow. The mothers also died very easily from cold, hunger, or sickness.

Thus it was that an unnamed woman sat alone on a rock on a cold winter day, weeping. In the distance, drums beat a sorrowful sound. Other members of her tribe gathered around the dead body of a woman. The unnamed woman—let us call her Noma—had lost her friend, her sister. How would she carry on? Life was so hard; she needed the help of her friend. She picked up a stone and felt the soft curves in her hand. She reached into her belt and found her flint rock. Slowly she chipped away at the stone. A large round curve in the front of the stone reminded her of her friend, who was pregnant when she died. This was a double sadness for all. That lovely rounded front meant life coming. Noma chipped and chipped. A smoothness comforted her hand. A small head emerged atop the rock body. Noma smiled. Her friend would live again. This lovely rock would bring her to life in a way. It was a promise.

Noma ran with the rock. She stood before the drum-beaters. They looked first at her tear-stained face, then at her tight fist. Slowly she opened her hand to show her treasure. Smiles crept onto the faces of the beaters. "Ah, ah," they said. Noma placed the worked stone figure of her friend softly on the skin wrapped around the dead body. When the sun rose, they would place her body into a hole in the ground, but with it the promise of another life. So beautiful it was.

Viewing the Art

Use some or all of the books that appear in the references following to show pictures of the various figurines carved by prehistoric peoples. If possible, try to include a picture of the *Venus of Willendorf*, the statue that is the subject of the story. Talk about how similar the figurines are even though they were found in different places in Europe. Note how many of them are featureless and are meant to represent the possibility of new life, fertility. Talk about what they were made of. Note the details of hair on some of them. Encourage the children's reactions.

Journal Writing

Have children write about what they have learned, their reactions, questions, etc., in a learning journal supplied for this course. If this is the first lesson of the year, give the journals out with much fanfare. Talk about them as a wonderful way for children to think about their learning and express their feelings about art. If the children have never kept a journal, do a class entry on the board or on chart paper. Continue to do this until you feel the children have an understanding of the kind of thing that can go into a learning journal and can make entries on their own. Each journal entry should begin with the date. Very young children can draw what they have learned if they are unable to write it. It is better for them to draw or write only a word or two rather than dictate their entry for you to write down. Encourage invented spelling and avoid making corrections in any journal writing.

Art/Drama Activity: Pantomime

Children truly enjoy pantomiming the story of Noma. You can have a storyteller (or several) tell the story, while some students prepare a body (another student or an imaginary one) for burial, some stand around the grave site, and some drum their sad dirge. Noma, of course, sits apart and carves her figurine, then races to share with the others what she has done.

LESSON 2: Cave Paintings

❑ The Story

Over a hundred years ago, in 1879, in Altamira, Spain, there lived a wealthy man named Marcelino de Sautuolo. He had heard about some tools and other objects found by archaeologists in caves in different parts of Europe, and he decided to explore one of the many caves near his home. He was very interested in such things and thought perhaps he would find something marvelous—some tools, a necklace—to show to the world. His little daughter Maria begged to go with him, and he agreed.

But once her father started poking around in the cave, Maria began to get restless. "Let's go home, Daddy. It's dark and cold in here!" Don Marcelino was too busy to pay attention to her. So Maria took a candle and began to move further into the cave. As she went further and further, she came to a place that was so small a grownup couldn't even stand up in it. But little Maria could, and she began to look all around her. All of a sudden she began to yell, "*Toros, toros. Papa, toros!*"

Now *toros* means "bulls" in Spanish. When her father heard Maria yelling, he came running to where she was, but he had to walk in all stooped over. Maria pointed to the ceiling. "Look, papa, *toros!*" And there Don Marcelino saw paintings of a herd of animals that looked just like bulls. They were painted in shades of red, yellow, and brown. Some were sitting, some were standing, and one was pierced by a spear. Maria's father was amazed. He had never heard of such paintings before. He returned day after day to study them. And finally he wrote an article all about them. He wrote that the paintings had been made by people living over 20,000 years before in the Stone Age. All the scientists who read the article laughed at him. "Those paintings are not old. Somebody got in that cave and painted them recently." And they called him a faker. Don Marcelino died nine years later, a very sad man.

But finally scientists began to pay attention to cave paintings and to understand that they were very old. In 1940, four young boys in France went rabbit hunting with their dog. The boys went to a hole where they thought rabbits were hiding, and the dog scampered into the hole to scare them out. But no rabbits came out of the hole. And no dog came out either! Then the boys heard barking that seemed to come from deep underground, and one of them decided to crawl down the hole to rescue the dog. He went sliding down, down, down, until he found himself in a deep, dark cave. He shouted to the other boys, and they went sliding down after him. When they lit matches to see where they were, they discovered paintings on the walls.

Since they really couldn't see very much, they decided to come back with flashlights the next day and do more exploring. They explored the caves for five days and found marvelous paintings of animals. And this time the scientists paid attention. Now we know about the wonderful art treasures in caves in Spain, France, and other parts of the world, and we can even visit some of those caves ourselves. Because these caves were sealed for thousands of years and no air was able to get in, the paintings are wonderfully preserved. But now we must be careful. Many countries only let a few people at a time into the caves because our breathing can destroy these precious paintings.

Viewing the Art

Use some or all of the reference books following to show pictures of the cave paintings. If you can obtain slides, this is preferable, since the children will be able to see more clearly how the cave artists used the natural formations of the rock in drawing their animals. Discuss the colors the artists used, what they used for paint, the kinds of animals pictured, and which ones are still on the earth and which are extinct. Talk about the positions of the animals and why some are shown with spears in their sides.

Journal Writing

Begin with a question: "When your parents hang pictures in your house, do they hide them, or do they put the pictures where everyone can see and enjoy them? Why do you think the cave artists drew these pictures, and why did they place them deep within the caves instead of right at the entrance where people could see them?" After they have finished writing, discuss the children's responses.

> Wednesday September 20, 1989
>
> I Thike They put The panTing in The back of The cave fcos The panTing Wer preshis

Art/Drama Activity: Cave Painting Ceremony

If you feel your community might object to the following activity on religious grounds you can easily make a few changes. Instead of having a child take the role of shaman, have the children gather around their cave animals once they have been taped to the wall. A clan leader can say something like, "Hunters, you see before you the animals that live around us. They are mighty and strong, but we are clever and strong. Go out now and hunt bravely for the sake of your people." The hunters ready their weapons and depart.

Materials
- Long strip of paper from a roll, preferably brown
- Pastels of the colors used by cave dwellers in their paintings: black, brown, yellow, red
- Drums

One possible explanation for the purpose of the cave paintings is that they were done for religious ceremonies. Perhaps the shaman, or religious leader, went before the pictures and recited special chants so the hunters of these animals would be successful. After all, the people's lives depended upon a successful hunting expedition. Assuming that this is a logical explanation, have the children pretend they are a clan of Cro-Magnon people. It is time for another hunt, and the artists have been requested to paint animals on the cave walls in preparation for a special hunting ceremony.

Spread the paper on the floor and allot a space for each child. Distribute the pastels. Ask each child to draw an animal that would have been alive during the Paleolithic period. Dinosaurs are definitely out! These are animals the Cro-Magnon people depended upon for their food and clothing. When the drawings are finished, tape the sheet of paper to a classroom or hallway wall so that it resembles a cave wall. Now you are ready to have a special ceremony for the hunt. Have one child volunteer to be the shaman, who will lead the group in a chant, whatever seems appropriate, such as, "O Great Spirits, give us good luck for our hunt!" Some children can beat a drum to this chant while the rest of the class repeats the chant after the shaman.

Curriculum Connections

Social Studies

- Prehistoric peoples
- Climate and geography of the areas talked about in the lessons

Science

- Animals of the Stone Age
- Insect and animal life in caves
- The formation of caves

Music

- Make up a melody to accompany the shaman's chant

References

Burenhult, Goran, gen. ed. Foreword by Donald C. Johanson. *The First Humans*. San Francisco: HarperSanFrancisco, 1993. First in a series of volumes that explore human history.

Covers the time up to 10,000 B.C. There is a chapter on prehistoric art. Three hundred color photos.

Chauvet, Jean-Marie, Eliette Brunel Deschamps, and Christian Hillaire. *Dawn of Art: The Chauvet Cave: The Oldest Known Paintings in the World.* New York: Harry N. Abrams, 1996. Discusses each work of art in the Chauvet cave discovered in 1994. Contains 94 full-color illustrations of these amazing works, believed to be over thirty thousand years old.

Clottes, Jean and Jean Courtin. *The Cave Beneath the Sea: Paleolithic Images at Cosquer.* Transl. by Marilyn Garner. New York: Harry N. Abrams, 1996. Discusses the many 27,000-year-old paintings discovered in 1991 in a cave sealed off by the Mediterranean at the end of the last Ice Age. Over 100 illustrations in color.

Grand, P.M. *Prehistoric Art: Paleolithic Painting and Sculpture.* Greenwich, CT: New York Graphic Society, 1967 o.p. Major works of Paleolithic painting and sculpture in different parts of the world. Large reproductions, many in color, suitable for viewing.

Leroi-Gourhan, André. *Treasures of Prehistoric Art.* Transl. by Norbert Guterman. New York: Harry N. Abrams, 1967 o.p. A magnificent book filled with large reproductions for viewing.

Ruspoli, Mario. *The Cave of Lascaux: The Final Photographs.* New York: Harry N. Abrams, 1986 o.p. After Lascaux was sealed in 1963, the author was allowed to do a final filming with a crew of six. This book is a record of the wonders within that cave. Includes information on hunting weapons and prehistoric peoples. Marvelous.

Children's Books

Aliki. *Wild and Woolly Mammoths.* Rev. ed. New York: HarperCollins, 1996. After discussing the discoveries of frozen mammoths in recent years, the author tells about these animals and the prehistoric peoples who depended on them for food and clothing.

Baumann, Hans. *The Caves of the Great Hunters.* Transl. by Isabel and Florence McHugh. Illus. by Hans Peter Renner. New York: Pantheon, 1962 o.p. Recounts the discovery of the great caves in a fictional narrative. Photographs and drawings.

Lessem, Dan. *The Iceman.* New York: Crown, 1994. In large picture-book format, the author tells the story of a 5,300-year-old man found frozen with his clothes, tools, and weapons in an alpine glacier.

Marcus, R.B. *Prehistoric Cave Paintings.* New York: Franklin Watts, 1968 o.p. Discussion of the discovery of cave paintings, Cro-Magnon people, and the meaning of the cave paintings.

Powell, Jillian. *Ancient Art.* New York: Thomson Learning, 1994. Simple presentation of the art of various ancient civilizations including cave painters, Africans, Egyptians, Greeks, and Romans.

Ruskin, Ariane. *Prehistoric Art and Ancient Art of the Near East.* New York: McGraw-Hill, 1971 o.p. Part of the Discovering Art series. Overview of prehistoric art, Egyptian art, and art in Mesopotamia. Good source of illustrations for viewing.

Samachson, Dorothy and Joseph. *The First Artists.* New York: Doubleday, 1970 o.p. Presentation of the lives and artwork of the first artists of Europe, Africa, and Australia.

Turner, Ann. *Time of the Bison.* Illus. by Beth Peck. New York: Macmillan, 1987 o.p. An eleven-year-old boy discovers that he is an artist and becomes an apprentice to the cave painter. Fiction. Can be an excellent read-aloud story.

Audiovisual Materials

The Caves of Altamira. Shows cave paintings of animals and mysterious symbols done thousands of years ago in the Altamira Caves in Spain. (Videocassette; 26 mins. Available from Films for the Humanities and Sciences.)

Nova: Mammoths of the Ice Age. Describes the life cycle of these ancient animals that lived beyond the Ice Age. (Videocassette; 60 mins. Available from WGBH, Boston.)

2 Ancient Egyptian Art

"Soldiers, forty centuries are looking down upon you."
—NAPOLEON BONAPARTE to his men
as they marched past the Egyptian pyramids

Background Information

The ancient Egyptians were a fascinating people who occupied a prominent place in antiquity for over 3,000 years. The land of Egypt in northern Africa was created by the Nile, which flows north from the center of Africa, forms many branches, and empties into the Mediterranean Sea. Until the Aswan Dam was built in the 1960s, the Nile overflowed each year, bringing rich mud onto the land. The lands bordering the Nile were the most fertile in the world, and Egyptian farmers prospered.

It has been difficult for scholars to determine the chronology of ancient Egypt, because the Egyptians had three calendars: one based on the movements of the star Sothis, one on the flooding of the Nile, and the third on the phases of the moon. Originally, the land of Egypt was divided into two kingdoms: the Upper Kingdom—which, ironically, was the lower half—and the Lower Kingdom, which was the land bordering the Mediterranean. In about 3100 B.C., Menes (sometimes called Narmer) united the two kingdoms, and pharaohs thereafter wore a double crown indicating complete authority over the entire land. With Menes began the first of over thirty dynasties, or periods of ruling families, which spanned 3,000 years. The first artist in recorded history was Imhotep, and he built the first Egyptian pyramid for Zoser, a pharaoh who ruled during the Old Kingdom, Egypt's classical era (2686–2181 B.C.). This period includes Dynasties III through VI. During this time, King Khufu built the Great Pyramid, the largest pyramid ever built, at Giza. Two other pyramids for Khufu's successors stand with it, and the Giant Sphinx stands guard over all three.

During the First Intermediate period (2181–2133 B.C.), comprising Dynasties VII through X, a social revolution took place in which the pharaohs lost power and the poor claimed possessions and property. Mentuhotep I of Dynasty

XI established reunification and ushered in the Middle Kingdom (2133–1786 B.C.) of Dynasties XI and XII. The pharaohs of the Middle Kingdom strived to recapture the grandeur of the previous centuries, and to revive art and culture, but toward the end of Dynasty XII, royal authority again weakened, invaders from Asia called Hyksos overtook the land, and the Second Intermediate period (1786–1650 B.C.) began.

When the Hyksos were finally driven out, art and culture were reborn, and the country attained its greatest military and political power. The era of the New Kingdom (1650–1085 B.C.) comprised Dynasties XVII, XVIII, XIX, and XX. Splendid temples and hundreds of monuments were built. This is the age of the famous pharaoh Ramses II; of Hatshepsut, a capable and powerful ruler who had herself declared "king"; of Akhenaten and his lovely queen, Nefertiti; and of King Tutankhamen whose tomb was uncovered intact in 1922. Although Tut was a minor pharaoh and ruled for only ten years, the riches found in his tomb give us some idea of the wealth that was buried with the ancient Egyptian pharaohs.

During the Late Dynastic period (945–332 B.C.), Dynasties XXI through XXX, Egypt began its final decline, with power moving back and forth between Egyptian rulers and their conquering enemies. First the Persians, then the Greeks under Alexander the Great and a succession of Ptolemy pharaohs, and finally the Romans ruled Egypt. Christianity came to the country in the second century A.D., and the Arab conquest occurred around 640.

Egyptian art is often referred to as the art of the dead. Ancient Egyptians believed that every person had a soul, or *ka*, which kept on living after the person died. In this life after death, the soul would seek out its body and continue to exist, using all the things it had enjoyed in life. Thus, the Egyptians went to great pains to prepare a body for burial so that it would be preserved for reunification with the soul. They mummified it by removing all the inner organs except the heart and preserving them in jars (they threw out the brain, which they considered of no importance). They washed the body inside and out with wine, stuffed it with cloths to keep its shape, and dried it out in natron, a type of salt, for forty days. The body was then smeared with resin, decorated with jewels, wrapped in linen strips, placed in elaborately decorated nesting coffins, and carried with great ceremony to a tomb. There it was buried with jewels, furnishings, and other treasures to be enjoyed in the next world.

Not every Egyptian had the means for an elaborate funeral, however. Such splendor was usually reserved for the pharaoh, whom the Egyptians believed to be a god and supreme ruler, and for important officials. Ancient Egyptian artists used their talents to decorate the magnificent palaces of their pharaohs, and the pharaohs' pyramid or place of burial. The huge pyramids took years to complete. The stones for these structures were probably quarried, loaded onto barges, and floated down the Nile. Then they were hauled to the building site. It took thousands of workers to accomplish these difficult tasks, and much of the work force was made up of farmers who built pyramids during the flooding season when they could not plant and tend crops. Since the ancient Egyptians did not use money, they often paid their taxes in labor for the pharaoh.

Egyptian artists made statues of the pharaoh and the royal family, painted pictures of the pharaoh, his family, and his servants on interior pyramid walls, and carved the story of the pharaoh's life and exploits in hieroglyphics on stone walls and pillars. They made magnificent funeral masks, jewelry, furniture, and other artifacts to be entombed with the pharaoh for use in the afterlife.

When we view Egyptian art, we are struck by how stiff it often looks. There is no evident movement, and the position is strange: heads, arms, and legs are in side view, while the eyes and bodies are in front view. That is because the artists had to work in accordance with a strict set of rules. Figures were drawn on a grid, measured out according to an exact formula from which they could not deviate. There was also no perspective or attempt to show depth. But during the reign of Pharaoh Akhenaten, who broke away from the powerful priesthood of the god Amun in the New Kingdom, some of the rules were relaxed, and there is a new movement and fluidity in the artwork.

Egyptian writing, or hieroglyphic, began about 3100 B.C. A hieroglyph is an individual symbol in hieroglyphic writing. At first only the names of important people such as pharaohs were written with their pictures or on statues. But by 2500 B.C., longer pieces of writing were being done. Only Egyptian professionals such as doctors, lawyers, government officials, or scribes learned how to read and write. A scribe, who could rise to high rank in government if his work pleased the pharaoh, began his studies at about age six and continued for ten years, practicing all day long until he learned about six hundred hieroglyphs. He learned how to paint or carve hieroglyphs on stone and to write on papyrus in hieratic, which is like a cursive in which the hieroglyphic symbols were joined. After many centuries, the hieratic writing became even simpler and was called demotic writing, the writing found on the famous Rosetta Stone discovered by Napoleon's soldiers in 1799. When the brilliant French scientist Jean François Champollion later deciphered the writing on this stone, he unlocked the secrets of Egyptian hieroglyphs, and, in turn, many secrets about the ancient Egyptian way of life.

LESSON 1: Art for the Afterlife

❏ The Story

Many, many years ago, Osiris ruled over all of Egypt. He was a just and kind king, and he and his wife, Isis, were very happy together. But Osiris had a brother,

Seth, who was very jealous. Every time Seth thought about how happy his brother's life was, he became angrier and angrier.

One day, Seth invited Osiris to a banquet. "How wonderful," thought Osiris. "Perhaps my brother and I can finally become friends." Little did he know that Seth had an evil plan! Seth had made a chest that was exactly his brother's size. During the banquet he said, "Let's have a contest. Anyone who can fit into this chest will win a prize." One by one the guests climbed into the chest. But no one fit—until Osiris tried. Of course, he fit perfectly, and the moment he was inside Seth slammed the lid shut. Once his brother had suffocated in the chest, Seth cut his body into fourteen pieces and scattered them all over Egypt.

But Isis's love for her husband could not be broken the way his body had been broken by his brother. She wept and wept for him and searched all over Egypt for the pieces of his body. With the help of Anubis, a god with the head of a jackal, she found every piece, and with her own magic, she put them together and brought Osiris back to life. But he could no longer be a king in this world. He became the ruler of the underworld instead. Meanwhile, Isis sent her son, Horus, to avenge his father's murder by Seth.

The ancient Egyptians believed that every pharaoh became the god Horus when he became ruler of Egypt. And when the pharaoh died, he would go to the underworld to be judged. There Anubis would be waiting with a set of two scales. On one scale, he would place the pharaoh's heart. On the other scale, he would place an ostrich feather. If his heart weighed more than the feather because he had lived an evil life, he was eaten by a monster. But if his heart weighed less than the feather because he was honest and good, he then became joined to Osiris and lived happily forever in the underworld, united once again with his soul, or *ka*.

Since his *ka* had to find him, the Egyptians made sure they preserved the pharaoh's body by mummifying it before they buried it in a huge pyramid. (Talk about mummification with the children.) They painted pictures of the pharaoh and his family on the walls of the pyramid and carved writing telling of all his wonderful deeds into the walls. They buried the pharaoh with all the things he would need for his life in the underworld: furniture, tools, weapons, jewelry. Much of the beauty Egyptian artists created was not for this life but for the life they believed was to come.

Viewing the Art

It is a simple matter to make ancient Egyptian artwork available for viewing. There are several videos and some wonderful books with very large prints. All of these are listed here. As you view the work, see if the children notice the unusual position of the figures: the head, arms, and legs appear in side view; the eyes and bodies are in front view. Have the children stand up and try to assume that position. Now have them pretend to be pharaohs, standing with their left foot forward.

Encourage the children's comments and observations. What strikes them? How does this art differ from art with which they are familiar? Talk about how Egyptian artists did their art according to a formula on grids, and how much of it appears stiff and flat. Ask the children to note the colors used in the paintings, to observe that the men are always a darker shade than the women and that important figures are larger than those of lesser importance. Discuss pyramid-building and the problem of modern grave robbers stealing the wonderful treasures buried in the pyramids.

Talk about Egyptian sculpture and relief carvings. There are three kinds of relief, low and high, and sculpture in the full round. You can demonstrate this very simply with a small piece of modeling clay. Mold the clay into a flat disk. Then, with a pencil point or other sharp instrument, carve a snake into it. This is low relief. Next, remove some of the background clay around the snake so that the snake appears raised on the clay. This is high relief. Finally, carve the entire snake out of the clay disk. This is sculpture in the full round.

Journal Writing

If you have shown the children any of the films or videos suggested here, they might write about what they have seen. What are some things they noticed about ancient Egyptian art? Would they like to have the job of a scribe in Egypt? Why or why not?

Art/Drama Activity: Mummy-making and the Arts of Egypt

Materials

- Newspapers
- Masking tape
- Papier-mâché mix
- Beads, macaroni, colored paper
- String
- Paper, cardboard
- Paints, markers
- Roll of paper for a mural

Have the children pretend to be artists hired by the pharaoh to decorate his pyramid and prepare his burial chamber. Divide them into groups to work on several projects.

Some can make a papier-mâché mummy. First, ball up old newspapers and shape them into a mummy-shaped body. Tape the pieces together. Next, rip sheets of newspaper into strips. Dip each strip into papier-mâché mix and layer the strips over the body. Make many layers until the body is strong and well-formed. Allow to dry several days. Paint in brilliant colors using some art books for models.

Jewelry makers can make Egyptian necklaces and bracelets from beads, macaroni, etc. They might wish to make jewel-encrusted furniture out of cardboard as well. They can use Egyptian portraits for models.

Painters can work on a mural depicting a scene in the pharaoh's life for the pyramid walls. Illustrations in the books referenced here can provide models. The students may wish to show the pharaoh in his palace with all his family and servants. Or they might like to picture the pharaoh on a hunt. Whatever the scene, they should make sure that the figure of the pharaoh is shown larger than all the rest to indicate his importance.

Children love to act out the story of Stolz's *Zekmet the Stone Carver* (see References). This is the story of how the Great Sphinx might have come to be. Read the story to the children and let them decide whether they would like to turn it into a play. Costumes are extremely easy for this production: white T-shirts with belts or sheets draped to knee length. The children enjoy making headdresses of cardboard.

LESSON 2: Hieroglyphics

❏ The Story

How many of you like puzzles? If someone were to buy you a 500-piece puzzle, how long do you think it would take you to put it together? Would you try to do it yourself, or would you ask for help? Well, this is the story of an incredible puzzle that took years to solve! It happened long after the ancient Egyptians whose artwork we have been enjoying had died. Almost two hundred years ago, which is not nearly as long ago as when King Tut was alive, a great French general named Napoleon Bonaparte marched his armies far and wide trying to conquer different countries for France. When he and his men went to Egypt, they took a group of scientists with them. Napoleon loved science, and he couldn't wait for the scientists to study all the wonderful carvings in the Egyptian pyramids and in the museums and to tell him about them.

But when the scientists went into the museums, they could not understand any of the writing they saw there. When they visited the pyramids, they couldn't read any of the writing on the pyramid walls. They had meetings with the Egyptian scientists. "Tell us what these writings mean," they said. But can you believe it? Not even the Egyptian scientists could read the ancient Egyptian writing!

Because so many countries had conquered Egypt since the days of the ancient Egyptians, the new Egyptian people stopped using their old language and spoke the language of their conquerors. By the time Napoleon got there, the people were speaking Arabic! Not a single person or government official or teacher could help the French scientists. Nobody could read or understand ancient Egyptian writing! Napoleon was very disappointed.

But then one day, while his soldiers were digging trenches, they found a large black stone with three kinds of writing on it. One language was Greek, one was Egyptian hieroglyphics, and one was a simpler form of Egyptian writing. They cleaned the stone and sent it to Napoleon, and Napoleon gave it to his scientists. "Now I'll find out about ancient Egyptian writing," he thought. But none of his scientists could figure out what the Egyptian writing said. They could read the Greek writing but not the Egyptian. It was like a secret code they could not break.

Years later, a nine-year-old French boy named Jean Champollion heard about the stone, which was called the Rosetta Stone because it was found in the Egyptian town of Rosetta. "I'm going to be the one to break that code," he said. "I just know I will!"

While he was growing up, Jean studied many languages, and by the time he was in his twenties, he could speak more than ten of them! He began working on the stone, and after years of effort he finally did crack the code. He figured out what the picture writing called hieroglyphics meant.

Now we know what the ancient Egyptians wrote on their walls and on their statues. And we know a great deal more about their lives. If you want to see the Rosetta Stone now, you must travel to a museum in London, England.

Viewing the Art

Show the children pictures of hieroglyphic writing. The ancient Egyptians usually wrote from right to left. But at other times scribes went from left to right. And when they carved on pillars or doorways, the writing went downward! Most ancient Egyptians did not know how to write and employed scribes to write for them. Describe the training and work of a scribe. Show them the print of the seated scribe (see *Art of Ancient Egypt* by Michalowski). What do the children notice about the hieroglyphs? Which are their favorite? Make certain they observe the oblongs encircling some of the figures. These are called *cartouches* and direct attention to the names of pharaohs and other important personages. Talk about writing on stone and a kind of paper called "papyrus" made from reeds that grow along the Nile.

Journal Writing

What is the children's reaction to the perseverance of Champollion and other scholars? How do they feel about writing? What if they lived in a country in which most people, including themselves, were not be able to write? How would their lives be different?

Art/Drama Activity: A Cartouche Necklace

Materials

- Plaster of Paris
- A sharp instrument such as the point of a scissor blade
- A copy of the Egyptian hieroglyphs
- Black paint
- Wax paper
- Masking tape
- Fine sandpaper
- Leather or string

Have children make cartouche necklaces for themselves or a family member. Give each child a portion of plaster of Paris to shape into a flat oval about one inch thick. Poke a hole through the top for a piece of leather or string to go through. Smooth it out and place it on wax paper to dry over several days. Tape the child's name on the paper. Sand the dry ovals and wipe smooth. Paint with black tempera paint. Have children practice writing their name or a family member's name in hieroglyphics on a piece of paper. They might prefer a description such as "strong one," "wise one," etc. When they can do this well, have them scratch the hieroglyphs vertically onto the cartouche. String and wear around the neck.

Curriculum Connections

Social Studies

- History of Egypt and its people
- Farming and irrigation methods
- Egyptian clothing

Mathematics

- Egyptian numerals and counting (see *Number Art* by Micklethwait in General Bibliography)

Science

- Egyptian inventions, such as the lever
- Papyrus

References

Michaeowski, Kazimierz. *Art of Ancient Egypt*. Transl. by Norbert Guterman. New York: Harry N. Abrams, 1969 o.p. Historical information interspersed with wonderful large prints suitable for group viewing.

Reeves, Nicholas. *The Complete Tutankhamun*. New York: Thames and Hudson, 1995. Illustrations depicting the glorious treasures found in Tut's tomb.

Scamuzzi, Ernesto. *Egyptian Art in the Egyptian Museum of Turin*. New York: Harry N. Abrams, 1965 o.p. Magnificent large prints of the art works in the museum in Turin, Italy.

Yoyotte, Jean. *Treasures of the Pharaohs*. Transl. by Robert Allen. Cleveland, OH: World Publishing Company, 1968 o.p. Egyptian art of different dynasties, with large prints suitable for group viewing.

Children's Books

Aliki. *Mummies Made in Egypt*. New York: Thomas Y. Crowell, 1979. Describes the process of mummifying bodies in ancient Egypt.

Bunting, Eve. *I am the Mummy Heb-Nefert*. Illus. by David Christiana. San Diego: Harcourt Brace, 1997. In this picture book, the mummified Heb-Nefert speaks from her glass museum case about her life as the daughter of royalty in ancient Egypt.

Clements, Andres. *Temple Cat*. Illus. by Kate Kiesler. New York: Clarion, 1996. A temple cat in ancient Egypt, tired of being pampered, escapes to live with a common fisherman and his family.

Cohen, Daniel. *Ancient Egypt*. Illus. by Gary A. Lippincott. New York: Doubleday, 1990 o.p. Describes in simple text the lives and accomplishments of the ancient Egyptians.

Crosher, Judith. *Ancient Egypt*. New York: Viking, 1993. Wonderful plastic overlays help to make this an excellent view of life in ancient Egypt.

dePaola, Tomi. *Bill and Pete Go Down the Nile*. New York: G.P. Putnam, 1987. Bill the Crocodile and his bird friend Pete go on a class trip down the Nile and encounter jewel thieves.

Der Manuelian, Peter. *Hieroglyphs from A to Z*. Boston: Museum of Fine Arts, 1991. An ABC book comparing the English alphabet with Egyptian hieroglyphs. Includes a stencil for writing Egyptian hieroglyphs.

Dexter, Catherine. *The Gilded Cat.* New York: Morrow, 1992. Maggie buys a mummified Egyptian cat at a yard sale and finds she has the power to make people do what she wants. But someone else has power over her as well.

Fleming, Stuart. *The Egyptians.* New York: New Discovery, 1992. Describes history of ancient Egypt, including a look at Egyptian art and architecture.

Gerrard, Roy. *Croco'nile.* New York: Farrar, Straus & Giroux, 1994. Readers get a good glimpse of ancient Egyptian life by following the zany trip Hamut and his sister, Nekatus, take along the Nile.

Giblin, James Cross. *The Riddle of the Rosetta Stone.* New York: Thomas Y. Crowell, 1990. The story of how the Rosetta Stone was discovered by Napoleon Bonaparte's men in Egypt and of the work of scholars over the years to decipher it.

Haslam, Andrew, and Alexandra Parsons. *Make It Work: Ancient Egypt.* New York: Thomson Learning, 1995. A wonderful book that presents a study of ancient Egypt with accompanying activities including making clothing, wigs, headpieces, death masks, toys, etc. Includes bibliography.

Katan, Norma Jean, with Barbara Mintz. *Hieroglyphs.* New York: Atheneum, 1984. Presents hieroglyphs found in ancient Egypt and instructions for writing them.

Lattimore, Deborah Nourse. *The Winged Cat.* New York: HarperCollins, 1992. The high priest denies killing a cat, though a serving girl has seen him. Both must go to the underworld to be judged. Wonderful story to read in relation to the story of Osiris and Isis.

Macaulay, David. *Pyramid.* Boston: Houghton Mifflin, 1975. Thorough discussion of the process of building a pyramid in ancient Egypt.

McMullan, Kate. *Under the Mummy's Spell.* New York: Farrar, Straus & Giroux, 1992. On a dare, Peter Harring kisses the mummy mask of Princess Nephia at the Metropolitan Museum of Art and is commanded by her to right a centuries-old wrong.

Millard, Anne. *Pyramids.* New York: Kingfisher, 1996. A beautifully illustrated book which discusses how and why pyramids were built in several ancient civilizations.

Morley, Jacqueline, Mark Bergin, and John James. *An Egyptian Pyramid.* New York: Peter Bedrick Books, 1991. Customs of the ancient Egyptians and a discussion of the process of pyramid-building.

Sabuda, Robert. *The Mummy's Tomb: A Pop-Up Book.* New York: Artists and Writers Guild, 1994. A very well-designed pop-up book about a tomb in ancient Egypt.

————. *Tutankhamen's Gift.* New York: Atheneum, 1994. Although Tut is the youngest of the pharaoh's sons, he does become king and makes an important contribution to Egyptian life. Beautiful linoleum-cut illustrations.

Scieszka, Jon. *Tut Tut.* Illus. by Lane Smith. New York: Viking, 1996. A Time Warp Trio fantasy. The threesome goes back in time to ancient Egypt.

Scott, Henry Joseph, and Lenore Scott. *Egyptian Hieroglyphs for Everyone.* New York: Crowell Junior Books, 1990. An excellent introduction to Egyptian hieroglyphs.

Stanley, Diane. *Cleopatra.* Illus. by Peter Vennema. New York: Morrow Junior Books, 1994.

Beautifully illustrated and written biography of the woman who tried to unite Rome and Egypt.

Stolz, Mary. *Zekmet the Stone Carver.* Illus. by Deborah Nourse Lattimore. San Diego, CA: Harcourt Brace, 1986. A stone carver comes up with an idea for creating the Great Sphinx of Egypt.

Tiano, Olivier. *Ramses II.* New York: Henry Holt, 1995. A fascinating look at ancient Egyptian life as it was throughout the long reign of Ranses II. Clothing, customs, pyramid-building, writing, and art are just a few of the topics contained in this very entertaining book.

Walsh, Jill Paton. *Pepi and the Secret Names.* Illus. by Fiona French. New York: Lothrop, 1994. Pepi lures dangerous animals to serve as models for his father, who is painting decorations for Prince Dhutmose's tomb. Beautifully illustrated, this book contains hieroglyphs for children to decipher.

Wilcox, Charlotte. *Mummies & Their Mysteries.* Minneapolis, MN: Carolrhoda Books, 1993. Discusses not only mummy-making in Egypt but throughout the world.

Wright, Rachel. *Egyptians: Facts, Things to Make, Activities.* New York: Franklin Watts, 1993. Crafts and activities related to the life and customs of ancient Egyptians.

Wynne-Jones, Tim. *Zoom Upstream.* Illus. by Eric Beddows. New York: HarperCollins, 1992. Zoom the cat climbs up a bookcase and follows a trail that leads to ancient Egypt and adventure.

Audiovisual Materials

Morgan's Adventures in Ancient Egypt. Children are transported to ancient Egypt where they learn about Egyptian life, customs, and the Egyptian alphabet. Includes teacher's manual of additional activities and resources. Ages 7–12. (CD-ROM for Mac and Windows, 1997. Available from HarperCollins Interactive.)

Nile: Passage to Egypt. Explores the art, architecture, culture and wildlife of Egypt on a trip up the Nile. (CD-ROM for Mac and Windows. Available from Library Video Company.)

Of Time, Tombs, and Treasure: The Treasures of Tutankhamen. The story of Carter's discovery of the tomb and presentation of its treasures. (Videocassette; 29 mins. Available from the National Gallery of Art.)

Pyramid. Video version of David Macaulay's wonderful book, with animated elements added. (Videocassette; 60 mins. Available from PBS Video.)

Treasures of Tutankhamen. Objects found in Tut's tomb. (Film; 5 mins. Available from the National Gallery of Art.)

Other Materials

Fun With Hieroglyphs. Inexpensive kit with rubber stamps for the different hieroglyphs. Available from the gift shop or catalogue, Metropolitan Museum of Art, New York City.

3 Ancient Greek Art

"Future ages will wonder at us, as the present age wonders at us now."
—PERICLES, ruler of Athens, 431 B.C.

Background Information

The life and art of the ancient Greeks have had a profound effect on humankind. The Greeks were lovers of beauty, philosophers and thinkers, mathematicians, champions of physical fitness and the human body. They gave us the *Iliad* and the *Odyssey*, Homer, Plato, Socrates, and Aristotle. The Greeks developed the first, albeit imperfect, democratic system of government. They loved drama and performed hundreds of plays, several of which survive to this day. Long before Columbus sailed the seas, Greek scholars knew that the earth was round, and Eratosthenes measured the earth's diameter with remarkable accuracy centuries before the sophisticated instruments we now use for this purpose were invented. The ancient Greeks initiated many of the disciplines we take for granted today: Herodotus wrote about the wars and other events in the lives of his people, and thus became the Father of History; Thales has been called the first scientist; Hippocrates, who tried to find cures for illness, is considered the Father of Medicine, and Euclid, the Father of Geometry. The Spartans with their vigorous training and austere way of life became geniuses at waging war, while most Greeks took honing and exercising the body seriously. The Olympic games originated in Greece in 776 B.C., and legend has it that the first marathon was run by Miltiades, who ran twenty-six miles at high speed to bring news that the Athenians had defeated the Persians. Greek sculpture and architecture, frequently created to pay homage to one or more of their many gods, have been unsurpassed by the work of any group of people before or since.

Although there were tribes of peoples speaking Greek in the lands surrounding the Mediterranean Sea as early as 1100 B.C., we take up their history in this lesson around 750 B.C., with Homer's writing of the *Iliad* and the *Odyssey*. At this time, the tribes formed city-states, the most famous of which was Athens. The earliest Greek statues sculpted around this time, the Archaic Period, were very much like those of the Egyptians. They were mostly of naked young boys, with the wide shoulders and narrow waists of the Egyptian statues, who stood stiffly with one leg forward. During this period, artists painted black figures on the natural clay color of jugs and vases. The lines inside the figures were made by scratching away some of the black paint. This pottery, and the pottery of later eras, is the only record we have of ancient Greek painting, since all the wall paintings have been destroyed.

The classical period (500–323 B.C.) ushered in a noticeable change in Greek art. Sculptors began to have a better grasp of the human form, and statues took on a new grace, beauty, and sense of movement. Greek sculptors emphasized perfection, giving their figures refined features and perfectly proportioned bodies. Painters left the figures on their pottery in the natural clay color and painted the background black, so they could draw interior lines and features with a brush rather than painstakingly scratching them in.

In ancient Greece, art and individual achievement were honored, and for the first time artists began to sign their works. We know the names of some of the pottery painters, and we know about the work of such marvelous sculptors as Praxiteles, Skopas, and Lysippos. During the classical period, the Greeks fought and defeated the invading Persians, and though the Persians destroyed the Acropolis, a hill in Athens on which stood temples to the gods, the Athenians pledged to rebuild their city and to clothe it in even greater splendor. Under its ruler Pericles, Athens entered into a Golden Age, or the Age of Pericles. Although this Golden Age did not last long because of Athens's devastating defeat at the hands of the Spartans in the Peloponnesian War, for the next forty years the city of Athens devoted itself to the arts.

To replace the temple to Athena, goddess of wisdom and patron of Athens, which had been under construction when the Persians destroyed it, Pericles hired two great architects, Iktinos and Callicrates. Greek temples were constructed in different styles, or orders, determined by the type of capital, or head, of the columns which supported them. The orders are the Doric, the Ionic, and most elaborate, the Corinthian. Athena's temple, the Parthenon, constructed in the Doric order, is considered to be one of the most beautiful buildings in the world. The architects built it in only fifteen years.

Designed to compensate for all possible optical illusions, there is not a straight line in the building, though to the observer it is perfectly proportioned. The great sculptor Phidias sculpted the enormous statue of Athena that was to be placed in the Parthenon. Standing on a twelve-foot base, the statue, made of wood overlaid with gold and ivory, rose another thirty-nine feet and held a six-foot statue of Nike, the Greek goddess of victory, in one hand, and a huge shield in the other. She was so grand she actually cost more than the temple that housed her! Unfortunately this statue, as is true of most ancient Greek statues, has been lost or destroyed, and all we have are Roman copies to apprise us of their splendor.

Alexander, called the Great, finally destroyed the much-hated Persian empire and extended Greek rule into Egypt and India. The period following his death in 323 B.C. is called the Hellenistic Age. It is during this time that Greek portrait statues began to shed their idealistic features and take on more individual characteristics. Finally, from 31 B.C. to A.D. 330, Greece fell under Roman rule.

❑ The Story

Long, long ago, there lived a group of gods high on a mountaintop called Olympus. These gods were very interested in what went on in the world of humans living far below them, so when the gods received news that a new city was going to be created, they had a big contest to see which god would be in charge of it. Two of the gods, Poseidon, who ruled the seas, and Athena, goddess of wisdom, led all the others in trying to gain control. Finally, the gods decided to act as judges. Both Poseidon and Athena were ordered to prepare a special gift for the people of the new city. Whoever thought of the best gift would win the contest. The other gods gave Poseidon and Athena time to think of what to offer the people. At last the day arrived for them to stand before the judges.

Poseidon strode proudly forth, and with one wave of his hand he created a thundering earthquake. The earth split at his feet, and out of the enormous crack rose a salt spring. "You see, I have created a body of water for the people. And since I rule the seas, I will make sure that these people are always powerful on water. They will have a mighty navy and defeat any enemies who come to attack them with ships."

The judges looked very pleased. "That is surely a fine gift, Poseidon. It is important that the people have the power to defend themselves. And you have shown yourself to be powerful enough to be their protector. Perhaps we should award you the city immediately. What could this woman do to compare with your gift?" And Poseidon laughed in agreement.

Meanwhile, Athena kept silent. She simply bent down and began to dig a hole in the earth. "Ha!" said Poseidon. "She digs a hole with the labor of her hands, while I was able to blast the earth apart. Is there any doubt who is more powerful?" But Athena again said nothing. She just continued to dig. Then she pulled a small bush out of a sack and planted it in the hole.

"That is your gift?" roared Poseidon. "A scruffy-looking little plant? How can that compare with my spring and with my power over the sea? Judges, you see for yourselves that I am the winner of this contest!"

Then Athena rose to her full height, though she was not nearly so tall as Poseidon, and looked her judges right in the eye. She spoke for the first time. "Honorable judges," she said, "this is no ordinary bush. It is an olive plant. When it grows into a fine tree, it will produce flavorful olives that will benefit all the people of the new city. They can use it as food for themselves. They can press the olives into oil to flavor their food and light their lamps when the day grows dark. They can travel across the sea and trade the olives and the oil for money or for the goods of other peoples. This plant will enable the people of the city to feed and support themselves for years and years to come. It will bring them gladness and joy." So saying, Athena stepped back to await the judges' decision.

The judges were truly surprised by Athena's gift. "This gift shows how very wise you are," they said. "Might on the seas is unimportant if the people are starving. So we award the new city to Athena. She will be a wise and helpful patron for the humans who will live there."

Athena called her new city Athens after herself, and the people remained her loyal and loving citizens. They built a marvelous temple called the Parthenon in her honor. It is one of the most famous buildings in the world, and we will look at pictures of it soon. When I show you those pictures, I want you to look closely at the statues the ancient Greek artists carved to decorate the temple. In the triangles formed by the roof, you can see statues of Athena and Poseidon having their contest. And all around the top of the building, artists carved a relief showing the procession the people of Athens had every four years to honor their goddess. Greek artists created statues of Athena and painted her picture on jugs and pottery. So let's enjoy some of the artwork of the ancient Greeks. It is among the most beautiful art ever created.

You can use the above story as an introduction to two lessons, one that has to do with painting, and the other with architecture and sculpture.

LESSON 1: Greek Painting

Viewing the Art

Point out to the children that since wall paintings have been destroyed, the only examples we have of Greek painting are what we have recovered from pottery and vases. Actually, many of the vessels we call "vases" are *amphora*, jugs the ancient Greeks used for carrying oil. Show several pottery paintings, being sure to include *The Banquet of Heracles with Athena* from the Andokides painter, *The Banquet of Heracles with Athena* from the Lysippides painter, and the beautiful painting of

Athena herself by the Berlin painter (all three included in Charbonneaux, et al., 1971).

The children should note that some paintings are done in black on red backgrounds, while others are the reverse. Point out the advantages of painting the figures in red. Talk about the different kinds and shapes of jars. Note the subjects of the pottery paintings: Greek gods and heroes, battles, animals. So much of what the ancient Greeks held dear is evident in these paintings—bathing, care of the body, physical prowess. Do the children have particular favorites? Can they tell a story from the paintings? Contrast the earlier forms done in black with the later ones, helping the children to see the increased movement and delicacy of the figures. If the children seem particularly interested, read some children's versions of the Greek myths and talk about the more well-known gods. How many of these gods can the children find in the pottery paintings?

Journal Writing

What have the children learned about Greek paintings? They can contrast the style of the older paintings with that of the new, talk about their favorite paintings, or recall stories of the gods they particularly enjoy.

Art/Drama Activity: Vase-painting and Myth-playing

Materials

- Several copies of outlines of each of different kinds of Greek jugs (or blank paper for the children to draw their own shapes from copies you provide)
- Black and reddish-brown colored pencils
- Scissors

Have the children assume the role of ancient Greek painters and draw stories of the gods or scenes of Greek life on their jug shapes. Perhaps they would enjoy drawing their favorite parts of the Athena myth they heard at the beginning of the lesson. They will either have red figures on a black ground or the reverse. If their figures are black, they should not make them too dark so that they can draw the interior lines in red. The children may wish to draw decorative borders around the top and/or bottom of their jugs. Have art books available so that the class can view the work of the original Greek painters.

If your students are older or especially capable, they might want to make their own Grecian vases as suggested in Wright's *Greeks* (see References).

Children love enacting Greek myths. I have been especially successful with stories of Athena, Perseus and Medusa, and Persephone. As with the Egyptian dramas, costuming is extremely simple: T-shirts and draped sheets. Enacting Greek myths is especially beneficial for children who might not wish to assume solo parts, since they can be part of a Greek Chorus. The chorus sits off to the side and, speaking together, either warns or encourages the main characters or tells the audience what is happening. For example, in an enactment of Perseus and Medusa, when Perseus is about to slay Medusa, the chorus can chant, "Beware, Perseus. Do not look upon Medusa!"

LESSON 2: Greek Sculpture and Architecture

Viewing the Art

Architecture

Show the children pictures of the three Greek capitals (Doric, Ionic, Corinthian) and show samples of each in Greek buildings. Have the children ever seen copies of these three orders in buildings or homes in their neighborhood? In public buildings? Discuss this and other ideas we have copied from the Greeks. Talk about the construction of the Parthenon by Iktinos and Callicrates and show as many pictures as you can of this marvelous structure. Mention that the triangles formed in the corners of the building by the roof are called pediments and contain scenes in the life of Athena, while circling the top of the building are statues depicting the marvelous procession the people of Athens had every four years in honor of their goddess. If the children were to visit Greece now, they would not see these statues on the Parthenon. In the nineteenth century, Lord Elgin had them moved to England to protect them from damage, and they can now be seen in the British Museum. Show close-ups of these beautiful "Elgin Marbles." Do the children see figures they recognize, such as centaurs?

Sculpture

Show the children early Greek statues of the mid-seventh century B.C. known as *kouroi*, naked male youth possibly representing Apollo, and *korai*, their female counterparts. Note how rigid and Egyptian-like these statues are in contrast to the work of later periods. Do the children notice the mysterious smiles on the faces of these statues?

Later sculptors began to realize that the human body does not always stand at complete attention and that any action such as putting forth a foot affects the muscles and position of other parts of the body. They began to consider how clothing is draped on the body and the shape of the body beneath the clothing. Have the children take various stances. What is the position of their hips when they take a step? What about the muscles in their arms when they reach back to throw something? How does their clothing move when they walk across the room?

Now look for these things in later Greek sculpture. We have no actual statues from this classical period, but there are Roman copies available for viewing. Show Myron's *Discus Thrower*; the revolutionary leaning ("hip-shot") stance in Praxiteles' *Hermes Holding the Child Dionysos* and his *Aphrodite*. Note the Greek emphasis on beauty in the perfect features, like the "Greek nose," which begins from the forehead and is finely shaped. Talk about how Greek sculptors, in their desire to portray perfection, avoided showing flaws like wrinkles or warts or crooked noses. View the work of Phidias, especially his colossal statue of Athena, created for placement in her special temple, the Parthenon.

Journal Writing

What are some of the most important things the children have learned about Greek sculpture and architecture? Which is their favorite statue? Why?

Art/Drama Activity: Athena's Feast Day

Have the children pretend to be ancient Athenians ready to celebrate a feast in honor of their goddess, Athena. They are making preparations for their great procession which takes place every four years. What gifts will they bring to her temple? Perhaps they will write poems in her honor and recite them before her statue. Create music for the occasion. The book *A Greek Temple* (see References) would be very useful in planning this procession.

Curriculum Connections

Social Studies

- Life and history of ancient Greece
- Geography of the Mediterranean region
- Democracy in Athens

Science

- Study the life and achievements of Thales, the first scientist, and Hippocrates, Father of Medicine.
- Research and discuss what the early Greeks knew about astronomy.

Physical Fitness

- Research the first Olympics in Greece in 776 B.C.
- Hold your own Olympic games or a physical fitness class in honor of the ancient Greeks.

Mathematics

- Talk about everyday uses of some of Euclid's geometric principles, such as angles.
- Construct some geometric shapes.
- Use *Number Art* by Micklethwait (in the General Bibliography) to practice making Greek numerals.

Language

- Practice making the letters of the Greek alphabet.

Literature

- Read biographies of famous Greeks. *The Librarian Who Measured the Earth* by Lasky is especially accessible for young readers.

References

Boardman, John, ed. *The Oxford Illustrated History of Classical Art.* New York: Oxford University Press, 1993. Written by different experts, each chapter discusses a different period of ancient Greek and Roman art.

Charbonneaux, Jean, R. Martin, and F. Villard. *Archaic Greek Art.* Transl. by James Emmous and Robert Allen. New York: George Braziller, 1971 o.p. Marvelous discussion and pictures of ancient Greek art from 620–480 B.C.

————. *Hellenistic Art*. Transl. by Peter Green. New York: George Braziller, 1973 o.p. Marvelous discussion and pictures of ancient Greek art after Alexander the Great (330–50 B.C.).

Liberman, Alexander. *Greece, Gods and Art*. New York: Viking, 1968 o.p. A discussion of Greek religious beliefs and their influence on art. Stunning close-up photographs.

Papaioannou, Kostas. *The Art of Greece*. Transl. by I.M. Paris. New York: Harry N. Abrams, 1972. o.p. Covers all the periods of ancient Greek art and includes very large pictures.

Children's Books

Chelepi, Chris. *Growing Up in Ancient Greece*. Illus. by Chris Molan. New York: Troll Associates, 1994. Discussion of various aspects of life in ancient Greece such as shopping, going to school, clothing, and festivals.

Cohen, Daniel. *Ancient Greece*. Illus. by James Seward. New York: Doubleday, 1990 o.p. Easily understood presentation of the major events and prominent figures of ancient Greek history.

Craft, M. Charlotte. *Cupid and Psyche*. Illus. by K. Y. Craft. New York: Morrow Junior Books, 1996. A beautiful picture-book retelling of the Greek myth about the god Cupid who, pierced by his own arrow, falls in love with the beautiful mortal, Psyche.

Fleischman, Paul. *Dateline Troy*. Cambridge, MA: Candlewick Press, 1996. Juxtaposes the legend of Troy with twentieth-century news stories. A tour de force!

Fox, Paula. *Lily and the Lost Boy*. New York: Orchard, 1987. Lily and her brother Paul meet a strange American boy during their family's vacation on the Greek isle of Thasos.

Lasky, Kathryn. *The Librarian Who Measured the Earth*. Illus. by Kevin Hawkes. Boston: Little, Brown, 1994. Describes how Eratosthenes, a Greek astronomer, measured the circumference of the earth.

Loverance, Rowena and Wood. *Ancient Greece*. New York: Viking, 1993. Very attractive presentation of ancient Greek life, complete with see-through overlays.

Macdonald, Fiona. *A Greek Temple*. Illus. by Mark Bergin. New York: Peter Bedrick Books, 1992. Describes the design and construction of the Parthenon and the ancient Greek feasts surrounding the worship of the goddess Athena.

McCaughrean, G., retel. *Greek Myths*. Illus. by Emma Chichester Clark. New York: Margaret McElderry Books, 1992 o.p. Delightful retellings of sixteen well-known Greek myths, accompanied by humorous illustrations.

Powell, Anton. *The Greek World*. New York: Warwick Press, 1987. Thorough but understandable presentation of the different periods of Greek history with a brief look at Greece today. Short bibliography.

Rockwell, Anne. *The One-Eyed Giant and Other Monsters from the Greek Myths*. New York: Greenwillow, 1996. Ten simple retellings of Greek myths featuring fabulous monsters. Delightful illustrations, pronunciation guide, and source notes.

Theule, Frederic. *Alexander and His Times*. New York: Henry Holt, 1995. An entertaining presentation of ancient Greek life, including such topics as food, clothing, wars, art, and religion.

Williams, Marcia. *Greek Myths for Young Children*. Cambridge, MA: Candlewick Press, 1992. Witty retellings of eight myths in this oversize book with illustrations resembling comic strips.

Williams, Susan. *The Greeks*. New York: Thomson Learning, 1993. Discusses ancient Greek life and culture. Includes glossary, important dates, and bibliography.

Wright, Rachel. *Greeks: Facts, Things to Make, Activities*. New York: Franklin Watts, 1992. Craft activities revolving around the lives and beliefs of the ancient Greeks. Glossary and list of some museums containing Greek art.

Audiovisual Materials

Athens and Ancient Greece. Shows daily life and customs of ancient Greece as well as 25 of the most significant buildings. (Videocassette. Available from Questar Video.)

The Greek Miracle. The achievements of classical Greece. (Eight study prints and 20 slides. Available from the National Gallery of Art.)

The Human Figure in Early Greek Art. The evolution of the human figure in Greek sculpture and reliefs of the early classical period. (Audiocassette and 18 slides. Available from the National Gallery of Art.)

Morgan's Adventures in Ancient Greece. Children are transported to ancient Greece where they learn about Greek life, contributions, gods, and the Greek alphabet. Includes a teacher's manual of additional activities and resources. Ages 7–12. (CD-ROM for Mac and Windows. Available from HarperCollins Interactive.)

The Search for Alexander. The life of Alexander the Great. (Audiocassette and 18 slides. Available from the National Gallery of Art.)

4 Ancient Roman Art

"Go, proclaim to the Romans it is heaven's will
that my Rome shall be the capital of the world."
—ROMULUS, legendary founder of Rome
as quoted in *Imperial Rome* by Moses Hadas

Background Information

Rome was founded in 753 B.C., when the various settlements of peoples living in the hill country of Italy united to form a city. Built on seven hills, Rome was originally ruled by a succession of Etruscan kings. By 509 B.C., the people, unhappy with the king's absolute power, established a republic ruled by consuls elected by the people of two political parties: the Patricians, representing the rich, and the Plebians, representing the common folk.

This Republican Age, which lasted until Octavian defeated Mark Antony around 27 B.C., was a time of great expansion under the mighty Roman army, which knew no equal. After three wars with the Phoenicians in Carthage, North Africa, fought over many years, Rome finally destroyed that city in 146 B.C. It was from Carthage that Hannibal crossed the Alps with thousands of men and some elephants to defeat Rome, but he received no help from the surrounding cities who were prospering under Roman rule, and was himself vanquished. Roman armies also conquered Gaul (now France), Macedonia, Greece, and various provinces in Asia Minor.

The Romans learned from and enriched the art and ideas of the peoples they conquered. Fascinated by Greek sculpture, Roman artists made hundreds of copies of these works. But while the Greeks created generalized or idealized portraits in stone, Roman sculptors of this period were able to capture the personalities of their subjects. Often portraits of venerated ancestors, these busts with their wrinkles and crooked noses seemed almost to speak! Romans experimented with Greek architecture as well, using the Greek orders to create temples to their gods, and they began working with a new material called concrete. Wall paintings and mosaics, many of which were recovered in the excavations of Pompeii and

Herculaneum, cities buried in volcanic ash in A.D. 79, adorned the homes of the wealthy and reveal a fine knowledge of anatomy and an attempt to convey depth on a two-dimensional surface. Artists painted pictures of the gods, battles, the occupants of the house, still lifes, and, for the first time, landscapes.

The Republic finally dissolved and the age of the Roman Empire began with the assassination of Julius Caesar and the rise to power of Octavian, (called Augustus), in 27 B.C. For the next five hundred years, Rome was ruled by emperors. "From this point on, Roman art and architecture were to be intimately bound up with propaganda for the state as guided by the imperial family" (Ramage, p. 80). Augustus's reign ushered in a Golden Age similar to that of Pericles in Greece, and he initiated an ambitious building program. The emperors who followed Augustus continued to use the arts to proclaim their own accomplishments and to win the support of the people. The Romans' skill with concrete and their perfection of the use of the arch enabled them to erect massive arenas for the sports and games the populace loved so well; public buildings in the heart of the city, known as the Forum; temples to the gods; and aqueducts, theaters, and bath houses. Roman architects developed the basilica, a rectangular, covered building of many uses. To rid the city of the spectacle of the emperor Nero's "House of Gold" in the midst of Rome's poor housing, his successor, Vespasian, built the Colosseum on its site. Infamous for the bloody gladiator fights and animal hunts that took place there, the Colosseum even today is an imposing edifice in the city of Rome.

The emperor Hadrian built the Pantheon, a beautiful temple perfectly preserved to this day, to honor all the Roman gods. A round building surmounted by a dome, the Pantheon's height equals its diameter. The Romans—unlike the Greeks, whose temples were meant to be seen only from the outside—paid great attention to interiors, and the interior of the Pantheon with its golden dome is magnificent. Roman reliefs on triumphal arches and especially the column of the emperor Trajan, under whom Rome achieved her greatest expansion, told the stories of their namesakes' victories.

Many emperors ruled Rome, some of them well and for long periods of time, and some of them badly or for only six months. In A.D. 330 Constantine transferred his palace to Constantinople, in what is now Turkey, and after the reign of Emperor Theodosius I, the empire was ruled by two separate emperors, one in Rome and the other in Constantinople. With its power divided and its empire far flung, Rome could no longer govern or defend itself and eventually fell victim to the attacks of barbarians from Russia and Hungary.

The Roman Empire ceased to exist in A.D. 476, but its influence continues to our own day. Our alphabet is Roman, and over 60 percent of our words come from Latin, the language spoken by the ancient Romans. We use the calendar devised by Julius Caesar. Roman numerals play an important part in our documentation. Our system of law, trial by jury, and republican form of government come from Roman traditions. Ancient Rome has given us such wonderful writers as Virgil, Horace, and Cicero. We look to Rome for its marvelous feats of engineering, its development of the arch, its massive structures made possible by the use of concrete. Truly, "All roads lead to Rome!"

❏ The Story

It was August 24 in the year A.D. 79 in the Roman city of Pompeii in Italy. (Show it on a map.) And it was hot—very hot. Ten-year-old Marcus was not anxious to get out of his bed, and the slave who came to his door with water for washing had to coax the sleepyhead to start moving. Father would be offering an early morning sacrifice in just a few minutes, and Marcus had to be ready. The boy stretched, splashed some water on his face, pulled a fresh tunic over his head, and left his bedroom. He went out into the atrium, a courtyard inside his home where there was a hole in the roof so light and air could come in. A small pool in the center captured the rainwater. Marcus took a few deep breaths of the early morning air and looked fondly at several portrait statues of his ancestors placed around the room. Then he went to join his parents and older sister before the shrine of the household gods.

"Bless this house. Protect all its people and let no harm come to anyone this day," prayed Marcus's father as he lit the incense before the shrine. After the short service, Marcus and his father left the house and headed for the Forum, the business center of the busy city. There Marcus was planning to watch the trials in the basilica and speak on behalf of a man accused of stealing. The more practice he got speaking in public, the more fit he would be to serve in the government when he grew to be a man. On the way, they passed some merchants opening their shops. Some were selling wine. Others were selling meat. The bakers had already prepared their dough, and the delicious smell of bread baking in the huge round ovens reached Marcus's nostrils. It made him hungry, and he looked forward to having a meal later in the day and a refreshing bath at the public bath house.

Just as they were coming within sight of the Forum, the earth began to shake and they heard a tremendous roar. Marcus began to scream in terror. The sky darkened and black ash began to fall everywhere. Marcus put his hand over his face to try to protect himself from the ash and fumes all around him, while his father picked him up and started racing back to the house. "We have to get your mother and sister and the servants out," he cried. Hundreds of people all around them were running, too. Bakers left their bread in their ovens and fled into the streets. Wool dyers left their cloth in the dying vats. Shopkeepers left their food on the shelves and didn't even bother to lock up. Everyone was looking for a safe place to escape the lava and ash spouting from the nearby volcano, Mt. Vesuvius.

When Marcus and his father finally fought through the crowd and reached their home, they found everyone in the household huddled in the cellar. "You'll be buried alive down there! Come, get the horses and wagons quickly!" cried Marcus's father. The servants ran to do his bidding, and in less than a few minutes everyone had climbed into wagons and was heading out of town. They passed neighbors on foot clutching the few valuables they could lay their hands on. Ash rained down so hard that it seemed black as night even though it was still early in the morning. The ash became so thick and heavy that it caved in roofs and piled deeper and deeper in the streets. It became harder and harder for the horses to pull the wagons through it. But Marcus and his family were among the lucky ones. They had enough money to have wagons and horses, so they were able to get out of Pompeii in time. They rode and rode until they had gone far enough to escape the falling ash and lava. As soon as they reached safety, Marcus and his family gave thanks to the gods for their protection.

But thousands of people weren't so lucky. Some were greedy and stayed behind too long trying to collect jewelry and other valuable things to take with them. Others couldn't run fast enough and were buried in the ash. Others choked to death on the poisonous fumes seeping out of the earth. Still others made the mistake of seeking shelter in their cellars and were buried there.

Marcus and his family never did go back to Pompeii to live. They never saw their house or the buildings and temples they loved again. The entire city and even a city nearby called Herculaneum were buried by the ash from the volcano. And believe it or not, they stayed buried for more than 1,500 years! Then, one day in 1594, a man named Count Muzzio Tuttavilla wanted to get water from the river to water his land. When he began to dig a tunnel, he cut right through the hidden city of Pompeii. It wasn't until two hundred years later that archaeologists began to dig carefully in the area and to uncover the lost city. What they found was simply amazing. The ash and lava had preserved many things just as they were. The archaeologists actually found bread still in the ovens. In the cellars they found the skeletons of people who had tried to escape. And they found jewelry and marvelous art works—wall paintings and mosaics in the homes of the rich, the Forum where Marcus and his father were heading on that terrible morning, temples, shops, public bath houses, theaters.

All the things the scientists found in Pompeii help us to know how the ancient Romans lived 2,000 years ago! The Romans had builders, architects, sculptors, painters, and makers of mosaics. They gave us ideas about making laws and deciding whether people are guilty or innocent of committing crimes. They showed us how to use concrete and a very special architectural form called an arch for large buildings. They even gave us our calendar and our alphabet! We're going to look at some pictures of ancient Roman artwork and building now. Some of the art I'm going to show you was found in the buried city of Pompeii, and you can see the original work in the uncovered city yourself if you travel to Italy some day.

LESSON 1: Roman Engineering and Sculpture

Viewing the Art

Begin by mentioning that the Romans copied many artistic ideas from the Greeks, whose country they conquered with their mighty army. But the Romans had some ideas of their own as well. Discuss the Romans' engineering genius, emphasizing their use of concrete and their development of the arch, which enabled them to build structures several stories high. Ask the children to hold their arms over their heads in the shape of a Roman arch so that they can experience its shape with their bodies. Using blocks, construct a simple arch. Then press down on it: The arch can withstand a great deal of weight and pressure. But push it sideways, and the arch tumbles over. The Romans solved this problem by covering their structures with a strong material called concrete and then putting a layer of stone or marble over them to make them look beautiful.

Show several pictures of structures that make use of the arch, especially the aqueduct Pont du Gard in Provence and explain the use of the aqueduct and what an incredible feat it was to span such vast distances. Show the Colosseum, triumphal arches, and a Roman theater as well. Discuss the purpose of the Colosseum. What similar structures do we have today (baseball and football stadiums)? Do the children have any arches in their own homes (over doorways, for example) or have they seen arches in churches or other public buildings? Show Roman temples and talk about the similarity of Roman and Greek gods. What ideas did the Romans copy from the Greeks in building their temples? Show the Pantheon and talk about its dimensions and its interior—a point of departure from the Greeks. Talk about the marvel of creating a dome, which is really a series of arches, that could enclose such a large space and how church builders in years to come would learn how to do this by studying Roman art. Depending upon the children's interest, show pictures of Roman baths and talk about the buildings in the Roman Forum.

Romans honored their ancestors by having busts of them made for display in their homes. Show the children some Roman busts. How do they differ from Greek statues? The Romans told their heroes' stories in relief sculptures. Show the class pictures of the magnificent Column of Trajan (see Ramage, *Roman Art*, for excellent detail prints), on which Roman sculptors carved the tale of their emperor's deeds.

Journal Writing

What are some differences between Greek and Roman sculpture and architecture? Some similarities? Do the children prefer the more realistic Roman busts to

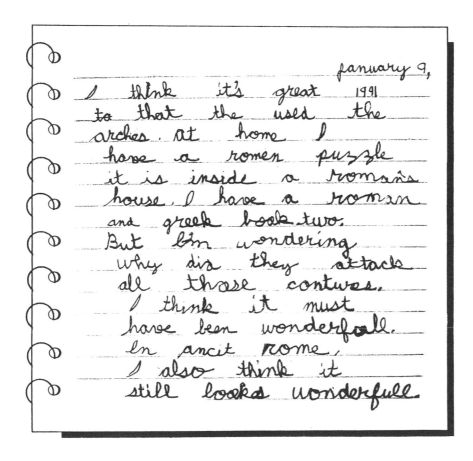

the idealistic statues of the Greeks? Why or why not? If they were having their own portrait done, which would they prefer? In what ways have the children seen arches used even today?

Art/Drama Activity: Trajan's Column

Materials

- Three or four sheets of poster board rolled and taped to form a column (wider at bottom, narrower at top)
- Strips of paper about six inches high and long enough to go around the column (these will be of different lengths, as the column decreases in width)
- Pencils

Divide the children into groups and have them create a column similar to Trajan's that tells the story of their class, or their school, or their town, if they prefer. Discuss the different things they would like their column to say. For example, if it is to represent their class, some ideas might be: depicting students doing various academic tasks such as reading or working on a science experiment; taking care of a class pet; planting a garden; playing at recess and/or sports; singing or playing instruments; doing artwork, etc. Give each group a strip of paper and have the children work together to create scenes around one of the topics agreed upon. When the groups have finished their work, tape the various strips around the column and display it in the room.

LESSON 2: Roman Wall Painting and Mosaics

Viewing the Art

We know a great deal about Roman painting and mosaics because of the art found in a wonderful state of preservation in Pompeii and Herculaneum. Many of the rich commissioned artists to fill their walls with paintings. Often their floors were covered with beautiful mosaics. Public buildings such as the baths also contained such artwork. Show the children examples of both. (See especially Feder, *Great Treasures of Pompeii & Herculaneum*.) Be sure to include some from the House of the Fawn, the Villa of the Mysteries, and the House of the Vettii, all in Pompeii. What colors are most often used by the Roman artists? Can the children describe how mosaics are made? What are the subjects of the paintings and mosaics?

Journal Writing

What have the children learned about Roman painting and mosaics? Have they seen mosaics in use today? If so, where? What are some things they notice about Roman wall paintings? How do the Roman paintings compare to the Greek pottery paintings?

Art/Drama Activity: Mosaics

Materials

- Large sheets of white paper
- Package of colored construction paper cut up beforehand into hundreds of small shapes
- Paste or glue

Have the children pretend they are Roman artists commissioned by a rich person to make a mosaic for a dining room floor. They must submit a copy of their picture or design for approval. Give each child a large piece of white paper, a pile of colored shapes, and a dollop of glue or paste on a piece of scrap paper. Have them work individually to create a mosaic. Make sure they understand that there should be a tiny white space between the pieces of colored paper and that they should use only the merest speck of glue or it will ooze out all over their paper. It helps to have a sample to show the children before they begin.

Curriculum Connections

Social Studies

- The history and customs of ancient Rome
- Foods and recipes of ancient Rome
- Geography of Roman conquests
- Farming and farm implements

Science

- The creation of the Roman calendar

Mathematics

- Roman numerals (see *Number Art* by Micklethwait in the General Bibliography)

Physical Fitness

- Learn about the games Roman children played
- Study Roman sports such as chariot racing, gladiator combat

Literature

- Find quotes from famous Roman poets and orators and copy them for display around the room.
- Read biographies of famous Romans and emperors.
- Make a game similar to Concentration in which you write the person's name on one card and a sentence describing something the person did on another. Players have to match the cards correctly.

References

Becatti, Giovanni. *The Art of Ancient Greece and Rome.* New York: Harry N. Abrams, 1967 o.p. Wonderful source of large reproductions.

Feder, Theodore H. *Great Treasures of Pompeii & Herculaneum.* New York: Abbeville Press, 1978 o.p. Exquisite large color reproductions of the paintings and mosaics found in these two cities.

Ramage, Nancy H., and Andrew Ramage. *Roman Art: Romulus to Constantine.* New York: Harry N. Abrams, 1991 o.p. Presents Roman art spanning 1,300 years. Very useful illustrations.

Children's Books

Avi-Yonah, Michael. *Piece by Piece! Mosaics of the Ancient World.* Minneapolis, MN: Runestone Press, 1993. Describes different mosaic techniques in the ancient and modern world including mosaics of Greece and Rome.

Baxter, Nicola. *Romans.* New York: Franklin Watts, 1992. Suggestions for crafts and activities related to the life and history of ancient Romans.

Bernard, Charlotte. *Caesar and Rome.* New York: Henry Holt, 1995. A delightful look at ancient Rome, including the life of a Roman soldier, fashions, government, the life of a slave, etc.

Clare, John D., ed. *Classical Rome.* San Diego, CA: Gulliver Books, 1993. Photographs featuring modern-day actors depict life in ancient Rome.

Connolly, Peter. *The Cavalryman.* New York: Oxford University Press, 1988 o.p. Describes the life of cavalryman Tiberius Claudius Maximus, whose tomb was found in northern Greece in 1965.

———. *Pompeii.* New York: Oxford University Press, 1990. Detailed drawings of such things as baths, theaters, and temples help students understand daily life in Pompeii in the first century.

Corbishley, Mike. *Ancient Rome.* New York: Facts on File, 1989. An atlas history of Rome that enables children to see where events took place.

———. *Growing Up in Ancient Rome.* Illus. by Chris Molan. New York: Troll Associates, 1993.

Presents different aspects of life in ancient Rome including going to school and getting married.

Goor, Ron, and Nancy Goor. *Pompeii: Exploring a Roman Ghost Town*. New York: Thomas Y. Crowell, 1986. Explores life in the ancient city. Even contains a recipe for garum, a fish sauce for which Pompeii was famous.

Guittard, Charles. *The Romans: Life in the Empire*. Transl. by Mary Kae LaRose. Illus. by Annie-Claude Martin. Brookfield, CT: Millbrook Press, 1992. Describes the creation of the Roman Empire and discusses such topics as table manners, travel, and entertainment. Dates to remember, glossary.

Hadas, Moses. *Imperial Rome*. New York: Time-Life, 1965 o.p. Explores the civilization of ancient Rome.

Hicks, Peter. *The Romans*. New York: Thomson Learning, 1993. Fairly simple presentation of the culture and history of ancient Rome.

James, Simon. *Ancient Rome*. New York: Viking, 1992. Presents life in ancient Rome. Transparent overlays help readers see into a variety of Roman buildings.

Morley, Jacqueline, and John James. *A Roman Villa*. New York: Peter Bedrick Books, 1992. Very readable account of life in a wealthy person's villa outside Rome. Includes time chart and glossary.

Odijk, Pamela. *The Romans*. New York: Silver Burdett, 1989. Civilization of ancient Rome, including such topics as medicine, clothing, and laws. Contains time lines, glossary, and short biographies of famous emperors.

Sabuda, Robert. *Saint Valentine*. New York: Atheneum, 1992. A simple biography of Valentine, a Roman physician who lived in the third century A.D. Exquisite mosaic illustrations by the author.

Seidelman, James E., and Grace Mintonye. *Creating Mosaics*. Illus. by Harriet Sherman. New York: Macmillan, 1967 o.p. Instructions for creating a variety of mosaics from different materials.

Audiovisual Materials

Roman City. Examines how the Roman Empire linked Western Europe, the Middle East, and North Africa. Based on David Macaulay's book. Uses animation and live footage. (Videocassette; 60 mins. Available from Library Video Company.)

Rome & Pompeii. Depicts ancient Roman life in these two cities. (Videocassette; 60 mins. Available from Questar Video.)

Other Materials

Roman Arch Block Set. Helps children understand how an arch stays up by enabling them to construct a Roman arch with this set of wooden blocks. (Available from the Metropolitan Museum of Art New York.)

Part II
Arts of the
East and Africa

5 The Art of China

"Human eyes are limited in their scope.
Hence, they are not able to perceive all that is to be seen;
Yet with one small brush I can draw the universe."
—WANG WEI, painter, in *Treasures of China* by Annette Juliano

Background Information

The Chinese civilization is one of the oldest on earth. The ancient Chinese were, in many ways, centuries ahead of the rest of the world. They invented paper and printing long before Gutenberg developed his movable type. They used herbs and acupuncture to treat illnesses. By the end of the Han dynasty (A.D. 220), the Chinese were able to measure earthquakes and had come to the conclusion that a year was about 365 days long. They had accurate measuring tools and farm implements that were superior to those in the West.

While humans began populating China as early as half a million years ago, the first period in recorded history was that of the Shang dynasty in 1500 B.C. During this dynasty, or period ruled by one family, the Chinese developed a system of writing, begun as questions carved on bones. Many years later, Chinese writing would become standardized, which enabled the Chinese to maintain unity and continuity in a vast country inhabited by people who spoke numerous dialects. The actual formation of the characters of Chinese writing became prized as an art form in itself, called calligraphy. Chinese paintings were often accompanied by characters drawn in calligraphy, and works of literature were valued as much for the care with which the characters were set down as by the content of the pieces. It was during the Shang dynasty as well that the Chinese developed bronze, a mixture of copper and tin, and their bronze figures, made in molds, are lovely works of art. Many bronze and pottery models of ritual vessels, furniture, farms, houses, servants, and animals were buried with the dead, for the Chinese, like the Egyptians, believed that the dead person would need them in the afterlife. Archaeological digs have uncovered exquisite bronze and pottery pieces.

Jade, prized by the Chinese even above gold, appeared in Neolithic times

52

and continues to hold a special place in their art up to the present day. First used in the making of tools, jade became a favorite material for creating ornaments such as jewelry and figurines. Because of its hardness it is difficult to carve, and jewelry pieces are often formed by constant rubbing and polishing.

The first Zhou king overthrew the Shang dynasty around 1027 B.C., ushering in the longest period of dynastic rule in Chinese history. During this feudal period, the iron and salt industries developed, and the Chinese began to use lacquer, made from the sap of a tree, to coat their art works. Even the lacquer itself, hardened when exposed to air, was carved and decorated with paint. Ancient lacquer-coated objects, unearthed by archaeologists, are as brilliant today as when they were first created. Two of the greatest Chinese philosophers, Confucius and Lao-tze, were born during the Zhou dynasty.

In 221 B.C., Ying Zheng, the king of the feudal state of Qin, conquered the neighboring states, united them into the first Chinese empire, and declared himself the first emperor. Using half a million workers, he built the Great Wall of China to protect the empire from the hordes of nomads to the north. He used even more workers to construct an elaborate tomb for himself, complete with a terra cotta army of thousands of life-sized soldiers to protect him in the afterlife. The terra cotta army was unearthed by farmers digging a well in a field in 1974, and new treasures are continually being excavated from the site, although Zheng's actual burial chamber has yet to be found.

The short-lived Qin empire gave way to the Han dynasty in 206 B.C. A civil bureaucracy grew up during this time, and the creation of civil service exams led to the development of an elite educated class that ruled the country. For centuries one of the few peoples who knew how to raise silkworms, the Chinese developed a bustling silk trade during this period. In A.D. 220, central authority gave way to three kingdoms: Wu, Wei, and Shu. These then split into the northern and southern kingdoms, with one dynasty after another coming into power, until the country was reunited under the Sui dynasty in A.D. 581. Buddhism as a religion took firm hold among the people, and many Buddhist sculptures and temples appeared. Wall paintings in palaces, tombs, and temples began to flourish at this time.

The Tang dynasty, one of China's most glorious eras, began in A.D. 618. Comparable to the Golden Age of Athens, it is the era of great works of art. During this period, the empress Wu Hou, while treating her competitors cruelly and even murdering her own daughter, generously supported the arts. Although the Chinese had been working in pottery since prehistoric times, it was during the Tang dynasty that they developed porcelain by combining kaolin, a fine white clay, with feldspar, a crystalline rock. The famous Blue-and-White porcelain dates from the early Tang dynasty. Chinese porcelain figures and bowls eventually became so famous that their name has become synonymous with fine tableware—china. Increased production of silk and paper contributed to the development of painting and the rise of landscape artists like Wang Wei.

The Tang dynasty collapsed in 907, and after a series of dynasties, the Song emperors reigned in the south. Under them, art became softer, more delicate, and rendered in more muted tones, and painting flourished as an art in itself rather than a means of decoration. The Mongol leader Khublai Khan defeated the Songs, taking the dynastic name Yuan. It is to Khan's court that the Venetian trader Marco Polo made his historic visit, linking East and West for the first time.

In 1368, a monk named Chu Yuan-chang drove the Yuan dynasty out of Peking and became the first Ming emperor. China turned inward in rebellion against foreign influences and, like the Renaissance artists in the West, looked back to ancient art for inspiration. Sixteen Ming dynasties ruled until 1644, when the Manchu or Qing dynasty took over. The Qing dynasty lasted 268 years, until 1912, when a period of unrest began until World War II, and the Communists gained control of the country. In all that time—almost 600 years—it was the art and thought of the ancients that held sway. China's worship of ancestors; her Great Wall, which locked traditions in and foreigners out; her symmetrical Forbidden City with its unchanging Imperial Palace as home of an emperor whose task it was to maintain harmony between his people and all of nature; her temples to Confucius and Buddha—all of these reflect China's everlasting link to her past. All of them have spawned China's art: masterpieces of pottery and bronze buried with the dead; figures of porcelain, lacquer, jade, and ivory; palaces and temples with their distinctive sloping roofs; and exquisitely delicate paintings and calligraphy.

❑ The Story

The emperor of China had a pet nightingale. After a long day governing his kingdom, he loved to listen to it sing in the evening The people called the emperor the Son of Heaven, for he was their bridge between earth and heaven. It was his job to preserve harmony among his people and all of the earth, to keep drought and famine and war from them. All day long he listened to the reports of his ministers, judged disputes, made decisions. It was exhausting work! No wonder, then, that he prized his gentle, sweet-singing nightingale above all his possessions.

"What would I do without the soothing song of my nightingale?" he thought as his servant brought the bird in her gilded cage to him. The more the emperor considered his nightingale, the more he loved her and wanted to show others what a marvelous creature she was. So one day he issued a decree to all the painters in his kingdom. "I wish to have a painting of a nightingale to place in the main hall of the palace. Whoever of you paints the most perfect picture of this glorious creature within one year's time will be declared official artist to the emperor and rewarded with a fine silk robe embedded with jewels."

You can imagine that when they heard this news, all the artists of the kingdom were very excited, for each hoped he would be the one appointed artist to the emperor. They spent hours studying nightingales. They viewed nightingales sitting on tree branches, nightingales in cages, nightingales flying through the sky, nightingales singing, nightingales sleeping. Day and night they practiced their brush strokes, searching for the perfect line, the perfect shape, the perfect proportion to create a bird to the emperor's liking.

There was activity everywhere—except on the work table of one artist. Oh, his helpers were working. They showed their master pictures of nightingales. They captured nightingales and brought them as models for their master to paint. They talked about the shape of a nightingale's body, the color of its feathers, the length of its beak. But the master never picked up his brush. After six months had gone by like this, his helpers began to worry and to question their master.

"Sir," they said, "time is passing swiftly while you sit here idly. Are you ill? Is there any way we can help you that we have not already considered? Perhaps we should fashion new brushes for you out of the finest animal hair and wood. Shall we get you new inks?"

But the master painter assured them all was well, and he continued to sit quietly at his work table day after day. No ink touched paper or silk scroll. And the helpers waited, growing more impatient with every passing day. When the master's work table remained empty even through the last month of the contest, his helpers spoke out again. "Master, there are but a few weeks remaining. Would you like one of us to try a painting in your name?"

But the master painter replied, "There is still much time left. When the hour is upon us, the emperor will have his painting." So they continued to wait, trying not to show him how uneasy they were, for he was a kind and thoughtful master and they did not wish to show distrust.

Finally, on the morning all the artists were due at the palace, the master painter bathed in water scented with sweet lotus blossoms. He put on his finest robe and smoothed his topknot. At last he sat at his work table, and with a few strokes of his brush, painted a nightingale. Before the ink was hardly dry on the page, he left for the palace accompanied by two of his helpers.

When they arrived, the palace guards placed them in a large room where they waited with all the other artists to appear before the emperor. Each painter kept his painting rolled in a long scroll, to be revealed before the eyes of the emperor alone. One after the other the artists went into the throne room, but each one came out as quickly as the last. None of their paintings had been found pleasing. At last, the master artist appeared before his ruler and slowly unrolled his scroll. There on the paper was the most perfect of all nightingales. The emperor was stunned into silence. The two helpers could hardly believe their eyes.

"This is the finest painting I have ever seen!" exclaimed the emperor. "From this moment forward, you are appointed special painter to the emperor." Then, turning to his servants, he said, "Come, bring the ceremonial robe here." And he placed the robe over the artist's own garments and bade him go home to pack his belongings so that he could move into the palace. Bowing low, the delighted painter and his helpers left.

While they walked back, the two helpers questioned their master. "Surely, sir, you painted that bird long ago after many attempts and kept it hidden to surprise us. No one could have painted such a perfect picture in so brief a time." And the master replied, "Of course I did not just paint the nightingale in the moments before we left for the palace. I have been painting it in my mind all year. I have been studying nightingales—their song, their flight. I have seen nightingales in my sleeping, in my waking, in my eating. The few strokes I put on the paper today are the result of my working hard all year long, of my finally being one with the nightingale so that I could imagine it as perfectly as it is in nature."

The artist's fame spread throughout the kingdom from that day on, and when he came to live in the emperor's palace and to paint pictures there, the emperor learned never to scold him for appearing lazy, but to wait for the artist to become one with his subject.

We are going to study the work of Chinese artists who believed that there is a harmony, a oneness, between people and nature. We will try to discover that harmony as we view their work. Like the artist in our story, these artists did not paint with an object in front of them but held a picture of the object in their heads. Then they painted quickly, using ink which could not be erased, so they had to be quite sure of their subject before they began.

LESSON 1: Chinese Painting

Viewing the Art

Try to show examples of the three kinds of Chinese painting: figures, landscapes, and birds and flowers. (Painting on vases, bowls, etc., is the subject of the following lesson.) Many Chinese paintings were done on silk or paper scrolls. The earliest painter to whom specific works can be attributed is Gu Kaizhi of the fourth century. Show his *Nymph of the Lo River* and *Admonitions of the Instructress to the Court Ladies*. The children might also enjoy Wu Tsung-yuan's *Procession of Taoist Immortals to Pay Homage to the King of Heaven, Duke Wen of Chin Recovering His State* by Li Tang, and *Eighteen Songs of a Nomad Flute* by an unknown artist.

After viewing several landscape paintings with the children, ask them what they see in almost every painting. They should notice mountains and water. Tell them that the Chinese word for landscape means "mountain water" pictures. The Chinese painter does not try to paint an actual scene as a Western painter might. Rather, the painter works from memory and is more interested in depicting the forms of things. Observe the minimal use of color in these paintings. Finally, show some scenes of flowers, birds, and other animals. What kinds of animals appear in the paintings? Observe how some paintings have fine delicate lines while others consist of broad, smudged brush strokes.

While you view the different types of paintings, point out that Chinese characters often appear on them, for calligraphy is directly related to painting. Both use a brush, require prior contemplation, and are done quickly. Often the characters on a painting are a poem related to the scene depicted. The Chinese have thousands of characters, and the art of calligraphy is an exacting one. The children might enjoy this admonition from the calligrapher Wang Hse-chih to his pupils:

> The shape of the character should not be too wide at the top [nor] too narrow at the base. The strokes should not be crowded together or the character will look as though it is plagued by a hundred ailments. The strokes should not be too elongated or it will look like a dead snake hanging from a tree. It should not be too squat or it will look like a frog floating on a pond. (Froncek, p. 120).

Wan-go Weng's *Chinese Painting and Calligraphy* (see References) has wonderful reproductions to use with this lesson.

Journal Writing

Of the three kinds of paintings viewed, which did the children like best and why? What did the children learn about observation from the Chinese artist? Encourage the children to write about the Chinese method of contemplating the subject beforehand and then painting from memory to capture the essence of the thing. Have they ever studied anything for a long period of time in order to be able to picture it in their heads? Would they like to try? What advantages do they think this would have over copying the object as it appears before them?

Art/Drama Activity: Chinese Painting

Materials

- Thin brushes
- Black ink (if you are concerned that the ink will stain clothing, substitute watered-down black tempera paint)
- Long pieces of paper that can be rolled horizontally into scrolls
- Newspaper to cover work surfaces
- Books containing scenes of mountains, water, birds, and flowers (if it is not possible to view these outdoors)
- Examples of Chinese characters (if children are interested in trying to draw them)

While Chinese figure painting may be too difficult for the children, they can probably succeed very well with the other subjects in this lesson. Give them a choice of painting a landscape, a bird, or a flower/plant. If weather permits, take the class outdoors and invite them to choose a scene, a bird, a flower to study intensely and silently. Give them as much time to do this as possible. How many ways can they see the object they are viewing: its size, shape, weight, color? If it is not possible to go outside, provide books for the children to study. After they have studied their subject sufficiently, invite them to paint it from memory on the paper provided. Talk about the experience after the children have finished their painting. What was it like trying to capture an object in their minds and put it on paper? How was the experience different from the times they copied an image onto paper?

In another lesson, the children might wish to learn the Chinese characters for bird, flower, etc., and to add those characters to their scroll.

LESSON 2: Chinese Porcelain

Viewing the Art

Explain to the children that the Chinese made pottery from the very earliest times, in the Neolithic era (5000–2000 B.C.), and that many marvelous pieces have been found in tombs uncovered by archaeologists. Then gradually they began to develop a new kind of ceramic called porcelain, 700 years before Europeans figured out how to do so. Porcelain is made by combining kaolin, a fine white clay, with feldspar, a crystalline rock. It is shaped on a potter's wheel and then fired at very high temperatures. It can be very thin, as in delicate cups and dishes, and you can actually see through many of the pieces when they are held up to the light. But it is really quite strong, and very beautiful.

The Chinese formed statues, vases, and dishes from porcelain. Through the centuries, they experimented with many styles and glazes, reaching a height of production and perfection during the Ming dynasty (1368–1644). During that time, porcelains reached enormous proportions and included huge vases five and six feet high, large dishes, and tall statues. Probably among the best known are the blue-and-white porcelain patterns, called simply Blue-and-White. During this time, the Chinese discovered a fine white clay that did not have a grayish tinge as the clay they had formerly been using did, and this made all the difference. To make Blue-and-Whites, the Chinese artists painted designs in blue, made from expensive cobalt, on their unfired pieces of white clay. Sometimes they even carved flowers and designs in paste and stuck them onto the figures. Then they covered them with a glaze that was almost colorless and resulted in a shiny, smooth appearance, and fired them in ovens reaching more than 1250 degrees centigrade. Many European countries, such as Holland with its Delft, have imitated these Blue-and-Whites. Show as many of these as you can. (See several exquisite examples in Weng and Boda, *The Palace Museum: Peking*).

Also show porcelains of different glazes. Ask the children to note the patterns painted on the porcelain. What kinds of borders do the plates have (often intertwining leaves and flowers)? What are the subjects painted on the pieces (birds, fish, dragons, flowers, water plants)? A trip to a museum to see some porcelain pieces first-hand would be an excellent way to truly appreciate their beauty.

Journal Writing

If the children have had an opportunity to visit a museum, encourage them to write about the experience. Otherwise, ask them to respond from their experience of the art in books. Which pieces did they like best and why? What figures did the Chinese artists paint on their pieces? What might some of these figures mean to the Chinese?

Art/Drama Activity: Pottery Design

Materials

- Paper
- Blue paint or colored pencils
- Brushes
- Newspapers to cover work surfaces

The Chinese prized porcelain, and during the Ming dynasty, when porcelain pieces proliferated, everyone used it. Chinese emperors collected porcelain pieces:

> In the year 1544 . . . . the imperial household alone ordered 26,350 bowls with 30,500 saucers to match, 6,000 ewers with 6,900 wine cups, 680 large garden fish bowls, and 1,340 table services of 27 pieces each. (Burling, p. 153)

Have the children pretend that they work for a famous potter, and the master has just received an enormous order from the emperor. Their job is to design a set of Blue-and-White tableware for the emperor's household. What design will go around the border of the plates? What figures will be painted on the porcelain? Have them work in groups or alone to design a pattern, being faithful to the types of figures found on Chinese porcelain: dragons, birds, flowers, etc. When the children have finished, either discuss which design they like best, or allow them to decide to make the dishes in several different patterns.

Curriculum Connections

Social Studies

- Study the history and culture of China.
- Geography: Find China on a world map. Then use a map of China to locate principal cities.
- Research the Great Wall of China, the only structure on Earth visible to astronauts in space. Why and how was it built?
- Discuss Chinese government today and Communist rule.
- Talk about Chinese customs and clothing.
- Discuss some broad principles of Confucianism and Buddhism.
- Study Chinese farming methods, tools, and crops.
- Discuss Chinese food and prepare a Chinese feast.
- Invite a parent or other speaker of Chinese origin to talk to the class.

Mathematics

- Learn to count from one to ten in Chinese. Learn to write some of the numbers in Chinese characters. (See *Number Art* by Lucy Micklethwait in the General Bibliography.)
- Demonstrate the use of the abacus. Students may enjoy making their own.

Science

- Discuss acupuncture and its uses.

- Study plants and animals native to China. Students may particularly enjoy learning more about the panda. Read *The Year of the Panda* by Miriam Schlein, listed above.

- Study Chinese inventions, such as paper and a system of printing, gunpowder and fireworks.

- Why is the Chinese calendar and celebration of the New Year different from that in the West? Investigate the names for the different years such as Year of the Lion, etc. Where do they come from? What do they mean?

- Study the growth and care of silkworms and their contribution to Chinese life and economy. Use *The Silk Route* by John S. Major (see References) to discuss the production and trade of silk.

- Study the contributions of archaeology in revealing information about the ancient Chinese. Children might enjoy reading *The Terra Cotta Army of Emperor Qin* by Caroline Lazo (see References).

Language Arts

- Read some Chinese poetry. Use *Maples in the Mist* by Ho Minfong (see References). Encourage the children to write poems to accompany some of the paintings viewed during the art lesson or the paintings they made during the art activity.

- Study Chinese characters and practice making them.

- Read biographies of famous Chinese such as Confucius. Read *A Young Painter* by Zheng Zhensun and Alice Low (see References).

- Read some Chinese folktales. Several are listed in the References, and many more are available. The children may wish to dramatize one or more of them or learn to tell them for a storytelling event.

Music

- Listen to Chinese music. How is it different from what the children are used to hearing? What instruments are particular to China?

Artists

• Visit a potter at work.

References

Barnhart, Richard M. *Along the Border of Heaven*. New York: Metropolitan Museum of Art, 1983 o.p. Excellent source of large reproductions suitable for viewing the different kinds of Chinese painting. Accompanied by poetry and sayings.

Choy, Rita Mei-wah. *Understanding Chinese*. San Francisco, CA: China West Books, 1989. A guide to the usage of Chinese characters.

Fazzioli, Edwardo. *Chinese Calligraphy*. New York: Abbeville Press, 1987. Explanations of and step-by-step guide for forming 214 essential Chinese characters.

Fong, Wen C., and James C. Y. Watt. *Possessing the Past: Treasures from the National Palace Museum, Taipei*. New York: Harry N. Abrams, 1996. Issued in conjunction with the exhibition of Chinese art at the New York Metropolitan Museum of Art in 1996, this huge book contains essays and beautiful color reproductions of Chinese art treasures, including many porcelains and paintings.

Hibbert, Christopher. *The Emperors of China*. Chicago: Stonehenge Press, 1981 o.p. Source of large beautiful colored pictures of Chinese art, including porcelains and paintings.

Juliano, Annette. *Treasures of China*. New York: Richard Marek, 1981 o.p. A discussion of China's art and thought as seen through her walls, gardens, temples, tombs, and art treasures.

Kerry, Rose, ed. *Chinese Art and Design: Art Objects in Ritual and Daily Life*. New York: Viking, 1992. Full-page photos of nearly 7,000 years of sculpture, ceramics, painting and weaving, including objects made of porcelain, jade, lacquer, and silk.

Kleiner, Robert L. *Chinese Snuff Bottles*. New York: Oxford University Press, 1994. Illustrations of various kinds of snuff bottles.

Kwo Da-wei. *Chinese Brushwork*. Montclair, NJ: Allanheld & Schram, 1981. The history, esthetics, and techniques of Chinese brushwork accompanied by examples.

Loehr, Max. *The Great Painters of China*. New York: Harper & Row, 1980 o.p. Master painters of the different periods of Chinese history. Examples of the three categories of painting mentioned in the viewing section.

Miyagawa, Torao. *Chinese Painting*. Transl. by Alfred T. Birnbaum. New York: Weatherhill, 1984. Chinese painting up to the Qing dynasty. Some large color reproductions.

Rawson, Jessica, Ann Farrer, Jane Portal, Shelagh Vainker, and Carol Michaelson. *The British Museum Book of Chinese Art*. New York: Thames and Hudson, 1993. Explanations of various kinds of Chinese art, including excellent chapters on ceramics, calligraphy, and painting.

Sullivan, Michael. *The Three Perfections: Chinese Painting, Poetry and Calligraphy*. New York: George Braziller, 1980. Explains why the Chinese write on their paintings.

Weng Wan-go. *Chinese Painting and Calligraphy*. New York: Dover Publications, 1978. Brief discussion of Chinese painting and calligraphy styles throughout the ages followed by wonderful full-page reproductions.

Weng Wan-go and Yang Boda. *The Palace Museum: Peking*. New York: Harry N. Abrams, 1982 o.p. Art treasures of the Forbidden City, including architecture, paintings, and figurines. Gorgeous large reproductions.

Zhu Jiajin, comp. *Treasures of the Forbidden City*. New York: Viking, 1986 o.p. Origins, development, and characteristics of Chinese bronzes, painting, ceramics, minor arts, and textiles as well as descriptions of 100 pieces chosen to represent them. Beautiful large pictures for group viewing.

Children's Books

Ashabranner, Brent. *Land of Yesterday, Land of Tomorrow*. Photography by David Paul and Peter Conklin. New York: Cobblehill Books, 1992 o.p. Photographs and text describe the Chinese province of Xinjiang.

Bohlke, Dorothée. *Mr. Chang and the Yellow Robe*. Adapted by Elizabeth Bradford. Ada, OK: Garrett Educational Corp., 1991. Mr. Chang wishes to have a yellow robe so that he will be considered as important as the ruler of Canton.

Demi. *Buddha*. New York: Henry Holt, 1996. A beautifully illustrated short biography of the spiritual leader.

———. *Buddha Stories*. New York: Henry Holt, 1997. A collection of ten tales from Buddha, each ending with a moral. Outstanding illustrations done in Chinese gold ink on vellum.

———. *The Dragon's Tale*. New York: Henry Holt, 1996. A fable about each of the twelve animals of the Chinese zodiac. Demi's wonderful illustrations were rendered with paints made from plants, minerals, and a touch of powdered jade.

———. *The Empty Pot*. New York: Henry Holt, 1990. When Ping is the only child who admits that he could not grow a flower, the Chinese emperor rewards him.

———. *The Magic Tapestry*. New York: Henry Holt, 1994. When a Chinese mother sends her three sons out to retrieve her beautiful tapestry, only the youngest son perseveres in the task.

Fang, Linda. *The Ch'i-Lin Purse*. Illus. by Jeanne M. Lee. New York: Farrar Straus & Giroux, 1995. A collection of nine ancient Chinese stories.

Flint, David. *China*. Austin, TX: Raintree Steck-Vaughn, 1993. Chinese life and culture presented through a study of geography.

Goff, Denise. *Early China*. Illus. by Angus McBride, Karen Johnson and Terry Dalley. New York: Gloucester Press, 1986 o.p. Presents the origins of China, religious beliefs, and family life. Glossary.

Ho Minfong, transl. *Maples in the Mist*. Illus. by Jean and Tseng Mou-sien. New York: Lothrop, Lee & Shephard, 1996. A collection of poems from the Tang dynasty (618–907). These poems and the brush paintings that accompany them are certain to appeal to children.

James, Ian. *Inside China*. New York: Franklin Watts, 1989. Presentation of Chinese life, agriculture and industry, with list of facts.

Lazo, Caroline. *The Terra Cotta Army of Emperor Qin*. New York: Macmillan, 1993. An account of Emperor Qin's life and accomplishments and the discovery of the 7,500 terra cotta statues buried in his tomb.

Lee, Huy Voun. *At the Beach*. New York: Henry Holt, 1994. A mother and son enjoy their day at the beach by drawing Chinese characters, many of which resemble the objects for which they stand, in the sand.

Major, John S. *The Silk Route*. Illus. by Stephen Fieser. New York: HarperCollins, 1995. The story of the trade route between China and Byzantium during the Tang dynasty.

Martell, Mary Hazel. *The Ancient Chinese*. New York: Simon & Schuster, 1993. Various aspects of ancient Chinese life including art, government, and religion. Glossary.

Odijk, Pamela. *The Chinese*. New York: Silver Burdett, 1991. Discussion of China's history, culture, religion, and contributions. Chronology of dynasties, glossary, illustrations.

Schlein, Miriam. *The Year of the Panda*. New York: Thomas Y. Crowell, 1990. When a Chinese boy rescues a panda, he learns more about them and the efforts to keep them from extinction.

Tompert, Ann. *Grandfather Tang's Story*. Illus. by Robert Andrew Parker. New York: Crown, 1990. A grandfather tells a story about shape-changing fairies. Tangrams, ancient Chinese puzzles, are woven into the story, and directions for making them are included.

Wang, Rosalind C., retel. *The Fourth Question*. Illus. by Chen Ju-hong. New York: Holiday House, 1991. Yee-Lee visits the Wise Man to discover why, despite his hard work, he remains poor.

Williams, Brian. *Ancient China*. New York: Viking, 1996. Double-page see-through spreads reveal the customs and daily lives of the ancient Chinese. Key dates and glossary.

Yee, Paul. *Tales from Gold Mountain*. Illus. by Simon Ng. New York: Macmillan, 1989. Eight stories about Chinese immigrants to America and their role in the gold rush, the building of the transcontinental railway, and the settling of the West Coast.

Yep, Laurence. *Tongues of Jade*. Illus. by David Wiesner. New York: HarperCollins, 1991. A retelling of seventeen Chinese folktales from various Chinese communities around the United States.

Yolen, Jane. *The Emperor and the Kite*. Illus. by Ed Young. New York: Philomel, 1988. The emperor's smallest daughter rescues him from his jailers.

Young, Ed. *Lon Po Po*. New York: Philomel, 1989. A Chinese version of Red Riding Hood in which three sisters outwit the wolf. Stunning illustrations.

————. *Voices of the Heart*. New York: Scholastic, 1997. Using collage art, award-winning artist Ed Young explores 26 Chinese characters, each describing a feeling or emotion, and each containing a symbol for the heart.

Zheng, Zhensun, and Alice Low. *A Young Painter*. New York: Scholastic, 1991. The fascinating story of a young Chinese woman who began painting at the age of three.

Audiovisual Materials

The Chinese Past: 6000 Years of Art and Culture. Objects from the Neolithic period through the Yuan dynasty. The program is divided into four units: Two units contain narration to accompany the 48 slides, and two units contain traditional music, poetry, and a discussion of Chinese philosophies. (Available from the National Gallery of Art.)

The First Emperor of China. Reveals the spectacular art treasures of the first emperor of China. Film footage of the original archaeological dig, tour of museums, Great Wall. In English and Chinese. (CD-ROM. Available from Library Video Company.)

Splendors of Imperial China. Presents more than 475 of the finest works of art in the National Palace Museum, Taipei. Special features include close-up details, audio pronunciations of Chinese terms and names, and the opportunity to unroll precious handscrolls. (CD-ROM for Mac and Windows. Available from the Metropolitan Museum of Art).

A Young Painter. The story of Wang Yani, a young Chinese woman who began painting at the age of three. (Videocassette; 25 mins. Available from Scholastic Publishers.)

Other Materials

Chinese Brush Painting. A beginner's guide to Chinese art techniques. Set includes an instruction booklet by I-Ching Hsu, ink palettes, brushes, an ink-stone, an ink stick, a spoon, a mixing dish, and 32 pages of Chinese painting paper. Available from Putnam & Grosset Publishers.

6 The Art of Africa

"Listen, then, Children of Africa, we have had a glorious past
and it presages a promising future."
—HERB BOYD, *African History for Beginners*

Background Information

Africa, the second largest continent, is a land of great beauty and harsh contrasts; of deserts and rain forests; of intense tropical heat and bitter cold; of level plains and steep snow-topped mountains; of busy cities and dense jungles; of wild game preserves and cultivated farmland. There is archaeological evidence that the first humans appeared in eastern Africa about two and a half million years ago. The first art to arise in Africa, as discussed briefly in chapter 1, are the rock paintings, begun over 8,000 years ago and discovered in 2,000 sites throughout the continent. Often pictures are superimposed on one another, and the scenes, while containing some human figures, are overwhelmingly of animals. Prehistoric African artists painted their pictures on rock walls or incised outlines into the rock, either with dots or a solid line.

Egypt, in northern Africa, whose art and culture we discussed at length in chapter 2, was established and prospered as early as 4500 B.C. South of Egypt, a kingdom called Kush arose about 2000 B.C. and lasted until about the fourth century A.D. Kush became a major center of trade, learning, and art and developed one of the world's earliest alphabetical scripts. In the eighth century B.C., Phoenician traders from the region that is present-day Syria established the city of Carthage, and Africans living in Numidia (now Algeria) and Mauretania (now Morocco) opposed them. By the end of the first century, Rome controlled the northern coast of Africa, and when, in the third century, Christianity became the official Roman religion, it spread to North Africa as well. As the rivers in the Sahara region gradually began to dry up, converting the area into desert, the people living there traveled south, bringing with them two advances that were to have a dramatic effect on the development of the continent: knowledge of farming and raising cattle, and the production of metal tools and weapons. Some of

66

the kingdoms formed by this resettlement of peoples became so famous or spawned leaders so legendary that they remain fascinating to us hundreds of years later.

Much has been written about the kingdoms of Ghana, Mali, and Songhy in West Africa. There were such rich gold deposits in Ghana that entire houses were made of the metal and the area became known as the Gold Coast. The Ashanti in Ghana made gold weights in the shape of animals and birds which they used for trade. Sundiata, a Mali hero, was once a cripple who overcame his infirmity, became king, and united his kingdom. While he ruled harshly, he was fair, and he led his people to prosperity. Mali rose to even greater glory under the reign of its greatest ruler, Mansa Musa, between 1307 and 1332. In Timbuktu in Songhy, a university was founded in the thirteenth century that attracted noted Muslim scholars from as far away as India. Some of the most ancient art in all of Africa was produced in early Nigeria. Nok pottery sculptures date from 500 to 200 B.C. and evince great imagination and beauty. The British brought almost 2,000 bronze, ivory, and wood pieces from Benin in southern Nigeria to Europe in the nineteenth century. The people of the sacred city of Ife in southwest Nigeria created bronze statues using the lost-wax technique.

Trade with other countries for needed commodities, especially salt, introduced the Muslim religion into northern Africa, where it spread into the western kingdoms below the Sahara. The creation of abstract bronze statues and masks was the result, in part, of the Muslim prohibition against exact likenesses. Muslim influence was also felt in education, for the Muslims taught reading and writing in Arabic to many Africans and established religious schools that attracted students from many parts of the continent.

Bantu-speaking peoples moved southward from what is now the Nigeria-Cameroon border region into the forests of central Africa, eventually settling throughout central and southern Africa. Population increased rapidly in the Congo forests, and the kingdoms of Kongo and Ngola became powerful rivals. The kingdom of Bakuba in the Congo was said to have had 124 kings in its long history, and artists carved a seated statue in honor of each king during his lifetime.

Great Zimbabwe, the largest of a series of stone-walled enclosures built in one of the wealthiest kingdoms of southern Africa, is so spectacular that it now gives its name to the country. The outer wall of the enclosure is sixteen feet thick, 825 feet long, and thirty-two feet high. The stone was fitted together without mortar. These structures are so sophisticated and magnificent that early nineteenth-century explorers refused to credit them to the African people. Later archaeologists have since proved that Great Zimbabwe is the work of ancestors of the people who still live in the area.

The first Europeans to land in Africa were the Portuguese when Vasco da Gama traveled around the southern tip of the continent in 1497. Traders and missionaries soon followed. By the sixteenth century, slave traders from Spain, Portugal, and England began capturing Africans with the cooperation of some African rulers and sending them to work as slaves on the plantations of the Caribbean and the Americas. This slave trade continued into the nineteenth century, and the capture of millions of Africans led to the decline of many of the ancient kingdoms. In the mid-seventeenth century, Dutch farmers went to the Cape of Good Hope as employees of the Dutch East India Company and settled in Cape Town. After the Cape became a British colony in 1806, tensions between the Dutch farmers, or Boers, and the British increased and escalated into a war. The Union of South Africa was created in 1910.

In the nineteenth century, European countries, especially England, France, Portugal, and Germany, entered Africa's interior regions and carved her lands into colonies that they exploited for their rich mineral deposits and natural resources. Only Liberia and Ethiopia escaped this foreign domination, which lasted for eighty years. Today Africa is made up of fifty-two independent countries, and its story is still being written. Ethnic strife may create still different borders. One of the greatest triumphs of the African people has been the establishment, after years of agonizing struggle, of majority black rule in South Africa.

It is a mistake to think of the African people as a single group. There are many different tribes and races, and they speak over 1,000 different languages. Each tribe has its own distinct culture, beliefs, and customs. Even occupation, dress, adornment, and housing are different. The people of Africa range from the small Pygmies living in the tropical rain forests of Zaire to the incredibly tall Tutsi living in Burundi and Rwanda. Their skin colors vary from a yellowish tan to light brown to rich ebony. It is into this amazingly diverse world with its ancient and rich heritage that we enter when we study the art of Africa, for African art is intimately connected to the lives and religious beliefs of its creators.

To appreciate it fully, we need to "read" these works of art as we would read a book, for

> in the absence of written documents, Africans often preserved their beliefs and values and conveyed them from generation to generation through their art. The significance of each work, therefore, derives not merely from its tangible form or its esthetic merit, but equally from the concepts and beliefs that it embodies. (Robbins and Nooter, p. 11).

As we view these works, we will come to know why they had a powerful place not only in the lives of their creators but also in the art world beyond the borders of Africa where they have influenced the work of Picasso, Brancusi, Modigliani and many others and spawned such art movements as Cubism, Expressionism, Fauvism, and Surrealism.

❏ The Story

(This story is meant to describe no particular tribe but is the combination of the initiation rites of several different groups of people. Some of the more graphic details of the pain inflicted on initiates in some cultures have been eliminated so the story can be told to young children.)

Koti could hardly keep his mind on his duties. The more he tried to focus on the cattle that his family depended upon for their food, clothing, and even their ranking in the tribe, the more his mind wandered. For in a few days he would leave his tasks behind and gather with other boys his age to prepare for one of the most important events of his life. Koti was twelve years old, and if he could prove himself worthy to leave behind the ways of childhood, he would enter into a special ceremony to make him an adult member of the tribe. He was excited, but also a little frightened, for he would have to show his elders he could bear responsibility and even pain. Koti shivered as the sun began to sink on the horizon and streaks of pink stretched across the sky overhead.

Five days later Koti's father led him to the outskirts of the village. As they walked, other boys Koti had played with all his life and their fathers met them on the path, so that before long they formed a solemn procession. There was no running or teasing now, only whispered comments among the boys while their fathers walked tall and proud before them. Soon they came to a round thatched hut set apart from everything else. Three tribal elders stood there to welcome the boys and send the men away. Koti watched his father leave, and a lump formed in his throat. He would not see any members of his family again until seven days had passed and he performed the special ceremonial dance that announced to everyone that he was an adult member of the tribe.

The boys gathered on the ground while the elders turned toward the altar set in front of them. The altar was a wooden table covered with a cloth woven and dyed in beautiful colors by the women of the village. On the cloth were placed several large statues. Koti knew those statues well. They were images of his ancestors, the great ones who had governed his tribe wisely in past generations. "Oh, fathers," prayed the elders when quiet had settled over the group, "send your spirit into these young people. Open their ears so that they may hear and receive instruction during these special days. Open their minds that they may know and understand the ways of our people. Open their hearts that they may be filled with the courage to accept the pain and challenges that lie before them." As the elders prayed, Koti could feel a deep peace come over him. Yes, his ancestors were with him. He could feel their presence, and he was anxious to join himself to them and to the members of his tribe still living so that he could contribute his strength and his talents for the good of everyone. And so evening came that first day.

Every morning after that, the boys were awakened early and made to cleanse themselves in a nearby stream. Then they spent the rest of the day listening to instructions. They were told what was expected of them as adult men and husbands. They heard of the deeds of those who had gone before them, and the statues of the ancestors surrounded them with their spirit and life. Koti and his friends were allowed food only once a day, a thin gruel that did not fill them but enabled them to keep their strength up. With each passing day, they grew leaner and more determined to succeed.

Finally the test of bearing pain came. The skin of each boy's forehead and cheeks was cut in a design that was the special mark of the tribe. Koti stood with his fists clenched during the cutting, neither flinching nor crying out when he felt the knife sting his flesh. Then tree sap was rubbed into the cuts so they would stand out in relief and reveal the decorative pattern. How proud Koti felt to be wearing the mark of his tribe! From this moment onward, everyone who saw him would know to whom he belonged. He was no longer only an individual but part of a group of people all living and working together. Koti felt like jumping and shouting for joy, but he knew he must remain serious and calm before the elders. This was his last night as a child. He would spend it in quiet meditation before the altar of the ancestors.

At dawn on the seventh day, the whole tribe gathered before the thatched hut while the young boys filed out in front of them. The sky was just beginning to fill with color. "My people," said the first elder, "behold these young men. They have proven themselves intelligent and brave. They have been instructed in our ways and have promised to remain faithful to them all their days. Witness now their final movement away from the days of childhood and welcome them into the tribe with open hearts. Share with them your wisdom and courage and allow yourselves to receive their strength when your limbs become weak with age. They are our future and our glory!"

One by one, the elders placed a beautiful ceremonial mask on each boy's head. The masks were heavy and completely covered their faces, for they were no longer only single individuals but joined to each other and to everyone else in the tribe. Slowly the musicians began to play their instruments. Koti could hear his uncle play the *sansa*, an instrument with wooden strips his uncle plucked. He could hear the drummers playing on animal skins and gourds and the trumpeters blowing through animal horns. His feet began to move. Around and around he twirled, while the beat became faster and faster. Koti's feet became a blur as he kept up with the music. He soon forgot where he was and who he was. He knew only that he must dance and dance and that he could not stop even if his body cried out for a rest.

On and on the musicians played, until finally, with a loud blast of the horn, they stopped. Koti and the others threw down their masks as a sign that they were throwing away the days of their childhood. The elders came forward and stripped the boys of their clothes and made them wash one more time in the stream. "Wash away your old ways and put on the new life of a man," they said to each boy as they gave him a colorful new cloth to wear. Then they piled the old clothes in the center of the group and set them aflame, for those who wore them were boys no longer. They were men. There followed a big feast, for the women had been preparing for this special day all week. Koti joined his parents and his younger brothers and sisters, proud of his special face markings and his new adult clothing, and there was great rejoicing all that day.

Now we are going to enjoy some of the statues Koti and his people made of their ancestors and some of the masks they used for their special ceremonies. When we look at them, it is important to remember that most of these works of art were not made as decorations. They were made because of the beliefs of the people about a Higher Power and their own place in the world. So we must think about the ways these things were used and what they stood for, and not judge them according to more familiar Western ideas about what makes art beautiful.

LESSON 1: African Masks

Viewing the Art

African art is often called primitive art. This does not mean it is crude or substandard. It simply means that it is art created by peoples who have had little or no access to machinery or formal training, except by apprenticeship. Most African masks are made of wood. In humid areas of the continent, most wood pieces last only about two hundred years, but in arid regions, art works made of wood are many centuries old.

Some masks are made using the pole style, that is, the mask takes on the long shape of the tree trunk from which it is made. There is no attempt by the artist to make the finished piece smooth. Rather, sharp angles and features emphasize the fierce or frenzied nature of the ceremony for which the mask was intended. Other masks are made in the round style, the finished piece being rubbed smooth and even soaked in oils or other materials to give it a rich tone.

Some masks are painted. White often represents death or ghosts. Red is a celebratory color.

Show the children a variety of masks. You may wish to show the art by region—western Sudan, West African coast, Central Africa, eastern Africa, southern Africa—or you may wish simply to show a series of African masks. Whatever you decide, be sure to point out that African peoples live in many different countries and regions where climate and natural resources for creating artwork differ. Their customs differ as well. By discussing this with the children, you help them avoid lumping all Africans into a single group, and thereby increase the children's respect for these talented and diverse peoples. Some of the masks in *The African Kings* by Mary Cable (see References) are quite unusual. Or you may wish to view videos or slides (see References), which are particularly effective for showing African art. Try to include a variety of different masks in your viewing: animal as well as human forms, round and pole styles, painted and unpainted examples. The children may especially enjoy the small but incredibly beautiful ivory mask carved for the king of Benin.

Journal Writing

How do the masks make the children feel? Are some frightening to look at? Why do they think the artist made them that way? Perhaps some children would like to choose one particular mask and write about a ceremony in which they think that mask played an important part.

Art/Drama Activity: Mask-Making

Materials

- Pictures of African masks to serve as models
- Newspapers (whole sheets and sheets cut or torn into strips)
- Tape
- Papier-mâché mix
- Paints and brushes
- Glue
- Fabric scraps (or anything else the children may wish to put on their masks)

Roll several pieces of newspaper into a round or elongated oval shape (depending on the kind of mask) and tape in place. If the mask is an animal with horns, or if it has any other special characteristics, form those shapes with crushed newspaper and tape onto original shape.

Cut or tear the remaining newspaper into strips and coat with papier-mâché.

Cover the newspaper shape with several layers of strips, taking care to smooth them into place after each application. Allow to dry overnight or for several days.

Paint the mask, adding eyes, mouth, and other features. Glue on beads, fabric, feathers, etc., as appropriate.

LESSON 2: African Sculpture

Viewing the Art

Sculptures are made of various materials, including terra cotta, wood, ivory, and bronze. Some depict a tribe's ancestors, some represent spirits, and still others are fetishes believed to have magic powers to ward off evil and protect people from sickness. Often statues will exaggerate breasts and reproductive organs, bearing witness to the African emphasis on fertility. Show some examples of different kinds of statues. You may wish to show the artwork by region as previously suggested, or simply to show a variety of statues. Some figures you may want to include are the statues of kings from the kingdom of Bakuba in the Congo; the double male and female figures of the Dogon; the Nigerian leopard figures; Nigerian stone and bronze heads; the Bidjugo carved figures from the coast of Guinea; Dogon ancestor figures; Ashanti gold weights; Baluba ancestor figures; Baule figures; the guardian figures from the Congo; and stools from the Hemba and Zela of Zaire.

Journal Writing

Ask the children to pick one statue as their favorite out of those they have seen. Why did they choose it? What do they especially like about the statue? Does it give them any ideas about the people who created it?

Art/Drama Activity: Initiation Ceremony

Act out an initiation ceremony similar to the one described in the story above. The children can assume the parts of elders, parents, initiates, and musicians. Use the masks created in the first lesson for a ceremonial dance. The children can use some of the text from *Dancing Masks of Africa* by Christine Prince in choral reading to accompany the dance. They may also wish to make instruments to use in the ceremony.

Additional Activities

Several wonderful art activities are suggested by Judith Hoffman Corwin in *African Crafts*, and the children may wish to undertake some of them.

Curriculum Connections

Social Studies

- Using a map, show the continent of Africa, locate different countries, find countries where artworks viewed originated, or where children about whom you read live.
- Locate different natural wonders such as Mt. Kilimanjaro, Victoria Falls, Sahara Desert, etc.
- Talk about African history: the ancient kingdoms; European colonialism; the struggles for independence; the abolition of apartheid in South Africa; Africa's struggles for survival today.
- Discuss the different tribal customs, dress, housing, and ways of life of some African peoples.
- Help children to understand that Africa has major cities in where life is very much like their own, as well as remote villages where life has not changed for centuries.
- Talk about Africa's vast natural resources—metals such as gold, and valuable stones such as diamonds. What kinds of wood do Africa's jungles provide?
- Discuss the roots of African-Americans today—the history of slavery.
- Learn about some African foods. Have an African feast.

Mathematics

- Present some different kinds of African counting. Use *Count Your Way Through Africa* by Jim Haskins (see References) and similar books.

Music

- Play tapes or CDs of African music.
- Learn some African folksongs using *African Roots* by Jerry Silverman (see References).

- Study African musical instruments. Make some simple instruments to accompany your singing.

Science

- For zoology, study some of the wildlife living in Africa. Make a book or calendar featuring African wildlife. Which species are endangered? What can the children do about it?

- What medicines are obtained from African rain forests? How are these valuable areas being used? Preserved? Destroyed?

Literature

- Folklore is rich in stories from Africa. Anansi the Spider is a famous African trickster. Read many African folktales. (The books listed in the References are only a sampling of the hundreds that are readily available.) Encourage the children to learn some for a storytelling fest. Dramatize a few favorites.

- Read some biographies of famous Africans: Nelson Mandela, Shaka, Sundiata, etc.

- Read some poems by African Americans. (See *Soul Looks Back in Wonder* by Tom Feelings.)

References

Boyd, Herb. *African History for Beginners*. Illus. by Shey Wolvek-Pfister. New York: Writers and Readers Publishing, 1991. A poetic exploration of the history of Africa.

Cable, Mary. *The African Kings*. Chicago: Stonehenge Press, 1983 o.p. Beautiful color reproductions of art created for the African kings.

Courtney-Clarke, Margaret. *African Canvas: The Art of West African Women*. New York: Rizzoli, 1990. A beautiful book presenting the art of contemporary women living in West Africa who still live in the traditional way of their ancestors.

———. *Ndebele*. New York: Rizzoli, 1986. A beautiful book presenting the various kinds of art produced by the women of the Ndebele of southern Africa.

Leuzinger, Elsy. *Arte del Africa Negra*. Illus. by Isabelle Wettstein. Madrid: Tribal, 1992. Explains the meaning of African art and provides reproductions of the art of different regions of the continent. Available in English.

Newton, Douglas. *Masterpieces of Primitive Art*. Photographs by Lee Boltin. New York: Knopf, 1978 o.p. Presentation of the works in the Rockefeller collection of primitive art, among which are many African pieces. Excellent for viewing.

Robbins, Warren M., and Nancy Ingram Nooter. *African Art in American Collections*. Washington D.C.: Smithsonian Institution Press, 1989. An introduction to African art and reproductions of pieces housed in the United States. Excellent for viewing.

Shillington, Kevin. *History of Africa*. New York: Macmillan, 1989. A history of Africa from earliest times to the present. Discussion questions at the end of each chapter.

Children's Books

Aardema, Verna, retel. *How the Ostrich Got Its Long Neck*. Illus. by Marcia Brown. New York: Scholastic, 1995. A delightful pourquoi tale from Kenya, complete with sound effects for the children to do.

————. *Misoso: Once Upon a Time Tales from Africa*. Illus. by Reynold Ruffins. New York: Apple Soup/Knopf, 1994. Twelve folktales from different African peoples. Glossaries and bibliography.

————. *Traveling to Tondo*. Illus. by Will Hillenbrand. New York: Knopf, 1991. A civet cat allows his friends to delay him on the way to his wedding.

Appiah, Peggy. *Tales of an Ashanti Father*. Illus. by Mora Dickson. Boston: Beacon Press, 1967. A collection of 22 folktales from the Ashanti people of Ghana.

Ashabranner, Brent, and Russell Davis. *The Lion's Whiskers and Other Ethiopian Tales*. Rev. ed. Illus. by Helen Siegl. North Haven, CT: Linnet Books, 1997. Sixteen tales related by short introductions to the people and places of Ethiopia. Woodcut prints.

Ayo, Yvonne. *Africa*. Photographs by Ray Moller and Geoff Dann. New York: Knopf, 1995. A book in the Eyewitness series that discusses African history, beliefs, and customs. An excellent treatment of many aspects of African life.

Bohannan, Paul, and Philip Curtin. *Africa and Africans*. 4th ed. Prospect Heights, IL: Waveland Press, 1995. Excellent presentation of the land and its peoples.

Browne, Philippa-Alys. *African Animals ABC*. San Francisco: Sierra Club, 1995. Twenty-six African animals, one for each letter of the alphabet, are introduced with lovely drawings.

Chiasson, John. *African Journey*. New York: Bradbury Press, 1987. Text and beautiful photographs reveal life in six African regions.

Corwin, Judith Hoffman. *African Crafts*. New York: Franklin Watts, 1990. Supplies directions for making several items related to African life and customs.

Ellis, Veronica Freeman. *Afro-Bets: First Book About Africa*. Illus. by George Ford. Orange, NJ: Just Us Books, 1989. Very simple history of Africa for young children.

Feelings, Tom. *Soul Looks Back in Wonder*. New York: Dial, 1993. An award-winning book containing poems celebrating African Americans by 13 African-American poets.

Gelber, Carol. *Masks Tell Stories*. Brookfield, CT: Millbrook Press, 1993. Describes the use of masks in ancient and contemporary societies throughout the world. Includes African masks.

Halliburton, Warren J. *Celebrations of African Heritage*. New York: Crestwood House, 1992. Different religious and cultural celebrations held in both Africa and the United States. May spark some classroom celebrations.

Hartman, Wendy. *One Sun Rises*. Illus. by Nicolaas Maritz. New York: Dutton, 1994. A counting book which features African wildlife.

Haskins, Jim. *Count Your Way through Africa*. Illus. by Barbara Knutson. Minneapolis, MN: Carolrhoda Books, 1989. The author uses the numbers 1–10, presented in Swahili, to introduce the land, culture, and history of Africa.

Kreikemeier, Gregory Scott. *Come with Me to Africa: A Photographic Journey*. Racine, WI: Western Publishing Company, 1993. Readers follow the author on a trip to 13 countries of Africa. Gorgeous photos and text offer a view of the wildlife and variety of life on this continent.

Kessler, Christina. *One Night: A Story from the Desert*. Illus. by Ian Schoenherr. New York: Philomel, 1995 o.p. The story of a young boy living in the Sahara and the tests he must pass to become a man.

Kroll, Virginia. *Africa Brothers and Sisters*. Illus. by Vanessa French. New York: Four Winds, 1993. A picture book that simply describes various tribes living in Africa.

Kurtz, Jane. *Fire on the Mountain*. Illus. by E.B. Lewis. New York: Simon & Schuster, 1994. An Ethiopian tale about a shepherd boy who stays warm overnight by viewing the fire on a far-off mountain.

————. *Pulling the Lion's Tail*. Illus. by Floyd Cooper. New York: Simon & Schuster, 1995. A grandfather helps a young Ethiopian girl get used to her father's new wife.

Margolies, Barbara A. *Rehema's Journey*. New York: Scholastic, 1990 o.p. Readers see Tanzania through the eyes of nine-year-old Rehema.

McKissack, Patricia and Fredrick. *The Royal Kingdoms of Ghana, Mali, and Songhay*. New York: Henry Holt, 1994. Examines three kingdoms of the Western Sudan. Includes maps and bibliography.

Murray, Dr. Jocelyn. *Africa*. New York: Facts on File, 1990. Explains African history and describes the different tribes and countries in the continent.

Naylor, Penelope. *Black Images: The Art of West Africa*. Photographs by Lisa Little. New York: Doubleday, 1973 o.p. Full-page photos of West African art accompanied by appropriate African poetry. Lovely.

Olaleye, Isaac. *Bitter Bananas*. Illus. by Ed Young. Honesdale, PA: Boyds Mills Press, 1994. Yusuf devises a plan to stop the baboons from stealing his palm sap. Ideal for group participation and drama.

Oliver, Roland, and J.D. Faye. *A Short History of Africa*. 6th ed. New York: Facts on File, 1988. Complete history of the continent. Maps, bibliography.

Onyefulu, Ifeoma. *A Is for Africa*. New York: Cobblehill Books, 1993. An alphabet book in which each letter stands for something to do with African life. The stunning photos were taken in Nigeria.

————. *Ogbo: Sharing Life in an African Village*. San Diego: Harcourt Brace Jovanovich, 1996. In words and pictures, a young boy tells about his life in Nigeria. Excellent!

Prince, Christine. *Dancing Masks of Africa*. New York: Scribner's, 1975 o.p. A marvelous book in which poetical text tells the role of the many different kinds of masks used in West Africa. A perfect accompaniment to the dance activity suggested in the lesson.

———. *The Mystery of Masks.* New York: Scribner's, 1978 o.p. Presents the meaning and significance of different kinds of masks created by various cultures throughout the world.

———. *Talking Drums of Africa.* New York: Scribner's, 1973 o.p. Explains the different kinds of African drums and the messages they convey. Includes some Ashanti poems. A unique book.

Reynolds, Jan. *Sahara: Vanishing Cultures.* San Diego, CA: Harcourt Brace Jovanovich, 1991. Describes through text and photos the way of life of the nomads of the Sahara.

Seed, Jenny. *Ntombi's Song.* Illus. by Anno Berry. Boston: Beacon Press, 1987 o.p. Ntombi, a girl living in South Africa, proves she is not too small to earn money by herself and bring home groceries.

Silverman, Jerry. *African Roots.* New York: Chelsea House, 1994. African folk songs in English and the native language accompanied by music, pictures, and informational notes. A treasure!

Stanley, Diane, and Peter Vennema. *Shaka, King of the Zulus.* Illus. by Diane Stanley. New York: Morrow Junior Books, 1988. A wonderful picture-book biography of the powerful Zulu military leader. Glossary and bibliography.

Stock, Catherine. *Where Are You Going, Manyoni?* New York: Morrow Junior Books, 1993. Manyoni's walk to school gives readers a glimpse of the lovely landscape of Zimbabwe. Glossary of African words and listing of wildlife viewed in the book.

Tadjo, Veronique. *Lord of the Dance.* New York: J.B. Lippincott, 1988. An African folktale that recounts the story of the Senufo people of the Ivory Coast. Excellent to use with a study of masks or in conjunction with dramatization of a dance.

Tames, Richard. *Nelson Mandela.* New York: Franklin Watts, 1991. An account of Mandela's life and accomplishments up to his release from prison.

Wepman, Denis. *Africa: The Struggle for Independence.* New York: Facts on File, 1993. Recounts the various struggles for independence among the countries of Africa. Includes bibliography and index.

Williams, Karen Lynn. *When Africa Was Home.* Illus. by Floyd Cooper. New York: Orchard Books, 1991. When Peter and his family return to the United States, they long for the life they had in Africa and eventually go back.

Wisniewski, David. *Sundiata: Lion King of Mali.* New York: Clarion, 1992. Breathtaking cut-paper illustrations and text tell the story of Sundiata, ruler of Mali in the 13th century.

Audiovisual Materials

African Art. A review of works of African art in terms of their ritual usage and regional tribal characteristics. (Audiocassette and 77 slides. Available from the National Gallery of Art.)

African Art and Culture. Presents the art of different areas of Africa. (Videocassette; 52 mins. Available from Clearvue/eav.)

How the Leopard Got His Spots. A "Just So" story that introduces students to Kipling as well as the people and wildlife of Africa, with an *a cappella* soundtrack by a South African vocal group. For grades K–4. (CD-ROM. Available from Microsoft.)

Vieux Diop. Music by African composer Vieux Diop. (CD. Available from Triloka.)

Other Materials

African Mask Kit. Provides materials necessary for creating an authentic-looking African mask. Available from The Metropolitan Museum of Art.

Part III
Art of the
Middle Ages and
the Renaissance

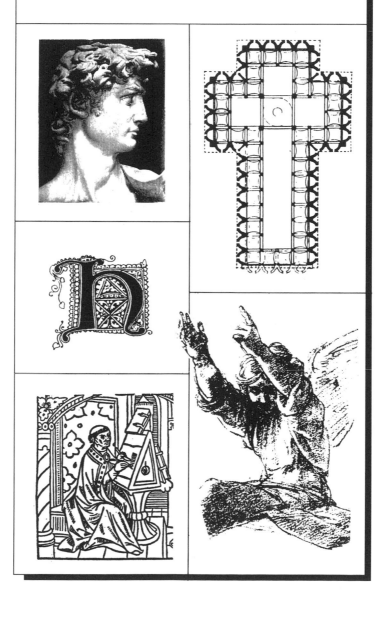

7 Art of the Middle Ages

As the third year that followed the year One Thousand was approaching, almost over the whole earth, but above all in Italy and Gaul, the churches were rebuilt. One might have thought that the earth was shaking itself to shed it skin, and was everywhere re-clad in a white coat of churches.
—RAOUL GLABER (eleventh century) in Sabbagh,
Europe in the Middle Ages

Background Information

The time from the fall of Rome in A.D. 476 to A.D. 1000 is sometimes referred to as the "Dark Ages," for most people lived in ignorance while education was the prerogative of the clergy and the rich. The term "Middle Ages" means that time in the middle, between A.D. 1000 and the birth of the Renaissance in Europe in the mid-fifteenth century. This is the era of building magnificent churches, of crafting brilliant mosaics, and writing illuminated manuscripts. Universities, businesses, banking, and trade and commerce among different cities and countries all flowered during the Middle Ages.

But life during the Middle Ages was harsh and difficult. While some people lived into old age, most did not see their fortieth year. Peasants and serfs worked long hours to eke meager harvests from infertile soil. Women had few rights and often died in childbirth, and noble women were pressed into marriage without their consent to increase the family holdings. There were wars such as the Crusades initiated by Pope Urban II in 1095 to wrest the Holy Land from the Turks, and the Hundred Years' war between England and France; the Black Plague, which wiped out a third of the population of Europe and even entire villages; and widespread famine. Indeed, life in the Middle Ages was not for the faint of heart!

The Church dominated medieval life, and religion was intimately connected to everyday existence. After the Roman persecution of Christians ceased with Constantine's conversion and proclamation of Christianity as the official religion in A.D. 392, Christianity spread. Charlemagne, called "Charles the

Great" as much for his stature (almost seven feet) as for his exploits, forced the conversion of all of Europe by the sword. Almost all the medieval art we celebrate is religious. Pagan temples were converted to Christian churches, and numerous cathedrals were built in the large cities with financing from clerics and nobles. Each village had its own less elaborate church, supported by the lord of the manor and the peasants, and its bell called the people to prayer throughout the day and to church services on Sundays and Holy Days. Church interiors were decorated with statues and paintings on the walls and ceilings, or beautiful mosaics such as those that adorned the Church of San Vitale in Ravenna.

In the first half of the Middle Ages, education was restricted largely to the wealthy or to boys destined for the priesthood, and books were rare. Priests taught in schools connected to the cathedrals. St. Benedict initiated monastic life for those priests who wished to live apart from the world in monasteries and follow a special rule, or way of life. Monasteries sprang up all over Europe, and some of the monks performed the invaluable service of copying and illustrating the Bible and classical writings by hand. "Books of Hours" containing the prayers the monks and priests said at different times of the day were also copied and lavishly illustrated. Many of these, such as the *Book of Kells*, are works of art in their own right. Thousands of pilgrims made arduous journeys to Rome, the seat of the Papacy (in 1309 the Papacy moved to Avignon, France, but returned to Rome once again in 1378), and to shrines to venerate the bones and relics of popular saints. Truly religion was the heart blood of all classes of medieval society.

The dangers of medieval life gradually gave rise to the feudal system, which began in France and, along with the Church, controlled Europe almost into the Renaissance. Under this system, the king granted land or a fief to his most influential lords or barons. They, in turn, promised to fight for him personally and with knights they supplied and equipped. Powerful lords built castles to protect their fiefs and might, in turn, have lesser lords also under their rule who managed the different parts of their fiefdom and fell to arms when they were needed.

These lords or barons were in charge of peasants who worked the land and gave to their lord a portion of their produce and livestock. The peasants, who lived in small cottages, often with their animals under the same roof, received protection from their lord in return. When crops were good, peasants were able to sell the surplus at market and to enter into trade. This gradually led to the rise of towns, especially in Italy, and the dissolution of the feudal system. Merchants and tradespeople populated the towns and lived comfortable lives, overseeing workers and apprentices. Some merchants became more prosperous than the lords in their fiefdoms! Trade with other lands, new inventions like the plow and new methods of irrigating the land, and most important of all, the printing press and the spread of education, led eventually to a new birth in art and thought called the Renaissance. But until this revolution took place, Europe was one in a common faith and an organization in which the rules were very clearly defined. Never again would this be so!

While we will concentrate only on church building and the illumination of manuscripts here, there is much about medieval life to capture children's interest and imagination. They may wish to study the construction of castles and to make their own models. This is the age of kings and knights and castles, of King Arthur and his Round Table, of armor and jousts, of fairs, jugglers, magicians, mummers' plays, crusades, and pilgrimages. There are a wealth of books of varying difficulty on this period and many possible activities to keep your students involved in an extended unit if you so choose.

❑ The Story

Almost a thousand years ago in France, in a time we call the Middle Ages, two baby boys were born. One baby's father was a poor peasant who had to work in the fields all day on land that was not his own. He had to give part of everything he grew to a great and powerful lord who lived in a castle and owned all the surrounding lands. In return, the lord would protect him and the other peasants on the property if enemies came waging war. The little baby was born in a thatched hut, kept warm by the bodies of the animals that shared the hut with his parents and brothers and sisters.

The child, whose name was Suger, grew to be strong and very clever—so clever, in fact, that his father began to consider something quite out of the ordinary: He would send his son to school. Now almost no peasants at that time went to school, nor could they read and write. The only exceptions were those boys who were to become priests of the Christian church—and that is what his father determined that Suger would be. So when his son reached the age of nine, he took the lad to a monastery near Paris, a special place where priests, called monks, lived, and asked that he be educated.

Next to the monastery was a church that was a shrine to St. Denis, a special patron saint of France. The monks took care of this shrine and welcomed visitors who came from great distances to pray there. Because the monks were among the few people who could read and write, they also spent time each day copying the Bible and other important books by hand and painting lovely pictures in them. These books were so beautiful that they were really works of art. And they were very precious, because there were so few books in the land. The monks created a wonderful library filled with the books they copied and started a school next to their monastery. They agreed to educate Suger and to train him in the things he must know to be a priest of God. Suger learned to read so quickly and worked so diligently that the monks were delighted that they had decided to take him in.

The other baby, named Louis Capet, was born in a palace and was the son of a king, King Philip I. He grew up attended by servants. He wore fine clothes and, of course, it was understood that he would be sent to be educated. For when his father died, Louis was destined to take his place as the next king. Certainly he would have to know how to read important documents and to write. And so when Louis turned nine, he was sent to the same monastery of St. Denis to be educated. He and Suger became best friends and remained so all their lives.

When both boys grew into manhood, Louis was crowned king on the death of his father, and Suger became a monk and lived at the monastery of St. Denis. Suger was the new king's adviser throughout the rest of the king's life and helped him gain power over enemies who tried to take away his throne. He was also elected to a special position as leader, or abbot, of the monastery when the old abbot died. As abbot, Suger had one great desire—to rebuild the Church of St. Denis because it was crumbling with age and was definitely too small for all the pilgrims who came to pray there each year. He saved as much money as he could from the donations the pilgrims made, and when he finally had enough, he gathered stonecutters and carpenters and artists and began work on the church.

Those of us here probably belong to many different religions. Some of us may be Jewish. Others may be Lutherans or Baptists or Methodists or Muslims. But when Suger lived, most people in the countries of Europe were Catholics, living under the authority of the pope in Rome. When the Roman Empire fell, the temples to the Roman gods were turned into Catholic churches, and many more churches began to be built. At first, the churches followed the ideas of the Roman builders. They used arches and had very thick walls to support those arches. But Suger had a new idea. He wanted to build a more graceful church with tall windows that would bathe the interior with light, and he wanted the spires of the church to reach up to the heavens like hands praying to God. No one knew how to build such a church, but Suger and his workers figured out some new designs that made it possible.

We're going to look at some of the marvelous churches built during the Middle Ages, churches that copied the ideas of the Romans, and churches built in the new style of the Church of St. Denis. We'll even see the church of St. Denis itself. And we'll also be looking at some of the marvelous books copied by the monks in their monasteries. For most of the art of the Middle Ages was done not simply to create beauty—it was Christian art done to honor God and the saints.

LESSON 1: Medieval Churches

Viewing the Art

While the churches in small medieval towns and villages were simple structures, huge cathedrals were often built in the large cities or where saints lay buried. Help the children understand that constructing such tall structures was an incredible feat at a time when most of the work was done by hand and architects were not always certain how to support them. It was not unheard of to have a church come crashing down several years after its construction. Ask the children to hold their hands over their heads in the shape of a Roman arch. This semicircular arch is very strong, for it can withstand a great deal of downward pressure. But it also requires very thick walls to support it. View some churches constructed with arches in the Roman style. This architectural style is called "Romanesque." Some examples of Romanesque churches are Saint Magdalene of Vezelay, the Church of St. Stephen at Nevers, the Church of St. Michael at Hildesheim, Worms Cathedral, Durham Cathedral, and the Church of St. Stephen at Caen. What are some things the children notice as they view these churches (arches, small windows, solid-looking walls)? View some church interiors. Note that the main apse, the side transepts, and the center nave form a cross. Invite the children to stand and form a cross-shaped church interior.

Abbé Suger's Church of St. Denis ushered in a new architectural style called "Gothic." Show pictures of the Church of St. Denis and other gothic churches such as Notre Dame in Paris, Chartres Cathedral, Canterbury Cathedral, and Westminster Abbey. What differences do the children notice (pointed arches, bigger windows filled with stained glass, flying buttresses, ribbed vaults)? The pointed arch placed less stress on the walls and enabled architects to use thinner and higher ones. The flying buttresses kept the thinner walls from collapsing under the weight of the roof, and since such solid masses of wall were no longer needed, the builders could create tall, stained-glass windows within those walls to light and beautify the structure. The ribbed vaults were a series of attractive intersecting arches on the underside of the roof. The film *Cathedral* (see References) explains all of these Gothic innovations and enables children to follow the long cathedral-building process from beginning to end.

Have the children put their arms over their heads in the shape of a Gothic arch, then a Roman arch. Intersperse pictures of Romanesque and Gothic churches and see if the children can tell the difference. Talk about the creation of stained-glass windows: making the glass from sand, lime, and potash; cutting and coloring the glass; fitting the glass together with lengths of lead to form a picture. Show examples of stained-glass and rose windows. Do any of the churches the children attend contain stained glass? Where else have they seen stained glass used?

Since so many people in medieval times could neither read nor write, the interior of the church, where they spent a good deal of their time, served to instruct them in their religion. It was a "book" everyone could read. Stained-glass windows, beautiful wall paintings, and statues told stories about God and the saints. If you wish, you can show the children pictures of some of the church paintings and statuary.

Journal Writing

What are some things the children have learned about Romanesque and Gothic churches? Which do they prefer? Why? Do they have any opinions about the huge sums of money spent building and decorating churches?

Art/Drama Activity: Stained Glass

Materials

- Sheets of brightly colored cellophane
- A large sheet of black construction paper folded in half for each child
- Scissors
- Glue or paste

It is helpful, especially if the children are very young, to have a model of a stained-glass construction to show the children. Have them cut shapes through both thicknesses of their black paper, keeping the fold intact and without going to the edges of the paper. In other words, they must poke a hole through the paper to cut their shapes. Demonstrate this, since it is difficult for some children to grasp. Some children may want to cut figures; others may simply want designs. It is important to have some black between the different shapes. Once this is completed, the children can cut pieces of colored cellophane to fit behind the cut-out shapes. They glue these pieces on the back of one half of the black paper, so that they are sandwiched between the folded halves. Finally, glue the black construction paper closed. Tape the finished pieces to the classroom windows so that the light comes through the cellophane the way that light comes through stained-glass windows in a church.

LESSON 2: Illuminated Manuscripts

Viewing the Art

It is quite effective to have a Gregorian chant playing softly in the background while viewing the art in this lesson.

Explain to the children what monks are and their role in medieval life. Do the children know of any monasteries near their homes? Have they ever visited one? Show pictures of a typical medieval monastery, pointing out the cloister and garden where the monks could walk and pray, the attached church, the work rooms, and especially the scriptorium. One of the most important functions the monks performed was the creation and preservation of books, rare treasures in the days before the printing press made multiple copies of books feasible. Explain how the monks drew beautiful pictures and designs in the books they copied so that these books became precious works of art. We call these books illuminated manuscripts, because the art seems to light them with beauty. Show as many examples of illuminated manuscripts as you can. Note that there are full pages of illustrations as well as decorative borders and even decorative letters—the first letter of a paragraph, for example. What colors are used? What are the subjects of the illustrations? Read *The Sailor Who Captured the Sea* (see References) so that the children can see that it took 100 years to create the *Book of Kells*! Mention that the libraries established by the monks were about the only places in Europe where books were available during medieval times.

Journal Writing

Have the children imagine a world without books, their own lives without books. What would life be like? What are their feelings about the heritage medieval monks have passed on to us? What do they think of the illuminated manuscripts they have viewed?

Art/Drama Activity: Illumination and Dramatization

As mentioned in the background notes, the art of the Middle Ages was mostly religious. Monks in their monasteries spent their days copying the Bible by hand and illuminating its pages with their exquisite artwork. However, depending upon your student population and the community in which you teach, the Bible need not be the subject of this activity. A selection from any important document would do just as well.

february 13, 1991

Every body learned from the church they had a lot of art in the churches like stain glass windolves they had stacheus and paintings on the wall the priest ment a lot to oll the people the inside of the church was an arch the monks had serten jobs.

Materials

- Copies of a selection from the Bible, a government document, or a famous quotation, printed in the center of one side of a large sheet of paper. Leave ample borders and the other half of the sheet blank so children can paint a larger picture there. Leave out the first letter of the selection so children can paint in a decorative one.

- Small paintbrushes

- Paints (make sure you include gold)

Invite the children to "illuminate" the excerpt with their painting. Have samples of illuminated manuscripts available so the children can see where the monks placed their paintings and borders. The children might wish to copy some border patterns or create their own.

Children love to dramatize medieval life, assuming the different roles of king, lord, knights, peasants, merchants, monks, cathedral-builders, artisans. In a series of scenes, have them move through a typical day: knights training for combat, king and his court seeing to affairs of state, lord visiting his peasants and overseeing the running of his fiefdom, monks in their scriptorium, merchants in their shops, etc. This can be a very simple way of summing up some discussions of medieval life, or a more elaborate play with costumes, scenery, and an audience.

Curriculum Connections

Social Studies

- History of the Middle Ages
- Maps showing the countries discussed
- Timelines for important events
- Beliefs and customs of the time
- Clothing
- Different members of medieval society: kings, queens, lords, clergy, peasants, merchants, etc
- Food: Find out about foods of the period. Prepare one of them.

Science

- Medical practices of the time: bleeding, herb medicines. What herbs are still in use for healing today?
- Illness and disease, especially the Black Plague
- Sanitary conditions: lack of plumbing and proper garbage disposal
- Inventions: armor, military weapons
- Astronomy of the time: Find out what people believed about the Earth, Sun, and other heavenly bodies.
- Farming methods: Find out whether there were methods more advanced than those of ancient peoples like the Greeks, Egyptians, and Romans.

Music

- Instruments: Find out what instruments were used. Some, such as the recorder and tambourine, are easily obtained in a school. Work with the music teacher to play or invent some medieval tunes, or have older students play for the class.
- Dance: Learn a medieval dance.

Literature

- Older children might enjoy some of Chaucer's *Canterbury Tales*, as adapted by Barbara Cohen.

- Read biographies of some famous people of the period such as Marco Polo, St. Benedict, St. Bernard, Dante, Robin Hood.
- Read a version of King Arthur's tales suited to class abilities.
- Practice medieval script using Henry Shaw's *Alphabets & Numbers of the Middle Ages*.

References

Duby, Georges. *History of Medieval Art, 980–1440*. New York: Rizzoli International, 1986. Especially useful for a section on medieval monks and the function of the monastery.

Favier, Jean. *The World of Chartres*. Photography by Jean Bernard. New York: Harry N. Abrams, 1990. Originally published in French under the title *L'univers de Chartres*, this is an exquisite collection of large photos of the interior and exterior of the cathedral. Especially useful for viewing vaults, flying buttresses, and stained glass.

Snyder, James. *Medieval Art: Painting/Sculpture/Architecture, 4th–14th Century*. New York: Harry N. Abrams, 1989. Wonderful pictures of churches, especially useful for church interiors, and pictures of stained glass.

Children's Books

Aliki. *A Medieval Feast*. New York: Thomas Y. Crowell, 1983. Preparations at Camdenton Manor for the visit of the king, queen, and their retinue. This simple picture book gives children an idea of the kind of food eaten in medieval times.

Anno, Mitsumasa. *Anno's Medieval World*. New York: Philomel, 1979. In beautiful pictures and simple text, Anno reveals the culture and beliefs of medieval times.

Arnold, Joan. *Medieval Music*. Oxford, England: Oxford University Press, 1985. Simple discussion of medieval instruments and music for different occasions such as music for the crusades, for monks and priests, for courts and palaces. Provides discussion questions and suggestions for activities.

Brown, Peter, sel. *The Book of Kells*. New York: Thames and Hudson, 1989. Color reproductions of details from the beautiful *Book of Kells*.

Caselli, Giovanni. *The Middle Ages*. New York: Peter Bedrick Books, 1993. Explains everyday life in the Middle Ages, including pilgrims and hospices, and trade fairs and markets.

Clare, John D., ed. *Fourteenth-Century Towns*. San Diego, CA: Gulliver Books, 1993. Photographs of live actors reveal life in a medieval town, including a look into a merchant's home and apprenticeships.

Cohen, Barbara, adapt. *Canterbury Tales*. Illus. by Trina Schart Hyman. New York: Lothrop, 1988. Four of Chaucer's tales, translated from the Middle English and adapted, with delightful illustrations.

Collins, Marie, and Virginia Davis. *A Medieval Book of Seasons*. New York: HarperCollins,

1992 o.p. Shows activities of medieval life related to the four seasons. Illustrated with paintings from the *Book of Hours* and other illuminated manuscripts.

Cushman, Karen. *Catherine, Called Birdy.* New York: Clarion, 1994. Humorous novel for older children in which Catherine, through her diary, tells of her efforts to avoid an arranged marriage.

————. *The Midwife's Apprentice.* New York: Clarion, 1995. This Newbery Medal winner tells the story of a poor girl who is taken in by a midwife. The book gives a wonderful insight into life in medieval times.

Fradon, Dana. *Sir Dana: A Knight.* New York: E.P. Dutton, 1988. When children visit the armor room in the museum, a suit of armor comes to life and talks about the Middle Ages. Presents a good deal of information in a humorous, playful way.

Howarth, Sarah. *Medieval People.* Brookfield, CT: Millbrook Press, 1991. Discusses in simple language the daily lives of 13 medieval people such as the doctor, the heretic, the merchant, the pilgrim, the herald. Very useful.

————. *Medieval Places.* Brookfield, CT: Millbrook Press, 1991. Describes various medieval buildings and places such as the peasant's cottage, the castle, the battlefield, the forest, the guildhall.

————. *The Middle Ages.* New York: Viking, 1993. An interesting look at the period including clothing, pastimes, disease and medicine, and the life of a noble. Plastic overlays.

Humble, Richard. *The Travels of Marco Polo.* Illus. by Richard Hook. New York: Franklin Watts, 1990. Picture book presentation of Polo's trip to the court of Kublai Khan and some of his lesser known journeys.

Hunt, Jonathan. *Illuminations.* New York: Bradbury, 1989. An illustrated book of such medieval terms as "coat of arms," "Black Death," "Excalibur," and "quintain."

Kent, Zachary. *Marco Polo.* Chicago: Children's Press, 1992. Describes Polo's travels and discoveries in the Far East.

Lattimore, Deborah Nourse. *The Sailor Who Captured the Sea.* New York: HarperCollins, 1991. A picture book that shows the incredible work involved in creating the beautiful *Book of Kells.*

Macaulay, David. *Castle.* Boston: Houghton Mifflin, 1977. Shows the planning and construction of a medieval castle.

————. *Cathedral.* Boston: Houghton Mifflin, 1973. Shows the planning and construction of a medieval cathedral.

Macdonald, Fiona. *A Medieval Cathedral.* Illus. by John James. New York: Peter Bedrick Books, 1994. Cutaway illustrations depict the building of a medieval cathedral. Excellent for viewing such elements as flying buttresses.

Mason, Antony. *If You Were There in Medieval Times.* Illus. by Richard Berridge. New York: Simon & Schuster, 1996. Enables young readers to experience firsthand what life was like in the Middle Ages. Includes a fold-out maze.

Mitgutsch, Ali. *A Knight's Book.* Transl. by Elizabeth D. Crawford. New York: Clarion Books, 1991. A squire tells of his adventures with his knight. Humorously written and accompanied by cartoon illustrations.

Morressy, John. *The Juggler*. New York: Henry Holt, 1996. A fascinating novel for older readers about a juggler living in medieval times, who gives everything he has to perfect his craft.

Needham, Kate. *The Middle Ages*. Illus. by Sheena Vickers and Dave Burroughs. Brookfield, CT: Millbrook Press, 1996. Presents life in the Middle Ages for young children.

Rockwell, Anne. *Glass, Stones & Crown*. New York: Atheneum, 1968 o.p. The story of Abbé Suger and the building of the Church of St. Denis.

Roth, Susan L. *Marco Polo: His Notebook*. New York: Doubleday, 1990 o.p. A picture book that contains a fictional account of Marco Polo's journeys in diary form. Based on his book *The Travels of Marco Polo* and other works about him.

Sancha, Sheila. *Walter Dragun's Town*. New York: Thomas Y. Crowell, 1987. Crafts and trade in the Middle Ages.

Shaw, Henry. *Alphabets & Numbers of the Middle Ages*. New York: Crescent Books, 1988. Provides models of letters and ornaments from the Middle Ages.

Skurzynski, Gloria. *The Minstrel in the Tower*. Illus. by Julek Heller. New York: Random House, 1988. Because their father died in the Crusades and their mother is seriously ill, young Roger and Alice set off on a perilous journey to find their uncle, a powerful baron. A short simple novel.

Talbott, Hudson. *King Arthur and the Round Table*. New York: Morrow Junior Books, 1995. A picture-book version of the King Arthur tale, accompanied by beautiful illustrations.

———. *Excalibur*. New York: Morrow Junior Books, 1996. In this picture-book story, young Arthur asks the Lady of the Lake for the sword Excalibur and promises to be deserving of it by performing deeds of valor.

Temple, Frances. *The Ramsay Scallop*. New York: Orchard, 1994. A wonderful novel about two young betrothed noble people who embark on a pilgrimage together. For older readers.

Williams, Brian. *Forts & Castles*. New York: Viking, 1995. Forts in different parts of Europe and the East. Plastic overlays.

Williams, Marcia. *King Arthur and the Knights of the Round Table*. Cambridge, MA: Candlewick Press, 1996. Comic-strip retelling of the tales of Camelot.

Wilson, Elizabeth B. *Bibles and Bestiaries*. New York: Farrar, Straus & Giroux, 1994. A marvelous presentation of illuminated manuscripts, how they were made, and the best-selling books of the time. Glossary.

Wright, Rachel, and Anita Ganeri. *Castles*. New York: Franklin Watts, 1995. Talks about castles of the Middle Ages and describes various activities for children such as making pulp and paper castles and tapestry.

Young, Bonnie. *A Walk Through the Cloisters*. Photographs by Malcolm Varon. New York: Viking, 1979. Shows the buildings and art collections at the Metropolitan Museum of Art's Cloisters museum.

Yue, Charlotte, and David Yue. *Armor*. Boston: Houghton Mifflin, 1994. Discusses knights and knighthood and the development of different kinds of armor.

Audiovisual Materials

Castle. Tours the castles of Edward I and explores medieval life through an animated story of the castle. Based on Macaulay's book. (Videocassette; 60 mins. Available from Library Video Company.)

Cathedral. Based on the book by David Macaulay, with animation. (Videocassette; 55 mins. Available from PBS Video.)

The Medieval Manuscript: Art and Function. Shows how manuscripts were illuminated in medieval times and what materials were used. (Videocassette; 30 mins. Available from Films for the Humanities and Sciences.)

My Make-Believe Castle. Children can manipulate medieval characters such as knights, princesses, dragons, etc. They can also design family crests, experiment with a catapult, and play songs on a harp. Grades K–2. (CD-ROM for Mac and Windows. Available from LCSI.)

Westminster Abbey: A House of Kings. A history of the cathedral begun in 1050. Includes views of the parts closed to the public. (Videocassette; 55 mins. Available from Public Media Video.)

Chant. The Benedictine monks of Santa Domingo de Silos sing Gregorian chants. Simply beautiful! Comes with program notes. (Angel; CD or audiocassette.)

Other Materials

Shepard, Mary B., and Fifi Weinert. *Fun with Stained Glass*. New York: Viking, 1996. A kit which contains everything needed to create colorful stained-glass panels. Comes with a 64-page book that explores the history of stained glass.

Crusader's Castle. A kit that enables students to make a medieval castle by mixing their own cement and using the miniature terracotta bricks provided. Includes turrets, battlements, a working drawbridge, and a secret passage. Cement is water soluble, so the castle can be taken apart and rebuilt. (Available from the Metropolitan Museum of Art.)

8 Art of the Renaissance

Thank God that it has been permitted to be born in this new age, so full of hope and promise, which already rejoices in a greater array of nobly-gifted souls than the world has seen in the thousand years that have preceded it.

—MATTEO PALMIERI (fifteenth century) in Hale, *Renaissance*

Background Information

As we have seen, Europe during the Middle Ages was in a state of almost constant war and deprivation. Most people worked so hard to survive that they had time for little else. The Church dominated life and thought, and her members obeyed almost without question. But by the fourteenth century, a number of changes began to take place that gradually ushered in a new era called the Renaissance, from the French word that means "rebirth."

Artists and scholars began to look back to the glorious days of the Greeks and Romans for inspiration and enlightenment. What they found in the ancient writings gave rise to a new movement called Humanism, in which the talents and worth of people in their own right were celebrated. Instead of yielding control solely to the Church, people began to question the Church's practices and to nourish a desire to control their own destinies. The clergy's amassing of wealth and selling of indulgences, believed to shorten a person's punishment after death, eventually gave rise to increased criticism. The monk Savonarola preached repentance and a stricter moralism in the Church, and urged Florentines to burn anything that hinted of the secular world. Another monk, Martin Luther, published a list of grievances against the Church and caused a split in her ranks in 1517. Never again would all of Europe worship with one voice.

Increased population of the cities and towns and the rise of a merchant class created a need for more widespread education, and the newly invented printing press made such education possible. Libraries—located mainly in the monasteries of Europe where the monks, often poorly educated themselves and prone to make mistakes, painstakingly copied books by hand—gave way to universities where businessmen could learn the intricacies of law they needed to enter into contracts and arrange trade agreements.

Increased trade, in turn, opened the door to new ideas and ways of life and created a need for more direct trade routes. Some countries sent brave men such as Prince Henry the Navigator, Christopher Columbus, Bartholomew Diaz, Vasco da Gama, Ferdinand Magellan, and Sir Francis Drake to seek such routes. What these men found were not only new passages, but entire continents! Such time-honored ideas as a flat world and the earth as the center of the universe shattered in the face of these explorations and the writings of astronomers like Galileo. Machiavelli's *The Prince* revolutionized ideas about governing while Luca Pacioli's *Arithmetic, Geometry, and Proportion* introduced double-entry bookkeeping to Italian merchants. There were important advances in medicine such as the establishment of hospitals, the quarantine of contagious diseases, and the recognition of typhus by the physician Girolamo Fracastoro.

It is not surprising that the Renaissance began in Italy, where a system of independent city-states had long before replaced the subservient system of feudalism in effect in the rest of Europe. Rich merchants and trading organizations called guilds often wielded great power in these states. In Florence, the Medici, a wealthy merchant and banking family that ruled for three generations, poured immense amounts of money into the arts. Although they suffered at the hands of the rival Pazzi family and Giuliano de Medici was assassinated, his brother Lorenzo spent the family fortune in commissioning artists to beautify not only his palace and gardens, but the city of Florence as well.

Under Medici patronage, artists flourished, and Florence embarked on a golden age similar to that of Athens under Pericles. Giotto, Botticelli, Brunelleschi, Fra Angelico, Luca della Robbia, Donatello, Ghiberti, Michelangelo, and Paolo Uccello are among the marvelous artists who were born and worked in Florence. And numerous others, not native to the city, were attracted there by the generous support and commissions of Lorenzo de Medici. The marvelous painter Masaccio, whose works showed a realism and skill with perspective that made them worthy of study by such artistic giants as Leonardo da Vinci, Michelangelo, and Raphael, spent time in this glorious city. Popes, too, supported the arts, and some gave more thought and money to the building and adornment of churches than to the care and instruction of the faithful.

Although he was born before the fifteenth and sixteenth centuries, which mark the Renaissance proper, Giotto is credited with initiating an artistic renaissance that was to gain momentum and culminate in the work of da Vinci, Michelangelo, and Raphael. Giotto's work, while lacking the sophistication and knowledge of anatomy and perspective of artists who would come after him, is filled with a realism unknown to his contemporaries, who were used to the stiff, decorative figures of the medieval world. His paintings were so revolutionary that he became famous in his own lifetime and raised the vocation of "artist" to a new dignity. Following in Giotto's footsteps, Renaissance artists continued on a revolutionary path, learning more about anatomy, the human figure, realism, and perspective. Sculptors moved from the low-relief sculptures in medieval churches to life-sized statues in the full round, and Donatello created the first nude since Greek times. Della Robbia developed the process of glazing terra cotta so that less expensive sculptures could be made available to those who wanted them. Architects worked on such magnificent structures as the church of St. Peter in Rome, the church of San Lorenzo and the baptistery, and the cathedral in Florence.

From Florence, the Renaissance gradually spread to northern Italy and then to the rest of Europe, but in no place did it take such a hold as in the glorious "city of the flowers." Even today, almost every street of that city bears witness to the genius of the Renaissance artists who built buildings, sculpted statues, and painted pictures within her walls. Eventually, the city-states became weaker, and toward the end of the fifteenth century, France invaded Italy. Italian nobility and prominent families could no longer afford to support the arts, and the era of the Renaissance came to a close. But its effects are felt even to our own day, and art will forever be judged by the standards set down in that incredible time.

To make study of this period more manageable, it can be divided into the Early Renaissance and the Late, or High, Renaissance, although this is an artificial division. Giotto, Filippo Brunelleschi and Donatello, and Sandro Botticelli are Early Renaissance; Leonardo da Vinci, Michelangelo Buonarotti, and Raphaello Sanzio are High Renaissance.

LESSON 1: Giotto (1266–1337)

❑ The Story

Once there was a young boy about eight years of age who lived with his family on a farm outside the city of Florence in Italy. Every day his task was to watch the sheep as they grazed on the hillside. Now the boy was happy to help his family in this way, but it was boring work. So to keep himself amused, every day after he had finished his lunch of bread and cheese, the boy would pick up a sharp stick and draw pictures on the ground. He drew the sheep, the trees, and the other things he saw around him.

One day, while the boy was packing his lunch and getting ready to set off for the hills with the sheep, an artist named Cimabue was getting ready to take a walk in the countryside. He was the most famous artist in all of Florence—so famous, in fact, that he was exhausted from all the jobs he was given to do. Wealthy people paid him to paint pictures in churches throughout the city. Cimabue had his own workshop, where he taught young boys called apprentices how to paint and gave them small jobs to do on the pictures he painted. But on this day, Cimabue was sick of working. "Some fresh country air will do me a world of good," he told his apprentices. "Take care of things until I return." And off he went.

After a few hours of walking, Cimabue came to the young boy's farm. Now the boy had just finished his lunch and was beginning a new drawing on the ground. The boy was so absorbed in his work that he did not hear the artist come up behind him. Cimabue watched for a long time without making a sound. Finally, he could stand it no longer. "Boy," he said, "who taught you to draw like that?"

Startled, the boy looked up and saw the man, but did not know who he was. He only knew that the man's clothes were much finer than any clothing he had ever seen, and he was afraid. But he answered with courage, "No one, sir."

"Come, come," replied Cimabue. "Someone must have taught you, for you show a good deal of skill. Who is your teacher?"

Again the boy answered, "No one, sir. I am a poor shepherd boy. My father could certainly not afford a teacher for me. I simply draw to pass the time while I guard the sheep."

Cimabue was amazed, for not even the boys he taught in his workshop every day did work as fine as this. "Take me to see your father," he said. So the boy led the sheep back to their corral and took Cimabue to the fields where his father was plowing.

As soon as he saw such a well-dressed man from the city on his property, the boy's father began to worry. Did he owe money on his taxes? Was he about to lose his land? Had his son done something to offend the man? For although Cimabue was famous, the boy's father did not know who he was either.

Then Cimabue spoke. "My good man, I am Cimabue, a painter in the city. My paintings appear in churches throughout Florence, and boys come from far off to study in my workshop. I have watched your son draw, and he has talent. You must allow him to come with me to Florence and live as an apprentice with the other boys. I will teach him all I know about drawing and painting."

The boy's father was deeply troubled by this. How could he afford to pay Cimabue to teach his son? And who would take care of the sheep if his boy were no longer there? "Sir, you flatter us," he said. "But I cannot afford to send my son to you. I am a poor man. And besides, I need him to care for the sheep."

"Sheep!" cried Cimabue. "Do you put sheep before art? Do you put your little farm before the glory of Florence? You must send the boy to me. A talent like his cannot be wasted! I will teach the boy for nothing and will provide his room and board. You need only free him from his work here."

And so the boy's father agreed to send him to Florence the very next day to study with Cimabue. The boy worked for the artist for several years, until he became even better at drawing than his master. Everyone was amazed by his pictures, for the people he drew actually seemed real. After a time he left Cimabue and started a workshop of his own with his own apprentices. Wealthy people and even popes gave him money to paint pictures in churches. One time a pope asked for a sample of his work and the artist, with one stroke of his brush, drew a perfect circle. The pope hired him immediately.

That boy's name was Giotto, and he started a whole new kind of art that was to change forever the way artists painted pictures. Painters came from all over Europe to study his work, and they still do today. When Giotto died, he was buried in the cathedral in Florence, where years before he had designed the baptistery tower. This was an honor reserved only for very important people. More than 100 years after he died, the people of Florence put a special medallion in the cathedral showing Giotto working on a mosaic. They considered him the grandfather of Italian art. The ruler of the city, Lorenzo de Medici, ordered that a plaque be placed under the medallion reading, "I am he through whose merit the lost art of painting was revived; whose hand was as faultless as it was compliant. What my art lacked nature herself lacked; to none other was it given to paint more or better. But what need is there for words? I am Giotto, and my name alone tells more than a lengthy ode."

Giotto's paintings were mostly Bible stories, for they decorated the walls of churches. We're going to enjoy some of them together now, and as I show them to you, see if you know any of the stories the pictures tell.

Viewing the Art

Show some medieval paintings and some work of Cimabue. Then show some of Giotto's paintings. His frescoes from the Scrovengi (or Arena) Chapel are especially appropriate, and their reproductions in Madeleine L'Engle's *The Glorious Impossible* are large and very fine. The reproductions in Basile's *Giotto: The Arena Chapel Frescoes* are even larger and there are many close-up details. What differences do the children see? Quote from Eimerl, *The World of Giotto*:

> Representations of the human face in earlier paintings had given it an expressionless stare; he [Giotto] invested it with grief, fear, pity, joy or other emotions to which the viewer could respond with instant

understanding. Above all, Giotto endowed his people with flesh and blood. (p. 9)

Do the children agree with this statement? Are they able to feel with his characters? The frescoes in the Scrovengi tell a story from the birth of Christ to the Ascension and the Last Judgment. Do the children know any of the stories these paintings tell?

Explain how a fresco was made:

1. The artist makes an outline, often called a cartoon, of the painting on a piece of paper. Small holes are pierced at intervals along the outline.

2. The cartoon is divided into squares, each square representing one day's work.

3. The whole wall on which the painting will be placed is plastered roughly to cover over bricks or other matter on the wall.

4. When the first coat of plaster is dry, a small portion of the wall, enough for one day's work, is plastered smoothly.

5. One square of the cartoon is placed over the wet plaster, and a bag containing charcoal is rubbed over it. The charcoal seeps through the holes pierced along the cartoon, leaving a black outline on the wet plaster. The dots of charcoal are then joined with paint and the underlying charcoal brushed away.

6. The picture is painted in using paints mixed beforehand. The painting process must be completed before the plaster dries so that the paint dries into the plaster, thus making a long-lasting work.

Making frescoes is very difficult, because the artist must know how long the plaster will take to dry under various weather conditions, and how long it will take to complete the painting. If he or she makes a mistake, the whole section has to be scraped off and replastered.

Show pictures of the bell tower of the Florence cathedral, designed by Giotto. A wonderful story to tell in connection with this bell tower is "The Rose of Midwinter" from the book *Elves and Ellefolk* by Natalia Belting. This story is guaranteed to keep Giotto's bell tower in the children's minds for a considerable time to come.

Whenever we do something for the first time, whether it's riding a bike or learning to write our alphabet, we do it imperfectly. It was the same for Giotto. No artist since the days of the Romans had done what he had. And so even though we know that Giotto's paintings do not have the movement and perspective of later works, he is important because he forged a new beginning and led the way for those who would come after him.

Journal Writing

What kinds of emotions do the children see on the faces of Giotto's characters? How does viewing these characters make the children feel? Invite the children to imagine that they are living in Florence in Giotto's time and seeing his work for the first time. They are not used to such pictures. What is their reaction? What do they like or dislike about Giotto's work, and why?

Art/Drama Activity: A Fresco Mural

Materials

- 4 very large sheets of paper, cut from a roll, if possible
- Colored markers

Divide the children into four groups and invite them to make a mural depicting how frescoes, a popular art form during the Renaissance, were made. Each group draws and labels a part of the process. In their drawings, which can be as simple as stick figures, the children should draw the artist and his apprentices working together. When the groups have finished their work, tape the pieces together to form a large mural for the classroom or hall wall. Keep the mural up throughout your study of the Renaissance. Suggestions for the group divisions and labels:

- Making the cartoon
- Plastering the wall
- Rubbing the cartoon with charcoal
- Painting in the picture

LESSON 2: Filippo Brunelleschi (1377–1446) and Donatello (1386–1466)

❏ The Story

Over six hundred years ago in Florence, a boy named Filippo Brunelleschi was born who would one day become one of the most famous architects who ever lived. His father was a notary. That meant that he witnessed the signing of documents for the wealthy and important businessmen in Florence. So Filippo's family had a good deal of money and were able to give him a fine education. His father hoped that Filippo would work for the government as he did, but Filippo was more interested in art, so the boy was sent to be an apprentice to a goldsmith. It wasn't long before people began to see that he was a sculptor of talent, and Filippo set up a workshop of his own. One day a young boy came and asked to be his apprentice. The boy's name was Donato, but everybody called him Donatello. Donatello's father was not as wealthy as Filippo's, for he was a wool comber. The wool trade was one of the most important businesses in Florence. Donatello was ten years younger than Filippo, but they quickly became good friends.

Now the Florentines loved contests, and they often gave jobs to artists who won them. When the city leaders decided the Baptistery of St. John needed new doors, Filippo and a sculptor named Ghiberti entered a contest to see who would be hired. The doors would be filled with golden squares, each square containing a sculpture of a scene from the Bible. Both Filippo and Ghiberti were told to do the same scene: the story of Abraham being stopped by an angel from sacrificing his son to God. Filippo and Ghiberti worked hard for months to make their bronze carvings as perfect as possible. But when the judges looked at the results, they gave the job to Ghiberti. Filippo was discouraged, but he had to admit that Ghiberti's work was better. And besides, he really didn't want to be a sculptor. His real love was designing buildings. So he decided to go to Rome, the land of the master builders, and learn all he could by studying the buildings of those ancient architects. Although Donatello was only about fourteen at the time, Filippo invited him to go too.

Both artists loved Rome. Filippo spent hours and hours in the Pantheon looking up at the dome. "How did the Romans get that huge dome up without having it come crashing down?" Filippo asked himself over and over again. In his city of Florence, there was a problem with the cathedral, Santa Maria del Fiore, St. Mary of the Flower. The builders had so enlarged it from its original design they could not figure out how to put a dome over it. No one had been able to solve the problem, and for years the cathedral stood unfinished. Filippo wanted to be the architect who would design a dome for one of Florence's greatest treasures. Donatello, meanwhile, studied the ruins of ancient sculptures. He saw how the Romans formed arms and legs and bodies so that they looked real. Never had he seen anything like these works of art!

When they finally arrived back in Florence, Filippo was given some very important jobs. He designed a hospital for orphans and some churches, and they were all quite wonderful, but he continued to think about a dome for the cathedral. The more he thought, the more convinced he was that he could design a dome that would work, and he began to make a model. His friend Donatello helped him.

Soon the Florentine officials held another big contest, inviting artists from all over Europe to bring their models for the cathedral dome. Filippo's model was finished, but he refused to show it to the judges. Only Donatello knew what it looked like. The judges became very angry and demanded that he present his model the way all the other architects did. But Filippo decided to teach them a lesson. He took a hard-boiled egg from his cloak and asked if they could stand it up without having it fall over. Of course, none of the judges could. Then he banged the egg on the table to flatten one end, and the egg stood perfectly without falling.

"Well, anyone could stand up that egg by smashing one end," said a judge.

"Of course," said another. "If we had only known that's what you were going to do, we could have done it ourselves."

"That's just my point," replied Filippo. "If you see my model, then anyone can copy my idea and build the dome. You must trust that I can do it and give me the job without seeing my model."

The judges didn't like that answer, but none of the other architects came up with an idea that would work, so Filippo was hired. Filippo's idea was to make two domes, one inside the other, so the two domes would strengthen each other and stay up without a central support until the building was complete. And he made the domes in the shape of a Gothic arch so that they wouldn't exert so much pressure on the walls. The dome was so high that Filippo designed special machinery to help the workers get up there safely and haul their materials up as well. What a celebration there was when Florence finally had its finished cathedral! In fact, even now, when Florentines leave their city or go away on vacation, they often say, "I miss my cathedral!"

Donatello, meanwhile, also worked on his own sculptures and amazed the city of Florence by his accomplishments. He carved marble statues of people in the Bible for churches in the city, and he made a bronze statue of David the giant killer that was the first nude statue since the time of the ancient Greeks and Romans! The people of Florence loved their sculptor, and they were sad when he spent a long time in Padua doing sculptures there. While he was in Padua, he carved the first person on horseback since the days of the Romans. When the people began to complain that he was taking too long, Donatello threatened to crack the statue's head. "If you do that, we will break *your* head," the people said. "I don't mind," answered Donatello, "as long as you fix my head as beautifully as I will fix the head of your statue" (Bennett & Wilkins, p. 31).

Filippo and Donatello remained friends all their lives. Filippo died at the age of sixty-nine and Donatello was an old man of eighty when he died—most unusual at a time when so many people did not live past forty. The Florentines loved him so much that even though he was too sick to make beautiful statues for them any longer, they rented a house for him and gave him money until his death. Today, if you go to Florence, you can see Filippo's dome rising gloriously above all the other buildings, and you can see Donatello's beautiful statues in churches and museums throughout the city.

Viewing the Art

(Some Renaissance sculpture recommended for viewing are nudes, as in Donatello's *David* here and some of Michelangelo's works further on. They are mentioned because they are masterpieces and well worth studying. Children who are prepared beforehand can usually handle themselves well. However, if you feel your community might object, simply omit them.)

Battisti's *Filippo Brunelleschi* and Poeshke's *Donatello and His World* are both incredibly rich sources of large, detailed reproductions of these two artists' work. Be sure to show Donatello's marble *David* and then his very famous bronze *David* (you may want to compare it to Michelangelo's *David* later if you teach that artist); his *Cantoria* for the Duomo (the children should especially love this); his wooden statue of *Mary Magdalene*; his bronze *Judith*; his equestrian *Monument of Gattamelata*; and his crucifix for Santa Croce. Tell the children that when Brunelleschi saw that crucifix, he told Donatello he didn't like it, and Donatello challenged him to make a crucifix himself and see if he could do better. Brunelleschi did, and the crucifix hangs in Santa Maria Novella (Bennett and Wilkins, p. 31).

After you show both crucifixes (both are in Poeschke), ask the children which they prefer and why. Mention how unusual it is for a sculptor to work in marble, bronze, and wood. Show Brunelleschi's and Ghiberti's sculptures of *Abraham* for the Baptistery doors. Which do the children like best and why? Also view the Foundling Hospital. Spend the rest of the time on the dome of the cathedral. Show individual views of the dome and then of Florence, with the dome towering above all else. It stands as a tribute to Brunelleschi's genius even to this day.

Journal Writing

Why was Donatello such an important sculptor? Of all the statues they studied, which is the children's favorite and why? After viewing Brunelleschi's *Abraham* sculpture and his crucifix, do the children think he should have continued sculpting, or was he wise to switch to architecture? If he had remained a sculptor, do they think he and Donatello would have remained friends? Why or why not? In what ways was the friendship of these two men beneficial to themselves and the world of art?

5/12/93

I really liked being
being narrator. It was
fun except the one
time I made a mistake
I never knew I could
speak so loudly. It was
lots of fun being the
bishop. I felt like I
really was the bishop
and the apprentice.

Art/Drama Activity: Writing a Book

Materials

- Large sheets of paper
- Pencils
- Markers

Divide the children into groups and invite them to make a book about the lives and work of the two friends Brunelleschi and Donatello. Each group can work on one phase of the artists' lives, writing a bit of text on one page with an illustration on the opposite page. When the work is complete, bind the pages together for a class book. Decide together on a title and a cover page. Some suggestions for book "chapters":

- Brunelleschi and Ghiberti showing their sculptures for the Baptistery doors to the judges
- Brunelleschi and Donatello journeying to Rome and studying there
- Donatello sculpting in his studio, mention some of his statues
- Several architects showing their models to the judges for the dome competition
- Brunelleschi and his workers building the dome
- The cathedral of St. Mary of the Flower

LESSON 3: Sandro Botticelli (1444–1510)

❑ The Story

Over five hundred years ago, a baby was born in Florence. He was the last of seven children, and his parents named him Sandro. Sandro's father was a tanner, and because there were so many children to feed, the family did not have much money. But when his older brothers and sisters left home to make their own way in the world, Sandro's parents were able to give him an education.

You would think Sandro would be grateful for the opportunity to learn and to have what his parents could not afford to give his brothers and sisters. But Sandro was a grumpy child, often sick, and a nuisance. His father was glad to be able to send Sandro off to his older brother's goldsmith shop as an apprentice, where he learned the skills of an artist. Sandro also studied for eleven years with a famous artist named Fra Filippo. "Fra" means "brother," for Filippo was a monk. Soon Sandro was doing paintings of his own, and his work was so good that the pope heard about him and invited him to Rome to paint some frescoes on the wall of a new chapel, called the Sistine Chapel, which he had just built. Other people began to hear about Sandro, too. One day he received a message from one of the most important men in Florence, Lorenzo de Medici. Lorenzo lived in a palace, and he spent thousands of dollars paying artists to paint and do sculptures for the churches and buildings of Florence. It was a great honor to be given a job by him, and Sandro went to the palace right away. He did many pictures for Lorenzo and remained his friend until Lorenzo died.

Remember what a cranky child Sandro was? He didn't change when he grew up. He lived by himself and never married. One day, he went to the house next door and complained to the weaver who lived there that the noise from his looms was driving him crazy. "I can't think. I can't even paint my pictures"! Sandro complained. The weaver paid no attention to him. "I can do what I feel like in my own house," he replied.

You can imagine how angry that made Sandro. He thought and thought about a way to get even with the weaver, and finally he had an idea. He got a ladder, climbed up to the roof of his house, and put a big boulder right on the edge. Sandro's roof was very high, higher than the weaver's next door, and slanted. If anything happened to shake the walls of the house, that boulder would roll off and go crashing into the weaver's house. When the weaver looked out his window and saw what his neighbor was doing, he became very frightened and went running to Sandro's house. When Sandro answered his knock, the weaver said, "You can't keep that boulder on your roof. It could roll off and damage my house. It could even kill me!" Can you guess Sandro's reply? Of course he said, "I can do what I feel like in my own house!" And from that day on, he never heard the weaver's looms again! (Vasari, also Burroughs, pp. 148–49).

As Sandro got older, he became very sick and could no longer paint. He even had to walk with crutches. He received no more jobs and was very poor. After he died at the age of sixty-six, people forgot about his work for three hundred years. But now we realize that he was one of the great artists of his time.

Viewing the Art

Botticelli painted not only religious pictures but secular ones as well. His *Primavera* and *Birth of Venus* are two of his most famous secular paintings. Be sure to show them to the children. Help the children to see that Botticelli's figures are elongated, or longer than figures would be in reality. Note his graceful lines, and the exquisite features on the faces. Tell the children that "primavera" means "spring." What signs of spring does Botticelli put in his picture? Tell the children the story of the *Birth of Venus* as you view the picture. Show some of Botticelli's portraits (*Giuliane de' Medici, Man with a Medal, Head of a Young Man*) as well as some of his religious paintings (*The Magnificat, Madonna of the Book, Madonna with the Pomegranate, The Annunciation,* and *Adoration of the Magi,* in which the tall figure in the gold cloak on the right is thought to be a self-portrait of Botticelli).

Journal Writing

Which of Botticelli's pictures do the children like best? Why? Why did he elongate his figures? What are some words the children can think of to describe Botticelli's paintings? Why do they suppose people neglected his work for 300 years?

Art/Drama Activity: Botticelli's Seasons

Materials

- Paper
- Colored pencils (make sure to have colors the children will need to represent the four seasons)

One of Botticelli's most famous paintings is his *Primavera*, in celebration of spring. But he also depicted *Autumn* and *Winter*. Show these two pictures to the children (Venturi, p. 12). Invite the children to choose a season and draw a picture to represent it. Perhaps they would like to begin by making a list of all the elements they can think of for their chosen season. For example, a fall list might include colored leaves, a rake, fall vegetables such as pumpkins and squashes, hay rides, bulbs for planting, soccer balls, etc. Once their list is completed, the children can consider how to incorporate some of the elements in their pictures.

LESSON 4: Leonardo da Vinci (1452–1519)

❑ The Story

"**A**ndrea, my good friend, how are you?" asked Ser Piero da Vinci as he entered the shop of the great artist Andrea del Verrocchio.

"Ah, fine, Piero, but so busy! Commissions for madonnas, portraits of our rich citizens here in Florence, sculptures . . . so busy. My apprentices and I can hardly keep up with the work."

"Well, look at these, then," said Piero. "They are a few drawings done by my son, Leonardo. You wouldn't believe that boy! Such talent! One day a friend of mine came in with a shield he wanted decorated with a painting. Leonardo took it and assembled dozens of creatures: bats, crawling reptiles, locusts—ugh, such ugly things! He studied them for days. Then he made a painting of one fantastic creature out of all of them. When I saw the shield with that hideous creature painted on it, I thought I was being attacked and nearly fainted. It was so real! Ever since we have moved here from our little town of Vinci, I have dreamed of apprenticing my Leonardo to a master like you. What do you think? Leo can learn much from you, and he would be a help with all the work you have here."

"Hmmm. These are good. Quite good for one so young. Send him to me, and we'll see what can be done with him."

And so Leonardo da Vinci came to Verrocchio's workshop and learned how to grind pigments for paints, and how to prepare walls for frescoes. He even got to paint in some clothing on the people Andrea drew. Then one day, Andrea said, "Leonardo, paint two angels in the corner of this picture of the baptism of Jesus I've just finished." Leonardo was delighted with this chance to paint real figures. He spent all his spare time walking the streets of Florence studying people—even ugly people, for he was fascinated with faces of all kinds. He would follow a person all day, sketching on the pad he always carried with him. But he did not make these angels ugly. He made them very delicate and graceful, and when he had finished, they were better than the figures his master had painted. "Never again will I work with paints," Andrea declared. "You can do it for me, while I turn my hand to sculpture which I love much more." Leonardo was only twenty years old when he painted those angels, and they were not perfect. He still had much to learn, but his reputation as a painter spread. And because he was so gentle, kind, and even handsome, people followed him and loved to be near him.

Since he started painting so young and lived a long life for those times, you would think that Leonardo did hundreds of paintings. But actually, he did very few—probably fewer than twenty. And even some of these are not completed. Can you imagine that? Do you think it was because he was lazy?

Actually, Leonardo never stopped working, but he worked at so many things, he never spent a long time in one single occupation. He was brilliant—some say one of the smartest people who ever lived—and he was interested in everything. Leonardo da Vinci was a musician who played the lyre, a popular instrument at that time, and sang beautifully. He wrote poetry. He was a scientist who studied the heavens, the muscles and organs of the human body, the movement of water, medicine, and flowers and plants. He also studied mathematics. Leonardo invented many things, including the parachute, weapons, a machine that was like our submarine, and even a flying machine that was not very successful. His mind was way ahead of the thinkers of his time, and we still use many of his ideas today.

Although we only have a few of Leonardo's paintings, we have hundreds of drawings that he made during his studies. He filled many notebooks with these drawings and notes, and we have about 5,000 pages of these still in existence. But if you tried to read them, you would have a hard time, because he wrote from right to left and reversed his letters. Some people say he did this because he wrote with his left hand and it was easier for him to write like that. Others think he was trying to keep his notes secret.

Leonardo was always conducting experiments. Some worked, but many were failures, and that is why some of his paintings did not survive. Once he was asked to paint a battle scene on the walls of a public building in Florence. He worked for months making beautiful drawings to get ready for the painting. But instead of doing a fresco the way the other painters of his day did, he used a new, thick paint mixture. Before he even got the painting finished, the paint began to run down the walls onto the floor, and he abandoned the project. While he was in the northern Italian city of Milan designing weapons for the ruler there, some monks asked him to do a painting in their monastery. He worked for years on that painting, and some say it is one of the greatest paintings in the world. It is called *The Last Supper* and shows Christ eating with his friends before he died. But again, Leonardo experimented with the paint, and the painting began to flake off the walls even in his own lifetime. The king of France loved that painting so much he tried to have the wall cut out of the monastery and brought to France, but it is still in Milan, and visitors still go to see it.

When he became old and ill, King Francis I invited Leonardo to come to France as his special painter. He gave Leonardo a beautiful house and paid him well. Leonardo's right hand was paralyzed, but since he could paint equally well with both hands, he could still work and teach. He lived four years in France and died there at the age of sixty-seven. He once said, "As a well-spent day brings happy sleep, so a life well used brings happy death." (McLanathan, p. 83). Truly, Leonardo had used his life well.

Viewing the Art

Mention that since Leonardo was so greatly admired, many artists copied his work, and it is only after careful study that scholars have been able to determine which pictures were actually done by him. Since so few of Leonardo's paintings exist, be sure to show the children as many of them as you can collect. A good place to begin is with Leonardo's angels in Verrocchio's *Baptism of Christ*. Then show *The Annunciation*, Leonardo's first complete work. This does not compare with the wonderful work of his later years. The children may enjoy hearing how someone else enlarged the angel's wings. Talk about the pyramid created by the figures in *Madonna of the Rocks* and *The Virgin and Child with St. Anne*. Note the many different hand positions in the *Madonna of the Rocks*. Show some of Leonardo's portraits: *Ginevra de Benci; Lady with an Ermine; Portrait of a Musician*; and, of course, his famous *Mona Lisa*. Tell the children that she may be smiling because Leonardo hired musicians to amuse her while he painted her picture. Discuss *The Last Supper*, showing details if you can so that the children can focus on the different faces of the disciples. In Leonardo's unfinished *St. Jerome* and *Adoration of the Magi*, note the expressions on the faces and the multitude of characters in the *Adoration of the Magi*. Perhaps here is where all of Leonardo's studies of people in the streets bore fruit.

As you view all of Leonardo's paintings, a major point to discuss is his use of light and shadow to produce depth, called *chiaroscuro*. The children love pronouncing this musical Italian word. Have them note examples of Leonardo's use of chiaroscuro in his work. From the paintings, move on to the notebooks and drawings. Also mention that Leonardo was one of the first to depict realistic landscape as an integral part of a painting. Be sure to show some of Leonardo's drawings of horses and cats, and mention his love of animals—he loved them so much he became a vegetarian. How many different areas of interest can the children find in the drawings?

Journal Writing

Which of Leonardo's paintings are the children's favorites and why? Because the artist was interested in so many things, he did not produce a great deal of work in any one field. How do the children feel about that? Would it have been better, in their opinion, to stick to one thing for a lifetime, or to investigate many as Leonardo did? What do they feel is his greatest contribution?

Art/Drama Activity:
Inventions, Geometry, and Mirror Writing

Materials

- Paper
- Pencils

Ask the children to think about the many conveniences we have now—all the result of people like Leonardo da Vinci, who experimented and asked such questions as "What if we could . . . ?" Or "What if we had . . . ?" We now have machines that wash our dishes and our clothing, fly us around the world and even into space, build our buildings, plow our fields, and harvest our produce. But we still need people to continue asking questions and dreaming dreams. Invite the children to do that very thing—to come up with a need we still have and to invent a machine to answer that need. You may want to brainstorm some ideas as a class to get the children started in their thinking. Allow time for them to share their inventions at the end of the session. They may want to bind them all into a book of fantastic ideas.

As an art activity, the children may wish to draw a picture in which the figures, buildings, or other objects form a pyramid shape.

Print some information about Leonardo da Vinci's life in mirror writing and have the children decipher it. They love this "secret code" activity, and it helps them remember his work.

LESSON 5: Michelangelo Buonarroti (1475–1564)— Painting and Architecture

❏ The Story

"**I** don't care what you want to do! Art is for lazy good-for-nothings. You have only been in school three years and you want to quit already. You can barely read and write Italian, let alone Greek and Latin as other boys your age can. You will finish school, become a merchant, and bring some money into this family. If I have to beat art out of you, I will do it," yelled Michelangelo's father.

The young thirteen-year-old boy had asked him once again if he might go and study art with the master Ghirlandaio in the city. Even though he was tired of begging and feared his father's repeated beatings, Michelangelo refused to give up. He was the most stubborn boy you could ever imagine!

"My father gave me up to the stonecutter's family when I was a baby. I grew up with marble dust in my veins. What did he expect? Of course I would want to carve marble for the rest of my life. And right now I want to study drawing like my young friend Granacci," Michelangelo thought to himself. Finally, his father gave in and brought the young boy to Ghirlandaio's workshop, where he promised that his son would work for the next three years. Michelangelo was already so fine an artist that the master agreed to pay him instead of the other way around. While he worked for Ghirlandaio, Michelangelo also had all of Florence as his school. The greatest artists in the world worked there, and Michelangelo studied their paintings. He made drawings of the frescoes Giotto had done many years before, and the frescoes of other Renaissance artists we've talked about.

While Florence was a beautiful city of churches and buildings filled with wondrous art works, Rome, a city south of Florence and home of the ancient Roman artists, was falling apart. Cattle and sheep grazed in what was once the beautiful forum, and even some of the churches were falling down. So when Julius II became pope in 1503, he decided to do something about it. He wanted to create new works of art for the city, including a magnificent tomb for himself. He wanted to rebuild St. Peter's church, the main cathedral of Christians throughout the world. It was over a thousand years old, and it was crumbling. Julius not only wanted to fix it, he wanted to make it even bigger. And he wanted to improve the Vatican, the special palace in Rome where the pope lives even now.

Julius was a warrior pope, often leading men into battle. He was filled with energy and determination, and when he said he was going to do something, he did it. He didn't care who stood in his way. He was already sixty years old, so he was in a hurry. And he wanted Michelangelo to be one of the artists involved in the work.

Now Michelangelo had already been working, carving statues for the pope's tomb. It was hard work, and there were many statues to be done. But in the middle of the job, the pope told him to stop, and he refused to pay Michelangelo the money he owed him. One thing we know about Michelangelo is that he could get angry and stubborn. He packed his bags and headed back to Florence in the middle of the night. Pope Julius sent messengers after Michelangelo, but they couldn't catch him. The artist was back in his beloved Florence.

Do you think Julius gave up so easily? Of course not. He sent a letter to the leaders of Florence saying that if they did not send Michelangelo back immediately, he would start a war! So back Michelangelo went, and when he got to Rome, he received quite a surprise. Instead of being asked to work on statues, which he loved doing, the pope took him into his own church in the Vatican, called the Sistine Chapel. He pointed to the ceiling, which was covered with blue paint and stars. "I want you to paint frescoes of Bible stories all across this ceiling," the pope said.

"But your holiness, I'm not a painter. I'm a sculptor. There are many fine fresco painters you could ask. How about Raphael? He is here in the city and is very talented. He has done other frescoes for you."

"I said I want *you!*" shouted the pope. "And I want you to begin immediately. I'm in a hurry to get the job done!"

Michelangelo had to obey, so he began making drawings to get ready for the tremendous work—5,800 square feet to be covered with more than three hundred figures! No wonder he called for assistants from Florence! But when he saw their work, he yelled, "No, no, this is terrible—not what I had in mind at all. Out, out all of you. I'll do it myself!" And so, Michelangelo was left in the huge chapel by himself to perform a task that seemed impossible. Every day he climbed a huge scaffold, where he had to lie on his back to paint the large figures. If he was working on the head, he could not even see where the feet would be. Paint dripped onto his face and into his eyes. And still he kept on. Every day Pope Julius would visit. "Have you finished yet?" he would ask.

Michelangelo moved his bed into the chapel and slept only a few hours a night. The rest of the time he painted. He even ate his meals up on the scaffold. The pope continued to press him "Are you finished yet?" Sometimes they would get into arguments, but Michelangelo kept working.

"I'll have you thrown from that scaffold if you don't tell me you're finished," shouted the pope one day. And so Michelangelo declared the work completed. It had taken him four years, an incredibly short time. The pope called for a big celebration. For years, people had been trying to get a look at what Michelangelo was doing, but he would allow no one into the chapel. Now, finally, the big moment had arrived. The crowd was amazed at what they saw. "This cannot be the work of a single artist," they declared. "Truly, his gifts are from God!" Pope Julius II died just four months after the ceiling had been finished.

Many years later another pope appointed Michelangelo as the chief architect of St. Peter's, because work on the church was still going on even after the death of Pope Julius II. Michelangelo was seventy-two years old! He studied the dome Brunelleschi had designed for his beloved cathedral in Florence. "I can't possibly make one more beautiful," Michelangelo said. "But it will be even larger." Today, St. Peter's is the largest church in the world, and Michelangelo's dome can be seen for miles around. It is a reminder of what an incredibly talented artist he was. Artists of every age study and marvel at his work.

Viewing the Art

Talk about how being a sculptor influenced Michelangelo's painting. His figures almost have the look of carved marble. Show the *Doni Tondo*, one of Michelangelo's early works. View scenes from the Sistine Chapel (many books have impressive fold-out inserts). Do the children know some of the Bible stories represented on the chapel ceiling? Mention that dirt and smoke from burning candles in the chapel had made the frescoes so dark you could hardly appreciate Michelangelo's colors. The ceiling was restored several years ago. You may want to show the film listed below about the restoration. What feelings does the picture of Adam and God evoke? Show the *Last Judgment*. Concentrate on the different positions of the figures, the expressions on the faces. This is an enormous cast of characters to ponder. Show some of Michelangelo's drawings. He believed that the best way to learn art is to draw as much as possible. Finally, show some pictures of St. Peter's, concentrating on the magnificent dome designed by Michelangelo. Show close-ups of the dome, both inside and out, and compare it to Brunelleschi's in Florence.

Journal Writing

Do the children feel Michelangelo should have listened to his father and pursued a career as a merchant? What do they think of Michelangelo's feat in painting the Sistine Chapel? Should he have accepted help? Is it good to dedicate almost every waking minute to a task? What is their favorite painting? Why? Compare the domes of St. Peter's and Santa Maria del Fiore in Florence. What did Michelangelo learn from Brunelleschi? How are the domes similar and different?

Art/Drama Activity: Scaffold Painting

Materials

- Large boards or pieces of corrugated cardboard covered on both sides with art paper—enough for half the class
- Tempera paint
- Paintbrushes
- Paper to cover the floor

Have the children imagine that they are Michelangelo, just given the enormous task of painting the Sistine Chapel. They are going to experience what it feels like trying to paint in such an awkward position. Cover the floor with paper, and divide the children into partners. Have one child hold a board or cardboard high off the floor, while the other lies on his/her back on the floor (scaffolding) with paint and tries to paint a picture on it. After a few minutes, turn the board over and reverse roles. Then discuss the experience. What does it feel like to paint in that position? How would it feel hour after hour? Day after day? Year after year?

LESSON 6: Michelangelo Buonarotti (1475–1564)— Sculpture

❏ The Story

If you had the most precious and rare seed in all the world—not another one like it anywhere—where would you plant it? (Invite children's responses.) Of course, you would prepare the richest, best soil you could. You would mix into that soil the best fertilizers and nutrients. You would choose the very best spot to put that soil, where it would receive just the right amount of sunlight and water, and then you would carefully plant that seed at just the right depth. You would probably even build a fence around it so no animals would dig it up or eat it. For if something happened to that seed, there would be no other to replace it. You would watch over it and nourish it and wait patiently for it to grow.

Well, Michelangelo was like that seed. Many people say he was the greatest artist who ever lived, even up to our own day. True, his father didn't care for his boy. He beat Michelangelo often. He never understood the boy's art, he never encouraged his art, and he never even thought it was good, even when kings and popes were so amazed they knelt down in awe in front of Michelangelo's statues.

But Michelangelo had the good fortune to be born at the perfect time in the perfect city—glorious Florence. The Florentines loved art and were happy to support artists. Michelangelo learned about painting from Ghirlandaio, one of Florence's greatest artists, and when Lorenzo de Medici saw Michelangelo's work, he invited the boy to live in his palace as his own son, to become the pupil of the great sculptor Bertoldo, and to create sculptures for the palace garden.

Lorenzo gave Michelangelo money for his work and treated him well, and Michelangelo produced some beautiful sculptures. After Lorenzo died only three years later, Michelangelo went to a monastery where the prior allowed him to cut open dead bodies and study the shape of muscles and tissues. This study would make him an even greater sculptor, but it was dangerous work, for it was against the law. To reward the prior for his kindness, Michelangelo carved a beautiful crucifix for the monastery.

Once Michelangelo carved a small cupid and sold it to a man for a very low price. The man knew that in Rome, people were very interested in the ancient art of the Greeks and Romans. So he took Michelangelo's little cupid and buried it for several weeks to make it look old. Then he sold it to a cardinal for more than six times what he gave Michelangelo. The cardinal thought he was buying an ancient statue, but some time later he discovered the truth. However, he still knew the statue was very good work, and he hunted and hunted until he found the artist who carved it: Michelangelo. He invited Michelangelo to live with him, and that's how the artist came to the second city in which he found jobs. All his life he would work mostly for art collectors in Florence and Rome.

While Michelangelo was in Rome, he did such wonderful carvings that another cardinal heard of his work. Now that cardinal wanted to give a work of art to St. Peter's church before he returned to his homeland in France, and he asked Michelangelo to carve a statue for him. It had to be a statue of the Virgin Mary holding the body of Jesus when he was taken down from the cross. This kind of statue is called a *pietà*, an Italian word that means "pity." The cardinal wanted the statue to be life-sized—and he wanted Michelangelo to finish it in exactly one year! Michelangelo was only twenty-three years old, and no one believed he could really do it. But he finished on time, and when people saw the statue, they were amazed.

One day, a big crowd was gathered in St. Peter's looking at the *Pietà*, and Michelangelo was hiding behind a pillar. "This work is so perfect, I know it was carved by our great artist in Milan. Only an old man with much experience could perform such a miracle with marble!" said an onlooker. Michelangelo was very angry when he heard that, so he came back to the church with his chisel in the middle of the night and on Mary's sash he carved the words, "Michelangelo Buonarroti the Florentine made it." It is the only work he ever signed. Today people still travel across the world to see that incredible statue.

Near the cathedral in Florence, there stood a huge block of marble. The Florentines used to laugh every time they saw it. "What good is that silly piece of marble?" they said. "It is very beautiful, but it is so narrow that nothing useful could ever be carved from it. It is good for nothing, perhaps, but to become a pillar."

"Give it to me," said Michelangelo, "and I will work wonders with it." So the leaders of the city gave Michelangelo the marble, and he built a wooden rectangle around it, hiding it from everybody. Then he set to work carving a statue of David, the young boy in the Bible who killed the giant Goliath with a simple slingshot. David reminded Michelangelo of Florence itself, like a small child defending itself successfully against larger city-states that were always trying to wage war against it. He knew the Florentines would love a statue of David for their city. For almost three years he chiseled away at the statue, and when it was finished, the Florentines were amazed. They placed it outside the palace of the city leaders where everyone could see it. Now it has been moved into a museum to protect it from the weather.

Michelangelo carved many other statues throughout his lifetime. When he died, just before his ninetieth birthday, his body, just as he had wished, was brought back to his beloved Florence. Michelangelo was a painter, a sculptor, an architect, and a poet. He had outlived the other two giants of the Renaissance, Leonardo and Raphael. He had accomplished incredible feats of art, many of which we cannot see because they have disappeared. People say he was the greatest artist who ever lived. What do you think?

Viewing the Art

Show the two works Michelangelo did as a teenager working for Lorenzo: *Madonna of the Stairs* and *Battle of the Centaurs*. What do the children think of such work being done by one so young? Note the twisted bodies of the centaurs and point out that Michelangelo loved to do such forms. Spend time on the first *Pietà*. What emotions does this sculpture evoke? Do the children notice Michelangelo's carving on the Virgin's sash? Talk about Italy's lending the statue, one of its most prized possessions, to the United States for a World's Fair exposition in the 1960s. What do the children think of the David? Discuss how Michelangelo's knowledge of anatomy is evident in this statue. What do they think of David's expression? Try to show close-ups of the face and hand. Call attention to the hand holding the slingshot. It is much larger proportionally than it should be because Michelangelo intended viewers to look up to his *David*. The hand is seen in the foreground by one looking up. Recall for the children what a difficult piece of marble Michelangelo had to work with. What is their opinion of the results?

View the statues that make up Julius II's tomb, especially the *Moses*. Note that the horns on Moses' head are the result of a mistake in the Bible translation (instead of light coming from Moses' head, the translation was "horns"). Moses is so real he almost seems to speak his anger at the disobedience of his people. In what ways do Michelangelo's statues *Day* and *Night* reveal those two times of day, or of life? Show Michelangelo's last works, especially the last two *Pietàs*.

Point out that Michelangelo did not do the figure on the left. Can the children note any difference between that statue and the other three? Call their attention to the fact that Joseph is a self-portrait and that Michelangelo smashed the statue in anger but allowed an assistant to repair it.

Journal Writing

If you have taught Donatello, the children might wish to compare his *David* with Michelangelo's. What kind of a person is each *David*? How does the artist show this? Which one do the children like best? Why? Invite the children to compare Michelangelo's three *Pietàs*. How are they alike? Different? What feelings do they arouse?

Art/Drama Activity: Biographical Drama

Invite the children to dramatize a scene in the life of Michelangelo. Some possibilities might be:

- Michelangelo begging his father to let him study art
- Michelangelo's being invited by Lorenzo to live in his palace and work in the sculpture garden
- Michelangelo obtaining the narrow piece of marble from the Florentines and carving the *David*
- Michelangelo and Pope Julius II arguing over the ceiling of the Sistine Chapel

LESSON 7: Raphaello Sanzio (1483–1520)

❑ The Story

"**P**apa, show me how to mix the paints. I know I can do it. Let me help you!" Young Raphael stood by his father, Giovanni, as he painted frescoes on the walls of the duke's palace in the town of Urbino, where Raphael and his parents lived. Raphael's father was a kind man, and realizing his son was interested in art, he taught him all he knew. But the boy was very talented, and before long, he became a better artist than his father.

"My dear," Giovanni said to his wife, "I am going to take our son to Perugia to work in the shop of the famous artist Perugino."

"Oh, you mustn't do that. He is so young, and he is our only child. I shall miss him so."

"But the boy has talent," replied Giovanni. "I have nothing left to teach him. He must go." And so Raphael became Perugino's apprentice, and in a very short time his work was as good as his master's. In fact, many people could hardly tell them apart!

While Raphael was studying with Perugino and doing a great deal of artwork on his own, he heard that many artists were traveling to Florence to study drawings made by two special artists, Leonardo da Vinci and Michelangelo. Everybody was buzzing about the battle scenes they had drawn for the walls of a building in Florence. The frescoes never were painted, but the drawings were available for study. So Raphael said goodbye to Perugino and went to study in another workshop, the city of Florence.

When Raphael saw Leonardo's and Michelangelo's drawings, he could hardly believe them! He copied them over and over again until he got them right. Then he began to study the other works of those two artists. He loved the way Leonardo used light and shadow in his paintings. He loved how Michelangelo showed nude people in different twisted positions. He drew Michelangelo's *David* many times. He copied Leonardo's *Mona Lisa*. Even though Raphael had been famous in Urbino, he was a student all over again. And he learned fast, not only from Leonardo and Michelangelo, but from many other great Florentine artists.

Raphael actually stayed in Florence for a few years, and although he never mastered painting nude people as well as Michelangelo, he learned so much that people were amazed by his work. Pope Julius II heard about him. You remember that Julius was busy fixing up the special place in Rome called the Vatican where the pope lives? He had already given Michelangelo the job of painting the Sistine

Chapel. Now he ordered Raphael to paint frescoes on the walls and ceiling of one room in the pope's special apartments.

Other artists were already busy painting frescoes in the other rooms. Raphael made many drawings to get ready for this tremendous job, and then he began work. Meanwhile, he kept wondering what was going on in the chapel, because Michelangelo wouldn't let anyone in except the pope—and he didn't even want the pope to bother him. But one day Michelangelo wasn't there, and Raphael sneaked in to see his work. He liked what he saw so much that he repainted one of his own frescoes in the pope's apartment. When the pope saw Raphael's work, he was so happy that he gave him two other rooms to do as well. "Paint over the other artists' frescoes," he ordered. "Your painting is much better than theirs."

Raphael's painting in the pope's chambers made him so famous that many rich people gave him jobs. They wanted their portraits painted. They wanted paintings for their chapels and their palaces. He painted many portraits and over forty pictures of Mary, the mother of Jesus. These paintings are called *Madonnas*. All of them are different and very beautiful. Raphael had so much work that he had many apprentices to help him. People followed him around wherever he went because he was so kind and handsome. Women especially liked him, and he had many girl friends, but he never married.

One day, just before his thirty-seventh birthday, Raphael became ill. In those days, when people became sick, doctors drained some of their blood, believing that if they got the bad blood out of the person's body, the person would get better. But that's just what Raphael didn't need. He needed strength, and draining his blood just made him weaker. He became so weak that he died a few days later, on his birthday. Some people say that when Raphael died, painting died with him. Leonardo was a genius at ideas, Michelangelo was a genius at sculpture, and Raphael, they say, was a genius at painting. After we look at some of Raphael's paintings, you can decide for yourselves.

Viewing the Art

Spend some time viewing Raphael's famous *School of Athens*, painted in the Vatican apartments. Note how well-balanced the painting is, with the two figures in the middle flanked by almost equal numbers of people on each side. Point out that some say the figure in red in the middle is Leonardo da Vinci, while the man writing in the foreground with his head in his hand is Michelangelo. Raphael has placed himself and his teacher Perugino on the extreme right. Notice the color and movement in this and all Raphael's works. If you have studied Greek art with the children, connect this painting to what they know of the ancient Greeks.

Study Raphael's *Deliverance of St. Peter from Prison*. Point out that since Raphael had to paint this in an alcove, he worked the alcove shape into his painting. Three parts of the story are told in this one painting: Peter's chains being released by the angel; the angel leading Peter out of prison; and the guards discovering Peter's escape. Notice Raphael's use of light and shadow, how the stairs appear to be part of the wall. Show Raphael's last painting, *The Transfiguration*, which was placed near his body at his death. Note the story taking place below—the boy being brought to Christ for a cure. Spend time viewing as many *Madonnas* as you can. Do the children recognize the triangular form in these pictures? From whom did Raphael learn this? (Leonardo.) Notice how well-balanced and graceful these paintings are, how beautiful the *Madonnas'* faces are. Finally, study some of the portraits, especially *Baldassare Castiglione*, *Angolo Doni*, *La Gravida*, and *Pope Leo X*. Note the Renaissance clothing, the position of the subjects.

Journal Writing

Raphael fit an enormous amount of work into a very short lifetime. What are some things he learned from other Renaissance painters and even surpassed them in doing? What is the children's favorite work and why? Do they agree that Raphael is a greater painter than Leonardo or Michelangelo? Why or why not?

Art/Drama Activity: Living Portraits

Divide the children into groups and give them several tasks that will allow them to experience in their bodies some of the things they have learned about Raphael's work. For example, encourage the children to use various objects in the room and pose themselves for a portrait so that they form a triangular shape. Or ask them to design themselves into a picture that shows the kind of symmetry evident in Raphael's paintings: the same number of children or objects on one side as on the other. Another possibility might be to encourage them to consider motion in their poses: freeze-frame themselves walking, talking, reaching out to someone, etc.

Additional Activities

My students have often chosen the Renaissance as the subject for their year-end play. There is such a cast of colorful characters from which to choose, and it is a wonderful way for them to recall some of the things they have learned about this important period in art history. Some possibilities for dramatization are:

• Giotto's discovery by Cimabue
• Brunelleschi's defeat in the contest for the Baptistery doors
• Brunelleschi's and Donatello's trip to Rome
• Brunelleschi's designing of the dome and his fight to keep his model secret
• Leonardo inventing new machines
• Leonardo following people to study different kinds of faces
• Michelangelo convincing the Florentines that he can carve something wonderful from the narrow block of marble
• Michelangelo arguing with Pope Julius II and painting the Sistine Chapel in secret, on his back
• Raphael sneaking into the Sistine Chapel to view Michelangelo's work

There are ways to simplify Renaissance dress to make costuming easy. For male parts, a long-sleeved shirt belted at the waist and worn over tights works well. If they can make a money pouch to hang from the belt, it is even better. They can wear ballet slippers or go without shoes. For female parts, it is easy to cut a long tunic with a scoop neck from material. Very little sewing is involved. Again, ballet slippers or feet in tights are fine. Those who are playing the parts of wealthier people can show this by wearing an elaborate hat. Make these by wrapping a pillowcase to resemble a turban. Wear it at a jaunty angle. Consult a book of costumes like the one listed in the bibliography for additional ideas.

Draw a large outline map of Italy on a piece of paper and display it to the children. With their help, put in some of the cities studied in the lessons on the Renaissance: Florence, Vinci, Rome, Urbino, Padua, Milan. Then put in the names of the artists who were born and/or worked in those cities. You could also list some of the art works created in those cities.

Curriculum Connections

Social Studies

• Read the history of the Renaissance.
• Geography: on a large world map, trace the routes of some leading explorers; locate on a map the various Italian cities in which Renaissance artists worked.

- Study the culture of the time of the Renaissance. What was life like for people in different segments of society?
- Find pictures of clothing of the time and point out its features. Why did people dress as they did? How does it compare with clothing today?
- Create a timeline of important events.
- Create a Renaissance town complete with a palace for the duke or leader, a guild, some apprentice shops, etc.

Science

- What were some inventions and medical practices of the time? How did they work? Do we still use them? Focus especially on the inventions of Leonardo da Vinci.
- Study the work of men such as Galileo. What did Galileo have to say about the relationship of the earth and sun and how did he suffer for his ideas?
- What were modes of transportation? Make a model of one of Columbus's ships.

Music

- Listen to Renaissance music: study polyphony, sacred music.
- What instruments were popular at the time? Draw them on a chart for display in the room.
- Learn a short piece of Renaissance music.

Mathematics

- Discuss double-entry bookkeeping and its influence on the way records are kept today.

Literature

- Read biographies of some famous people of the time: Galileo, Dante, explorers, Lorenzo de Medici, etc.
- Find some quotes from the poet Dante that the children can understand and post them on charts around the room.
- Read some of Michelangelo's poetry.

• Using a book such as *One Day in Elizabethan England* by G. B. Kirkland (see References), compare English expressions during Renaissance times with those of our own day.

References

Basile, Giuseppe. *Giotto: The Arena Chapel Frescoes*. London: Thames and Hudson, 1992. An absolutely beautiful book filled with commentary and large reproductions of the frescoes.

Battisti, Eugenio. *Filippo Brunelleschi: The Complete Work*. Transl. by Robert Erich Wolf. New York: Rizzoli. 1981 o.p. A marvelous source of large, detailed reproductions of all of Brunelleschi's works. Contains a large picture of his death mask.

Beck, James. *Raphael: The Stanza della Segnatura*. New York: George Braziller, 1993. A discussion of Raphael's frescoes in the Stanza della Segnatura in the Vatican Palace.

Bennett, Bonnie A., and David G. Wilkins. *Donatello*. New York: Moyer Bell, 1984 o.p. A discussion of Donatello's life and works.

Cole, Bruce. *Giotto: The Scrovegni Chapel, Padua.* New York: George Braziller, 1993. Commentary on Giotto's work and on each of the plates in the book. The plates are not overly large but suitable for group viewing.

d'Arcais, Francesca Flores. *Giotto*. New York: Abbeville Press, 1995. Nearly 400 large color reproductions of Giotto's frescoes and panel paintings.

Eimerl, Sarel. *The World of Giotto*. New York: Time Inc., 1967 o.p. A thorough discussion of Giotto's contribution to art. Many color reproductions, including a large selection of medieval works for comparison.

Hartt, Frederick. *Michelangelo: The Complete Sculpture*. New York: Harry N. Abrams, 1968. A discussion of each of the sculptures accompanied by wonderful large close-ups ideal for viewing.

Instituto Geografico De Agostini. *Leonardo Da Vinci*. New York: Reynal and Company in association with William Morrow, 1956 o.p. A huge book that presents the many facets of Leonardo's talent: anatomist, biologist, artist, engineer, etc. Excellent source of all his paintings, including hundreds of his drawings and notebook entries.

Labella, Vincenzo. *A Season of Giants*. Boston: Little, Brown, 1990. A discussion of the works of the three giants of the Renaissance: Leonardo, Michelangelo, and Raphael. Tied in to four-hour miniseries on Turner Network.

Lightbown, Ronald. *Sandro Botticelli: Life and Work*. Rev. ed. New York: Abbeville Press, 1989. Describes the artist's early life and apprenticeship and relates his paintings to the culture of 15th-century Florence. More than 217 color plates.

McCarthy, Mary. *The Stones of Florence*. Illus. by Evelyn Hofer. New York: Harcourt Brace, 1976. Discussion of art in Florence, with wonderful pictures of Florentine buildings and churches and large reproductions of the work of many Florentine artists.

Pietrangeli, Carlo, Michael Hirst, Gianluigi Colalucci, Fabrizio Mancinelli, John Sherman, Matthias Winner, Edward Maeder, Pierluigi De Vecchi, Nazzareno Gabrielli, and Piernicola Pagliara. *The Sistine Chapel: A Glorious Restoration*. Transl. by Lawrence Jenkens. New

York: Harry N. Abrams, 1992 o.p. A large book filled with close-ups of all the paintings in the Sistine Chapel. Marvelous for viewing. The book is a companion to the video mentioned below.

Poeschke, Joachim. *Donatello and His World.* Transl. by Russell Stockman. Photographs by Albert Hirmer and Irmgard Ernstmeier-Hirmer. New York: Harry N. Abrams, 1990. Contains very large photos of all of Donatello's works and of some of Brunelleschi's as well.

Vasari, Giorgio. *The Lives of the Artists.* Transl. by Julia and Peter Bondanella. New York: Oxford University Press, 1991. The lives of over thirty Renaissance artists. Filled with anecdotes and interesting information.

Venturi, Lionello. *Sandro Botticelli.* New York: Oxford University Press, 1937 o.p. Commentary and large reproductions of Botticelli's work, including wide pull-out reproductions of *Primavera* and *The Birth of Venus.*

Wasserman, Jack. *Leonardo Da Vinci.* New York: Harry N. Abrams, 1984. Leonardo's life accompanied by 139 reproductions.

Children's Books

Avery, Charles. *Donatello: An Introduction.* New York: HarperCollins, 1994. Examines Donatello's sculpture. Many illustrations, including four color plates.

Belting, Natalia M. *Elves and Ellefolk.* New York: Holt, Rinehart and Winston, 1961 o.p. Contains some wonderful tales which can be used for storytelling while studying the Renaissance. Note especially: "The Marvelous Doors" and "The Rose of Midwinter."

Bender, Michael. *Waiting for Filippo.* San Francisco, CA: Chronicle Books, 1995. A delightful pop-up book that tells the story of Filippo Brunelleschi and the building of the dome over the cathedral in Florence.

Brighton, Catherine. *Five Secrets in a Box.* New York: E.P. Dutton, 1987 o.p. Galileo's daughter, Virginia, tells about the secrets she finds in her father's special box. Very simple creation of the world of the Renaissance accompanied by beautiful illustrations.

Caselli, Giovanni. *The Renaissance and the New World.* New York: Peter Bedrick Books, 1986. The everyday life and culture of Europe during the Renaissance and its spread to the New World.

Corrain, Lucia. *Giotto and Medieval Art.* Illus. by Sergio with the assistance of Andrea Ricciardi. New York: Peter Bedrick Books, 1995. A large, colorful book that discusses life and art in thirteenth century Florence including information on Cimabue and some of Giotto's contemporaries.

Fisher, Leonard Everett. *Galileo.* New York: Macmillan, 1992. A picture-book version of the life of the mathematician, physicist, and astronomer. Beautiful illustrations.

———. *Prince Henry the Navigator.* New York: Macmillan, 1990. A picture-book biography of the Portuguese explorer, accompanied by beautiful illustrations.

Fischetto, Laura. *Michael the Angel.* Illus. by Letizia Galli. New York: Doubleday, 1993. A picture-book account of the life of Michelangelo. Simple, but contains some interesting facts about the artist's boyhood and work. Glossary.

Harris, Nathaniel. *Renaissance Art*. New York: Thomson Learning, 1994. A discussion of the major artists of the Renaissance. Includes glossary, index, and brief bibliography.

Howarth, Sarah. *Renaissance People*. Brookfield, CT: Millbrook Press, 1992. Describes thirteen types of professions from the Renaissance including craftsman, artist, banker, and mercenary. Includes glossary, bibliography, and index.

———. *Renaissance Places*. Brookfield, CT: Millbrook Press, 1992. Describes thirteen Renaissance places such as the chapel, the sculptor's workshop, and the monastery. Includes glossary and bibliography.

Kirtland, G.B. *One Day in Elizabethan England*. Illus. by Jerome Snyder. New York: Harcourt, Brace & World, 1962 o.p. Recreates a day in the life of two children living in an English manor house. Filled with expressions and customs of the time.

L'Engle, Madeleine. *The Glorious Impossible*. New York: Simon & Schuster, 1990. The story of Christ's life, beautifully illustrated with large reproductions from Giotto's frescoes in the Scrovegni Chapel.

Llorente, Pilar Molina. *The Apprentice*. Transl. by Robin Longshaw. Illus. by Juan Ramon Alonso. New York: Farrar, Straus & Giroux, 1993. In Renaissance Florence, Arduino, who wants to be a painter, is apprenticed to a famous artist and discovers a terrible secret.

Mathé, Jean. *Leonardo's Inventions*. Transl. by David MacRae. Paris: Minerva, 1989. Gorgeous close-up photos of Leonardo da Vinci's inventions and notebooks.

McLanathan, Richard. *First Impressions: Leonardo da Vinci*. New York: Harry N. Abrams, 1990. Very readable life of Leonardo from his birth to his death in France. Some reproductions.

———. *First Impressions: Michelangelo*. New York: Harry N. Abrams, 1993. Thorough discussion of Michelangelo's life for children, including pull-out of the Sistine Chapel.

Milande, Veronique. *Michelangelo and His Times*. New York: Henry Holt, 1995. A presentation of Michelangelo's sculpture, his painting of the Sistine Chapel, his travels, and interesting facts about Renaissance Italy. Includes cartoons.

Morrison, Taylor. *Antonio's Apprenticeship*. New York: Holiday House, 1996. An excellent fictional picture-book story of the steps involved in painting a fresco in Florence during the Renaissance.

———. *The Neptune Fountain*. New York: Holiday House, 1997. A companion book to *Antonio's Apprenticeship*. In seventeenth-century Rome, young Marco convinces a famous sculptor to take him on as apprentice. Readers will learn a great deal about Renaissance art in this picture-book story.

Muhlberger, Richard. *What Makes a Leonardo a Leonardo?* New York: Viking, 1994. Explores twelve major works by Leonardo and the elements that make his art different from all others.

———. *What Makes a Raphael a Raphael?* New York: Viking, 1993. Explores twelve major works by Raphael in terms of color, composition, and subject matter.

Peacock, John. *Costume 1066–1990's*. London: Thames and Hudson, 1994. Clothing of different eras is pictured and labeled. Includes bibliography.

Pinguilly, Yves. *Da Vinci: The Painter Who Spoke with Birds*. Transl. by John Goodman. New York: Chelsea House, 1994. Leonardo's life told in letters between a young girl and her uncle.

Provensen, Alice and Martin. *Leonardo Da Vinci*. New York: Viking, 1984. An ingenious pop-up book showing the various talents of the artist.

Richmond, Robin. *Introducing Michelangelo*. Boston: Little, Brown, 1992. Very readable biography of the artist accompanied by pictures of his major works. Filled with stories.

Ripley, Elizabeth. *Botticelli*. New York: J.B. Lippincott, 1960 o.p. Botticelli's life as told through his paintings. Valuable book to have when showing Botticelli's works to children.

Rockwell, Anne. *Filippo's Dome*. New York: Atheneum, 1967 o.p. The story of the cathedral of St. Mary of the Flower, and the design and building of Brunelleschi's incredible dome.

Romei, Francesca. *Leonardo da Vinci*. Illus. by Sergio and Andrea Ricciardi. New York: Peter Bedrick Books, 1994. A large book that explores the many facets of da Vinci's talents.

Sis, Peter. *Starry Messenger*. New York: Farrar, Straus & Giroux, 1996. This picture-book biography traces Galileo's life from childhood to his days as a prisoner of the Church. The story is enhanced by a great deal of sidebar information. A 1997 Caldecott Honor Book.

Skira-Venturi, Rosabianca. *A Weekend with Leonardo Da Vinci*. Transl. by Ann Keay Beneduce. New York: Rizzoli, 1993. In a first-person narrative, the artist tells the reader about his life and work.

Stanley, Diane. *Leonardo da Vinci*. New York: William Morrow, 1996. Stanley, an award-winning author of marvelous biographies for children, here gives a lively account of da Vinci's life. Wonderful illustrations.

Venezia, Mike. *Botticelli*. Danbury, CT: Children's Press, 1991. Although this simple biography is too brief as a sole reference, the reproductions are excellent.

Willard, Nancy. *Gutenberg's Gift*. Illus. by Bryan Leister. San Diego, CA: Harcourt Brace, 1995. A clever pop-up book that shows how Gutenberg made the first book using movable type.

Wood, Tim. *The Renaissance*. New York: Viking, 1993. Discusses the achievements of the Renaissance. Plastic overlays give inside views of a Florentine townhouse, the Santa Maria, St. Peter's, and a printer's workshop.

Audiovisual Materials

Donatello: The First Modern Sculptor. (Videocassette. Available from Video Opera House.)

Leonardo the Inventor. A multimedia exploration of the life and works of the great artist. (CD-ROM. Available from Future Vision Multimedia Inc.)

Leonardo: To Know How to See. A video that depicts the accomplishments of the artist, including his best-known paintings. Introduces viewers to some of Leonardo's contemporaries and to the Italian countryside. (Videocassette; 58 mins. Available from The National Gallery of Art.)

The Life of Leonardo da Vinci. The life of the artist. (Three videocassettes; 270 mins. Available from Questar.)

Michelangelo. Michelangelo's life and accomplishments in painting, sculpture, architecture, and literature. While meant for high school students, this CD will afford even younger children the opportunity to ponder his works close-up and at leisure. Over 500 colored images. (CD-ROM. Available from Educational Resources.)

The Renaissance of Florence. Uses the works in the Uffizi in Florence and the Louvre. Authentic Renaissance music. (CD-ROM for Mac and Windows. Available from A & F Video.)

Return to Glory: Michelangelo Revealed. Depicts the twelve-year process of restoring the Sistine Chapel. (Videocassette; 52 mins. Available from Crown Video.)

The Treasures of Italy: Florence—Video Portrait of a City. Presents the works of Michelangelo, Brunelleschi, Botticelli, Giotto, and da Vinci. Compares the *Davids* created by Michelangelo, Verrocchio, and Donatello. (Videocassette; 50 mins. Available from Library Video Co.)

The Trecento. Focuses on the work of Giotto, and also includes the art and architecture of Florence, Siena, Assisi, Padua, and Venice. (Videocassette; 26 mins. Available from Entertainment Video.)

Part IV
Five European
Masters

9 Jan van Eyck in Flanders

Here lies Jan, famous through his unparalleled talent.
In whom the art of painting was wonderful.
—FUNERARY MARKER

Background Information

Flanders (present-day Belgium) in the time of the Late Gothic Period (fourteenth and fifteenth centuries) was the scene of an artistic movement away from decorative art to a new realism that endeavored to present pictures as the eye saw them. Flemish artists set their subjects in landscapes of real vegetation. They showed the effects of air, which filters what the eye sees, and of light, which is absorbed by some surfaces and refracted or reflected from others. Although Giotto, in Italy, was experimenting with realism and making some attempt to use perspective, his work was unknown to Flemish artists, who struggled with perspective on their own. Even though there were many commissions for religious paintings in the still-Catholic country, painters introduced landscape and still life. In addition, the growth of mercantilism meant that a good segment of the population had the means to acquire portraits, causing portraiture to gain a new importance. Flemish artists also used oil in a new way. Instead of working with the thick, egg-based paints used by the Italians, they thinned their paints with turpentine and mixed them with clarified oil. They then painstakingly applied their paints in layers, using a transparent glaze as the final coat. The oil permitted the rich colors underneath to shine through, producing a more brilliant work.

The cities of Ghent and Bruges, in Flanders, were two of the busiest in Europe, centers of trade between the north and the south. Rich merchants populated these cities, and many were avid patrons of the arts. Add to this the fact that the Flemish court was the richest in Europe and employed many artists in its decoration, and it is little wonder that the arts flourished in Flanders at this time.

Jan van Eyck was born not only among a populace ready and willing to honor his talent but also into an entire family of gifted artists. His older brother

Hubert, with whom he probably worked on the famed Ghent alterpiece, was a painter of renown. It is generally believed that Hubert also painted four pages in the *Book of Hours of Turin* and the small painting *Marys at the Sepulcher*. Two other siblings—Lambert, and a sister, Margaret—were also painters.

The date of Jan's birth is uncertain, but he was probably born around 1390 in Maaseyck. In 1425, he entered the service of Philip the Good, duke of Burgundy, and remained in the duke's employ until his own death in 1441. Jan undertook many journeys on behalf of the duke, one of them to Portugal to paint Philip's bride-to-be, the Infanta Isabella, and bring her home to Flanders. As with many of Jan's paintings, this one of Isabella has been lost. In addition to his work for the duke, Jan did several religious commissions, the most famous being the altarpiece at Ghent, and some portraits. He married a woman named Margaret, whose portrait he painted, and had one, or possibly two children. Jan van Eyck died in Bruges on July 9, 1441, and was buried in the church of St. Donatian. He is considered by many to be one of the greatest Flemish painters and to have contributed enormously to the movement toward realism in painting.

LESSON 1: Jan van Eyck (1390?–1441)

❏ The Story

(While oil painting probably did not originate with Jan van Eyck, he did work wonders with oil. This story is meant to convey the contribution of the northern painters to the perfection of oil painting.)

It seemed to young Jan van Eyck that as far back as he could remember, he could crinkle his nose and smell the wonderful aroma of paint in the house. He knew the feel of brushes in his hands, thick brushes and thin, delicate ones. His older brother Hubert painted the most wonderful pictures, and Jan loved to watch him work. As he grew to manhood, Jan knew that he wanted to be an artist too, and he worked hard with his brother to learn all he needed to know to earn his living. Early each morning, he began work on his painting. He painted pictures of the things in his house: his room, his bed, bowls of fruit, tables. He painted pictures of his sister, Margaret, and his two brothers. He painted madonnas and saints. The more he worked, however, the more discouraged he became.

"What is wrong, brother?" asked Hubert one day. "Your painting is coming along nicely. Why don't you look more pleased with yourself?"

"Look at the sleeve of Margaret's dress," Jan replied, pointing to his sister, who was sitting on a chair across the room. "Do you see the delicate flowers in the pattern? Do you see the way the folds of the material hang just so?"

"Well, of course I do," replied Hubert. "What is the problem? Are you having trouble drawing Margaret's dress?"

"Oh, no. I love to draw such details. I try to notice everything just as it is and to put each thing I see into my painting. But the paint dries so fast that I do not have the time I need to capture every little detail! I need a different kind of paint. This egg we mix our paints with just doesn't work. The Italians living in their sunny country may like it, but in our cold climate, it is no good at all!"

From that moment on, Jan was determined to find a new way to mix paints. Day after day he experimented. He made his mixtures thicker, then thinner. He tried more egg, then less egg. But nothing pleased him. Frustrated, he decided to try a different medium to make the paint from, and he chose oil. The results were amazing.

"Hubert," Jan cried, "come here. Look at what oil allows me to do. I can make my colors glossy and put them on in layers. I can take my delicate little brushes and paint in all the tiny details I wish—and the paint stays wet for a long time!"

Hubert was just as excited as his brother. From that day on, the brothers mixed their paints with oil, and their fame spread throughout the city. Rich wool merchants, who thanked God for their prosperity by giving paintings to the Church, hired the van Eyck brothers to do art works for them.

When the duke of Burgundy heard about Jan's fine work, he asked him to become his special painter. Jan loved working for Duke Philip. Not only was he asked to paint pictures, but he was also sent on some secret trips. Once he even went all the way to Portugal to bring the duke's new bride back to Flanders. But only a year after Jan began working for the duke, his beloved brother Hubert died. Hubert had been working on a magnificent altarpiece, showing Jesus as the Lamb of God with crowds of people coming to worship him. Jan finished that work and today it is one of the most famous art works in the world. Whole books have been written about just that one picture. We will look at it and some of the other pictures painted by Jan van Eyck. Many of his pictures have been lost or destroyed, but the ones we have can show us what a marvelous painter he was.

Viewing the Art

In viewing van Eyck's work, it is important to choose books that provide details of the larger pictures, since it is the artist's exquisite rendering of the most minute facets of his subjects—the hairs on a dog, the fibers in a garment, the blades of grass in a field—that give such pleasure. *Hubert and Jan van Eyck* by Elisabeth Dhanens (see References) is excellent for this purpose. The CD-ROM *The Age of van Eyck* is also extremely useful. Try to show as many of van Eyck's paintings as you can since there are so few, but be sure to focus on two in particular: *The Adoration of the Lamb* altarpiece and *Wedding Portrait (Giovanni Arnolfini and His Wife)*. In the *Adoration of the Lamb*, call attention to the details in the vegetation, the buildings in the background, and the clothing on the crowds of people, especially the magnificent jewel-encrusted robes of the Christ. Children especially love the Arnolfini portrait. Many of the details in this picture are symbolic. For example, one candle in the chandelier represents Christ; the dog stands for faith, etc. (See Curriculum Connections: Literature for suggestions for a discussion on symbolism.) How many things can the children notice? Point out the clothing, the oranges by the window and the shrub outside, the shoes the couple have removed from their feet, the chandelier, the mirror with the ten scenes from the Passion and the two witnesses (one possibly the artist) reflected within, the rosary on the wall, the artist's signature, the chair with the statue of St. Margaret, and many other details.

How many can the children find on their own? If you show the portrait of the *Man in a Red Turban*, point out that this is possibly a self-portrait.

Journal Writing

Ask the children to choose one person or object from the pictures they have seen and try to list as many details as they can remember about it. For example, if they were to choose Arnolfini's wife, they might mention the lace bordering her veil, her necklace and other jewelry, the bands of gold around her wrists and waist, the folds of her dress, the fur around her mantle, etc. How do these details add to the overall effect of the picture?

Art/Drama Activity: Tiny Details

Materials
- Large pieces of paper
- Pencils
- Oil pastels

Ask the children to choose an area of the classroom such as a shelf, or a single object such as a chair or a book, and draw it large enough to fill their paper. They should include as many details as they can in imitation of the Flemish artists of Jan van Eyck's day. They can color their pictures with oil pastels if they wish.

Note: Curriculum Connections and References follow chapter 11.

10 Rembrandt and Vermeer in Holland

LESSON 1: Rembrandt (1606–1669)

> With the threefold skills of draughtsman, etcher and painter,
> Rembrandt created three separate worlds, each self-contained and
> autonomous.
> —F. SCHMIDT-DEGENER

Background Information

Rembrandt van Rijn, the ninth child of ten, was born into an era of prosperity and growth in Holland on July 15, 1606. Although the Netherlands was soon to wage a war with Spain for her independence—a war that would last for eighty years—the northern provinces of which Holland was a part formed an independent republic in 1609. The north differed from the Catholic south, too, in embracing the Reformation then spreading across Europe, but it was the doctrine of John Calvin rather than that of Martin Luther that held sway. Because Calvin forbade the use of images in church, the wealthy Dutch, who made their living predominantly from the sea around them, lavished their funds on artwork for their own pleasure: portraits of individuals as well as of members of the important guilds; landscapes that celebrated their beautiful countryside; and still lifes. Commissions abounded for artists of talent and industry, and Rembrandt was to profit enormously from this widespread largess.

Rembrandt's father was a miller, and because he had a good income, he was able to send his son to an excellent school. But when it became evident that Rembrandt's interest lay in art, he left school at the age of thirteen and worked as an apprentice to the artist Jacob van Swanenburgh. A few years later, he moved to the bustling city of Amsterdam, where he continued his study of art under Pieter Lastman. It was from Lastman that Rembrandt developed a love of painting the Bible scenes that were to become the subjects of his numerous etchings later on.

When he was ready to strike out on his own, Rembrandt teamed up with another young artist, Jan Lievens. They worked so hard and so well that they soon built up a fine reputation. Rembrandt came to the notice of the prince of Orange, and his work for the court made him one of the best known artists in the country, enabling him to charge far more than his contemporaries for his paintings. He did portraits of many Amsterdam notables, and group portraits for important organizations such as the Surgeons' Guild and the Amsterdam Civic Guardsmen. By his twenty-fifth birthday, Rembrandt was famous and wealthy. He married Saskia, cousin of an art dealer with whom he worked, and they had four children. Unfortunately, three of the children died before the age of two, and the fourth, Titus, died a year before his father at twenty-six. Saskia herself died before she turned thirty. Rembrandt's second wife, Hendrickje, also died young.

Rembrandt's years of prosperity and success did not last. He spent his money foolishly, collected art works and other extravagances, purchased a large house beyond his means, and his debts soon outweighed his income. In addition, he refused to accommodate his art to popular taste and moved from the flamboyant baroque style favored by his contemporaries to a more somber, introspective vision. His works were dark (though recent cleaning reveals they were not so dark as formerly thought), filled with the unexpected, and required thoughtful study in the face of the current penchant for predictable, uncomplicated scenes. Rembrandt also persisted in etching Biblical scenes when the Dutch of the Reformation were increasingly looking for secular art. This fall from favor, coupled with debt and the death of all those close to him, marked Rembrandt's later years with sorrow. (While he continued to receive some important commissions, his star never rose to the heights of his early career.) Yet Rembrandt never ceased working, and he left an incredible legacy: 600 paintings, over 1,400 surviving sketches (he probably did countless more), and 290 etchings. His mastery of chiaroscuro, "with a skill no other artist has ever surpassed" (Wallace, p. 25), and his poignant portrayal of human character, place Rembrandt at the top of almost anyone's list of the world's greatest artists. He has been so admired and so copied that historians are constantly separating "real" Rembrandts from imitations, and works once thought to be his are still being discredited. But when authentic Rembrandt works are identified, they sell for incredible sums. In 1995, his *Abduction of Europa* sold for thirty-five million dollars! Rembrandt needs no last name. His genius is simply enough.

❏ The Story

One day over three hundred years ago in Holland, a small crowd gathered outside town hall, where a special notice had been posted. Everyone was trying to read what it said, and there was much pushing and shoving. Finally, one of the burghers, or citizens, spoke above the crowd.

"Quiet down. Quiet down. I'll read it to all of you." And clearing his throat, he began. "On Friday next, the possessions of one Rembrandt van Rijn will be sold at auction to the highest bidder. Among the items available are: one book bound in black leather with the best sketches of Rembrandt; one *St. Jerome* by Rembrandt; one small painting of hares by the same; one small painting of a hog by the same . . ." (Wallace, p. 137). The voice droned on and on.

In all, seventy works of the painter known as Rembrandt would be auctioned off. His house—even some of his handkerchiefs—were on the list! The good citizens of Amsterdam were shocked. Rembrandt had not died. And even if he had, there was his son Titus to inherit his belongings. What had happened to the master painter?

The people were right to be asking such questions, for Rembrandt was one of the most famous painters in Holland. Rich Dutch businessmen paid him more money to paint pictures for them than they paid most other artists. He painted marvelous portraits of individual people and of members of important organizations. Some of his paintings were hung in places where they could be seen by almost everybody in the city. Why, he even painted pictures for the prince!

So what had happened? Well, Rembrandt spent his money even faster than he earned it, if you can believe that. He collected works of art from all over Europe, including some by important Italian Renaissance artists. He bought a house that was much too big and expensive. He bought fine clothes for himself and his wife. He ate fine food. Finally the day came when he owed people so much money that he had to sell things to pay them. Art collectors today, who would gladly pay millions of dollars for just one Rembrandt painting, are shocked at the small amount of money all of Rembrandt's paintings together raised—just 5,000 guilders or about $5,000—not even enough to pay all his debts!

Rembrandt rented a small apartment for himself, his wife, his son, Titus, and his daughter, Cornelia. Not only was he struggling with money problems, but his wife, and a few years later his son, both died. When he was a young man, Rembrandt's first wife and three other children had also died! In fact, his daughter Cornelia was the only one in his family to survive him. His life was certainly filled with sorrow, but he never quit working. He continued to do portraits and etchings of scenes from the Bible right up until his death.

And Rembrandt continued to paint in his own way, even though he could have earned more money if he had done what was popular at the time. The

Dutch wanted pictures that were easy to understand. They wanted pictures of themselves, and scenes of their beautiful country. But Rembrandt used light and dark in his pictures the way the Italian painters of the Renaissance did. In fact, he did it even better! The Dutch were not used to such pictures. So Rembrandt never again enjoyed the wealth he had as a young man. He would even do a portrait for free if he found someone with a face he really wanted to paint! When you look at a portrait by Rembrandt, you can see not only what the person really looked like but what the person *was* like inside.

Today, people say Rembrandt was one of the greatest artists who ever lived. And they say he was the greatest etcher in history. We are going to look at some of his paintings and etchings now. You can decide if you agree.

Viewing the Art

In showing Rembrandt's art, it is important to include some paintings, drawings, and etchings. Explain to the children how an etching is made:

1. Coat one side of a metal plate, usually copper or zinc, with a layer of acid-resistant wax.
2. Coat the other side of the plate with varnish to protect it from the acid.
3. Draw the picture by carving into the wax with an etching needle or other sharp instrument, exposing the metal beneath the wax.
4. Place the plate with its completed drawing in nitric acid. The wax protects the copper plate from the acid, except for the lines which have previously been carved out.
5. Remove the plate from the acid and take off the remaining wax.
6. Put ink on the plate.
7. Wipe the plate. Ink will remain within the lines "bitten out" by the acid.
8. Place the inked plate in a heavy press and lay a sheet of damp paper over it. Move the plate steadily through the press. When it emerges on the other side, ease the paper off the plate. The drawing will have been transferred to the paper.

Many critics feel Rembrandt has no equal in the art of etching, so be certain to show the children several of them. Some you may want to consider are: *Three Trees; Jan Six, Reading; Thomas Jacobsz. Haaring; The Descent of Christ from the Cross;* and *Christ Healing the Sick* (or the *Hundred Guilder Print*).

In discussing and viewing Rembrandt's oil paintings, mention his mastery of chiaroscuro in such paintings as *The Night Watch*, a portrait of some Amsterdam civic guardsmen. (Its correct title is *The Company of Captain Frans Banning Cocq and Lieutenant Willem van Ruytenburch*.) The children might be interested in the controversy surrounding this picture. When it was finished, those who had asked Rembrandt to do the painting were not pleased with it because he did not give all of them prominent places in the portrait and put extra people in it. Some other oil paintings you may wish to view: *Rembrandt and Saskia* (his first wife); *Hendrickje Bathing* (his second wife); *The Anatomy Lesson of Dr. Sebastiaen Egbertsz*; *The Anatomy Lesson of Dr. Tulp*; and *Titus at His Desk*. Show some individual portraits of people outside Rembrandt's family as well.

The children may also find it interesting to view some of Rembrandt's self-portraits. He did more of these than perhaps any other artist. An interesting exercise is to show them in chronological order, for they are an incredible testament to the successes and trials of Rembrandt's life. *Rembrandt: Self-Portrait* (see References) is an excellent source for these prints.

Although Rembrandt produced a wealth of drawings during his lifetime, only twenty-five that bear his signature are known. View some drawings with the children.

Journal Writing

Have the children choose one portrait and write about it. What kind of a person do they think the subject was? What makes them think so? Why do they think Rembrandt wanted to paint that particular portrait?

Art/Drama Activity: A Scratch-work "Etching"

While the children cannot make etchings (it would be wonderful if they could observe an artist working in that medium), doing a scratch-work project may at least give them an idea of what it is like to create a picture using a sharp instrument.

Materials
- Paper
- Black crayons
- Sharp instruments such as scissor points or compass points

1. Have the children cover their papers with a thick layer of black crayon to simulate the wax-covered copper plate.
2. Using the point of a scissor or other instrument, have them scratch lines through the crayon to create a picture. They may wish to create scenes reminiscent of Rembrandt's Holland: ships at sea or in the harbor; windmills; etc. They may even want to scratch in a person wearing the clothing in vogue in seventeenth-century Holland.

LESSON 2: Jan Vermeer (1632–1675)

> With apparent effortlessness he snatched an instant of reality and
> lifted it out of a static realism to preserve it in a dynamic world of
> space, light and color.
> —HANS KONINGSBERGER, *The World of Vermeer*

Background Information

Jan Vermeer was born in Delft, Holland, in October 1632, the same year Rembrandt's *Anatomy Lesson* became known in Amsterdam. His father was a weaver
and later took to inn-keeping and dealing in art. However, he never made much
money at either, and after his death in 1652, it took his family years to pay off
his debts.

Not much is known about Jan's early art training, but he could have studied
in Utrecht, where he may have learned of the work of Caravaggio, the Italian
realist painter, and where he met his future wife, Catharina Bolnes, a woman from
a well-off Catholic family. Jan converted to Catholicism to obtain permission to
marry Catharina. By the time he turned twenty-one, Jan was a member of the
Guild of St. Luke and a master painter, an indication that he had served an
apprenticeship for several years. In addition, he probably learned much from the
pictures his father handled as an art dealer, and from leading artists of the day.

While he began his career doing historical and Biblical paintings using a
rather dark palette, it is for his interior scenes of young women engaged in ordinary household tasks, his subjects flooded with light, usually from a nearby window, that Vermeer is well known. He and Catharina had fifteen children, eleven
of whom survived. Even though Jan worked as an art dealer as well as a painter,
the burden of providing for a large family, his country's war with France, which
drained the coffers so that even the well-to-do had no money to buy paintings,
and the constant haranguing of debtors took their toll. Jan Vermeer died in 1675
at the age of forty-three. His widow, left with large debts and eight children at
home, was forced to sell his paintings and other family assets.

Jan Vermeer produced only about forty paintings in twenty-one years, and
although he was never quite forgotten, he did not achieve fame until the nineteenth century. Today he is recognized as one of the truly great Dutch masters,
and some scholars consider

> the pearl as a perfect symbol for his work, not only because of the
> radiance of the young girls in his paintings or because so many of them

wear pearl earrings or other pearl jewelry. The paintings themselves suggest pearls. Each of them is a perfect world, closed within itself, secret, softly lit, full of luster. (Koningsberger, p. 126)

❏ The Story

(Although the camera was not invented until the nineteenth century, artists as early as Leonardo da Vinci's time had been using its precursor, the camera obscura—a device which allowed light to pass through a tiny hole and project an inverted image on the walls of a darkened room. When the camera obscura became small enough to be easily portable, its use increased. By reproducing a scene exactly, the camera obscura saved the artist from the tedious calculations, first devised by Brunelleschi, necessary to obtain the correct perspective. The artist simply had to trace the outlines of the scene projected by the camera obscura. In addition, by reflecting the scene exactly, the camera obscura saved the artist from the tricks his eyes might play on him. The camera obscura also showed "the 'circles of confusion' that occur around points of intense illumination when not every ray in a beam of light is brought into the sharpest focus." (Pollack, p. 13) Art historians generally agree that Jan Vermeer made wonderful use of the camera obscura, and this story describes the joy he might have had upon discovering it for the first time.)

Over three hundred years ago, during the same time that Rembrandt lived and even in the same country, Holland, there lived in the city of Delft a painter named Jan Vermeer and his family. One afternoon, Jan came bursting through the front door. "My dears, come and see what wonderful device I purchased when I went into town today!" Jan's wife, Catharina, and his five daughters (in the years to come, he would actually have eleven children) gathered around him as he carefully placed a large object on the table.

"What is it father?" asked Maria, the oldest.

"This," said her father, "is called a camera obscura." Maria wrinkled her nose at the strange-sounding words. But her excited father continued, "It is just what I need to help me paint wonderful pictures."

"How can a box help you paint? That's silly, father!" And Maria laughed.

You must remember that this family lived in the days before the camera was invented, so they had never seen anything like what their father had brought home. And it wasn't a camera like the ones we have now. "This is not just a box," Jan explained. "It is a special instrument which can actually show me things as they really are, not just as I think they look. Most important of all, it can show me how light hits objects and seems even to dance or bounce off them. Light. It is so wonderful and so mysterious." Jan became very quiet, and his wife and children somehow knew to keep silent, too, for they were used to seeing him sit for hours and think while he watched daylight stream through the windows of their house.

Finally, Jan remembered that his family was still waiting. "Elisabeth, bring me that candle and I will show you how it works." Elisabeth gave the candle to her father who placed it in front of the box. Right before their very eyes, the image of the candle appeared on the glass screen on top of the box.

They all began to talk at once. "Oh, it's magic, father!" "Let me try it." "Can we play with it?"

"No, it is not magic, children," replied Jan. "It is a scientific instrument that shows us how our eyes work. It makes pictures the way our eyes do. And it is not a toy, so you may not play with it. I must use it to help me understand more about light. Run along now so that I can begin my observations."

Day after day Jan studied light. He arranged a few objects in many different ways in the two rooms he used for his painting. "Will the room look bigger if I move the table back here?" he wondered. "What if I drape the cloth this way? Will the light reflect off the folds of material? "Maria," he called, "put on these pearl earrings and come stand by this window. Ah, yes. Now turn your head a little this way. Open your mouth ever so slightly. Perfect!" And Jan began to paint his daughter's picture.

Day after day he arranged and thought and painted. You would think that in the twenty-one years he was an artist, Jan Vermeer would have painted hundreds of pictures, for he was a very hard worker. But he only painted about two pictures a year, because each one had to be perfect. His camera obscura showed him how light sparkled in tiny specks. When he painted, Jan tried to get those sparkles just right. He layered his paints so that sometimes there were strokes that were barely the thickness of a single hair!

Some experts say no one has ever mastered light as well as Jan Vermeer did. We are going to look at some of his paintings now. Try to find the shimmering light in them. Notice how he arranged people and objects in his pictures. Then decide whether you agree with what people say about his work.

Viewing the Art

Since there are so few of Vermeer's works in existence today, try to show as many of them as you can, especially his two outdoor scenes, the magnificent *View of Delft* and *The Little Street*, and his renderings of women engaged in ordinary household tasks. When viewing Vermeer's interior scenes, show several to the children without saying anything. After a while, ask them what they have noticed. Among the things they should say are: all the scenes have women in them, either alone or with others; there is usually a window or source of light; the woman are doing ordinary domestic chores; many of the women wear and/or hold pearls; the same tile floor, drapery, wall paintings, and globe appear in many pictures; Vermeer uses blue and yellow often. It would be helpful to use books that provide details of the larger reproductions. Then you and the children can concentrate on the play of light in the pictures. Find the sparkles of light in such pictures as *Maidservant Pouring Milk, Officer and Laughing Girl,* and *Girl with a Red Hat.* These sparkles are achieved with dabs or points of paint and were Vermeer's attempt to paint the sparkles of light he saw in his camera obscura. Point out that although war was raging around him as France invaded Holland, Vermeer never made this violence the subject of his paintings. Nor did he ever paint young children, although he had eleven of his own.

Journal Writing

Which picture is the children's favorite? Invite the children to write as much as they can about that picture—what do they think is happening, what did they notice, how does the painting make them feel, etc.? Does the picture tell them anything about the kind of man Jan Vermeer might have been? Explain.

Art/Drama Activities: Pose a Vermeer and Make a Camera Obscura

Materials

Props to help the children pose pictures Jan Vermeer might paint. Some suggestions are:

- Material for draping
- Table
- Paper and writing instruments (no pencils or ballpoints!)

- Bowls, pitchers, fruit
- Musical instruments
- Pearl jewelry

Divide the children into groups (as many groups as you have materials to support the activity) and invite them to set up a picture for Vermeer to paint. Can they pose by a classroom window to have a source of light? How many people will be in the picture? What will they be doing? How will the scene look? Give

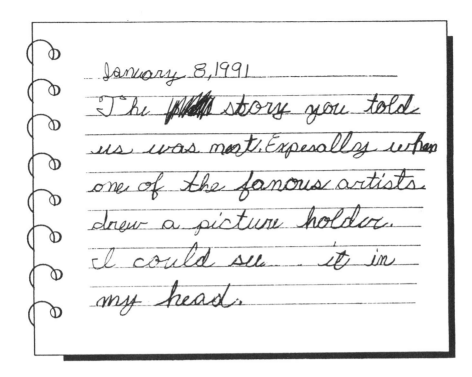

January 8, 1991

The ~~firs~~ story you told us was most. Expesally when one of the fanous artists drew a picture holder. I could see it in my head.

each group time to work with the materials, and then to pose their "picture" for each other.

You could also make a camera obscura and demonstrate how it works.

Materials

- A convex lens
- A mirror
- A cardboard box, the top of which is translucent (use a piece of clear plastic or glass)
- Scissors
- Tape
- A flashlight

(An inexpensive lens may be obtained from Edmund Scientific Company, 101 East Gloucester Pike, Barrington, NJ 08007-1380. Tel. (609)573-6250.)

1. Cut a hole in the center of one side of the box just large enough for the lens to fit in snugly.
2. Place the mirror inside the box on a slant.
3. Tape the glass or plastic onto the top of the box.

4. Place an object in front of the lens a short distance from the box.
5. Darken the room and shine only the flashlight near the lens.
6. The object should appear right side up on the glass or plastic.

See Koningsberger, *The World of Vermeer*, pp. 138–39 and Pollack, *The Picture History of Photography*, pp. 11–14 (both in References), for a more detailed explanation of the camera obscura. Also see a lengthy article in *The New York Times*, Jan. 14, 1996, p. E3.

Note: Curriculum Connections and References follow chapter 11.

11 Velazquez and Goya in Spain

LESSON 1: Diego Velazquez (1599–1660)

> His self-confidence and curious eye led him constantly down new
> trails, and he dared to paint subjects others shied away from.
> —CHRISTOPHER BROWN et al., *Rembrandt: The Master and His Workshop*

Background Information

In the fifteenth century, Spain was a dominant power in Europe. She had sent her explorers out to the New World to claim territories rich in gold and other resources. Her armada boasted over a hundred galleons and seemed invincible. Her coffers were filled. But in 1588, the English admiral Francis Drake defeated the Spanish armada, and Spain began a period of devastating decline. The Thirty Years' War fought in alliance with Austria, a war with France, and the eighty years' war to stamp out Protestantism in the Netherlands weakened the country still further.

It was into this dismal scene that Diego de Silva Velazquez was born in Seville in 1599, the oldest of seven children. His parents were of low nobility but had sufficient funds to provide him with a good education. His early desire to become a painter was fulfilled with an apprenticeship to Francisco Pacheco, one of Seville's most prominent artists. He married Pacheco's daughter, Juana, in 1618 and they had two daughters, only one of whom survived to adulthood.

Velazquez was so talented that his work soon outshone the lifeless canvases of his master. Although he distinguished himself early on with his religious paintings and pictures of ordinary people eating and making merry, it is for his work in the Spanish court of Philip IV that Velazquez is most famous. When Velazquez was only twenty-four, the king's advisor, Count Olivares, invited him to court, where he quickly became the young king's chief painter. Over the years, and throughout the mounting vicissitudes of the king's forty-three-year reign, Velazquez became his friend, and confidant as well, until eventually Philip refused to allow any other artist to paint portraits of him or the members of his household.

During his years at court, Velazquez made two trips to Italy, stopping in Venice to study the work of Titian and other Venetian painters, and in Rome, where he was welcomed into the pope's own apartments and allowed to copy the works of Michelangelo and Raphael. While there he painted one of his most famous portraits, that of Pope Innocent X. From his studies in Italy, he perfected his mastery over space and three-dimensionality.

Velazquez served Philip until his own death in 1660, receiving ever-higher ranks and promotions, culminating in his knighthood in the Order of Santiago in 1659. Velazquez was the only major artist of his time who painted primarily secular subjects in the face of a highly charged religious atmosphere (Brown, p. 92). His works are a chronicle of the Spanish working man, and of court life and fashion in the seventeenth century. Famous and respected in his own lifetime, Diego Velazquez today is considered one of Spain's greatest painters.

❏ The Story

Diego Velazquez, the artist, worked for King Philip of Spain. He lived in a beautiful house with his wife and little daughter. He had fancy clothes and fine food, and the king usually paid him well, though not always on time. All day long he worked on pictures of the king and the king's family. And he did other jobs, such as making sure rooms were ready for the king when he needed them.

It sounds like a great life, doesn't it? It was, most of the time, but Diego was restless. He wanted to see the work of other painters and learn new things. So he asked the king for permission to go to Italy and study the great Italian master painters. The king didn't want to let Diego go, but he wanted his favorite artist to be happy, so he finally agreed.

Diego had a wonderful time in Italy. He went to the museums and copied famous paintings. He visited Venice and Rome. And because he was such a famous painter, the Italians treated him well. But one day he received an urgent message from King Philip's special counselor. The poor messenger who delivered it was exhausted from hours and hours of riding. "Come back to Madrid as soon as possible," the message read. "I am building a new palace for the king, and you must fill the huge Hall of Realms with pictures of the royal family and battle scenes that show Spain's victories over her enemies. King Philip is feeling sad about all the things that have been going wrong in the kingdom lately, and this new palace will cheer him up. Hurry! There is much work to be done!"

Diego packed his things and set off the next morning. When he saw the size of the room he was to decorate, he was amazed. It was enormous! How would he ever finish in time for the grand opening of the palace? Quickly he called his assistants together. "The king wants pictures of twelve battle scenes," he said. "That is far too many for me to be able to finish in time. I will draw up a list of the scenes I would like done, and you will do eleven of them. The twelfth I will do myself. In addition, we will need portraits of the royal family."

Diego's assistants scurried to obey, while the painter sat and thought about what scene he would do. Lately he had heard an amazing story. Spain had been fighting with the Netherlands for many years. Finally, to put an end to the war which was costing lives and a great deal of money, King Philip sent one of his best generals, Ambrosio Spinola to fight the Dutch general, Justin. Spinola and his men cut off the Dutch army's food supply. But Justin and his soldiers didn't give up for almost a year. You can imagine how the Spanish felt when the Dutch finally surrendered! "Spinola will show them," said the soldiers. "He'll think of some cruel punishments." But Spinola did not. He admired the bravery of the Dutch commander and his men and asked them only to surrender. He didn't even want them to feel embarrassed.

Diego was very impressed by the way Spinola acted and decided to paint this story. In the picture, Justin is handing the key to the city of Breda to the victorious Spanish general. But instead of showing Spinola looking proud and haughty, Diego painted him putting his hand on Justin's shoulder. It seems as if he's saying, "You put up a good fight. You should be proud of yourself. My men and I will not make you suffer any longer."

Diego was worried that perhaps the king and the Spanish people would think the painting made Spain look weak. But he was wrong. The king and everybody who saw it loved the painting because it showed how dignified and noble a Spanish general could be. In fact, the king liked his work so much he gave Diego a promotion. Diego also worked on some wonderful pictures of the king and his family for the Hall of Realms. In all of them he gave the country and the world an honest picture of the rulers of Spain. The king made Diego a knight, and the Spanish people consider him to be one of their greatest painters.

We are going to look at some of Velasquez's paintings now. As you look at them, see if you can figure out some of the things the artist was trying to tell us about the people whose pictures he painted.

Viewing the Art

Show the children some portraits of the royal family, making sure to include several of King Philip. What changes in the king do the children notice as he ages and as the fortunes of the country continue to deteriorate? Show the equestrian portraits of the king, Queen Isabel, and young Prince Balthasar Carlos.

Notice the brushwork evident in the horses' manes, the detail in the queen's dress. Study the outlandish dress and wig in the portrait of King Philip's second wife, Queen Mariana, and the dresses on the Infanta Margarita and Prince Felipe Prospero. Spend considerable time on Velazquez's most famous royal portrait, *Las Meninas* (*The Maids of Honor*). You may wish to read *The Princess and the Painter* (see References) as you show this marvelous painting. This picture book gives children an idea of what the Infanta Margarita's day might have been like and her possible friendship with Velazquez. In *Las Meninas*, the young princess has just announced that she does not wish to pose. Point out that Velazquez has put himself in the painting on the left. Show the children the portrait of the king and queen in the mirror. Where does this reflection come from? Choose, if you can, a book that includes details of this picture. The royal family loved to surround themselves with dwarfs. One is evident in *Las Meninas*. Show Velazquez's portraits of other dwarfs. Is he making fun of them or treating them sympathetically? Finally, show some paintings Velazquez did of people outside the palace, especially the subject of the story above, the *Surrender of Breda*. What do the children think the Spanish soldiers on the right and the Dutch soldiers on the left are saying among themselves? What are the two generals saying? In *Pope Innocent* X, look at the pope's eyes. What kind of a man was he?

Journal Writing

King Philip was not a very handsome man, yet Velazquez always showed him looking kingly and dignified. What are some things the children noticed in the portraits that give them the impression Velazquez wanted people to be proud of their king when they saw his portrait. Are there portraits of other people the children would like to write about?

Art/Drama Activity: Costume Design

Materials

- Paper
- Crayons
- Costume books

The costumes of the Spanish court in the seventeenth century were incredibly elaborate and impractical by today's standards. Have the children pretend they are royal tailors commissioned to create clothing for the rulers to wear to the grand opening of their royal palace. First, the tailors must put their designs on paper and present them to the king's counselor for approval. Using Velazquez's portraits as models and/or other costume books, ask the children to design clothes for a member of the royal family: the king, queen, prince, or princess. Some may wish simply to design a wig for the queen. When the children have finished their designs, one of them might assume the role of the counselor surveying the results.

LESSON 2: Francisco Goya (1746–1828)

> I am still learning.
> —FRANCISCO GOYA, captioned sketch

Background Information

Spain's lengthy wars for European dominance squandered the riches brought in from her North and South American colonies and left her monarchs with little energy to manage affairs at home. The country had no basic services such as education, waste removal, road systems, or effective police. The Catholic Church was a major force in Spanish society, but it used its power more heavily on the side of evil than good, stamping out any who disagreed with its tenets through the Inquisition and bleeding the poor. Industry hearkened back to feudal days, and farming methods were so bad that the soil barely yielded a living. It was into just such a poor farming village, Fuendetodos, in the province of Aragon that Francisco Goya was born on March 30, 1746. The family had gone to the village because his mother had inherited her family's land, but conditions were so severe that they could not eke out a living and moved to Saragossa around 1760. There Goya's father took up his trade as a master gilder.

Not much is known about Goya's early years. He studied drawing with a third-rate painter named Luzan for a time and after a brief stay in Madrid, he returned to Saragossa to establish his reputation before beginning his painting career in earnest. He married Josefa Bayeu and the couple had numerous children, only one of whom survived to manhood. While Goya was drawn to the ornate and energetic Baroque style of painting, his desire for success and acceptance forced him at first to conform to the styles of Giambattista Tiepolo and Anton Mengs, then popular painters in Madrid. Later Goya developed his own style, based in part on the principles of the Enlightenment which emphasized truth in nature. Many of Goya's patrons were leading proponents of Enlightenment philosophy.

Goya began his career in Madrid painting cartoons which the weavers used as designs for their work in the royal tapestry manufactory. Over his lifetime, he did sixty-three of these paintings, which celebrate the Spanish people engaged in pastimes and festivities. He also painted many portraits of wealthy patrons and was so successful that he finally attained the position for which he longed: first painter to the king. Unlike the king he admired, Charles III, who had ushered in a period of peace after many devastating wars and was intelligent and likable, his successor, Charles IV, was dull-witted and incompetent. Goya did not hide his disdain for this royal family in any of his portraits of them, but they kept him in their employ.

Charles IV's incompetence, coupled with the ferment generated by the revolution in France, left Spain vulnerable. When Napoleon invaded the country, he met with little resistance from the royal family, who were too busy quarreling over power to realize what was happening. Napoleon seized the throne, but the Spanish people resisted and plunged into a six-year war. The horrors of this war were to transform Goya from portrait artist to the rich to chronicler of disaster.

When the war ended Charles IV's evil and incompetent son, Ferdinand, took the throne. Conditions did not improve in Spain, and a disillusioned Goya moved from Madrid to a house in the country where he painted his famous "black paintings" on the walls. In 1824 he left Spain for France and died there in 1829, an old man of eighty-two who had remained an active painter until his brief final illness. Painter of frescoes on church walls, portrait painter of royalty and the rich, etcher of society's foibles, lithographer—in his long lifetime, Goya never ceased to experiment both with media and styles, and to express his inner vision and even his torment in his work. His astonishing accomplishments have rightfully earned him the reputation of being one of Spain's greatest artists, and his daring and innovative brush work have gained for him the title of Father of Modern Art.

❏ The Story

Francisco was in a good mood. He had just finished painting the portrait of his friend Sebastian Martinez, and Sebastian had liked his work. Now he was on his way back to the city of Madrid, where he was First Painter to the king. An artist couldn't get a higher position than that, and Francisco Goya was proud.

Just as he sat back in the carriage pulled by two big black horses, the artist began to get dizzy. "I guess I've been working too hard," he thought. He wanted to get out his handkerchief to wipe his sweating forehead, but he couldn't move his hand! He began to pound on the floor of the carriage with his right foot, the only foot he could move.

The coachman stopped the horses. "What is the matter, sir," he asked, looking into the carriage. What he saw really frightened him. Francisco sat slumped over, unable to speak. The driver quickly covered him with a blanket, got back up on his seat, and turned the horses around. "Faster, faster!" he called to them, cracking his whip as he raced back to Señor Martinez's house.

Of course, Sebastian was amazed when he heard his friend's coach return, and he ran outside, only to see the coachman trying to lift Francisco out of the carriage. The two men carried him up to bed. For weeks he lay there, visited by the doctor every day. "Will he recover, doctor?" asked the worried Sebastian. "Only time will tell," replied the doctor, shaking his head. "This is a very strange illness, and I don't know its cause."

Weeks went by, then months, and slowly Francisco began to gain strength. Some days he would be able to move his hands. But on other days, he could hardly move his head. And every day he heard nothing but loud buzzing in his ears. Sebastian came to talk to him. Other friends came. But he could hear none of them. He had become completely deaf! Francisco lay in his bed and thought about his career. He remembered the days when he painted pictures for the weavers to copy when they made rugs for the royal tapestry factory. He thought about the beautiful paintings he had made on the walls and ceilings of churches. He thought about the wealthy families who asked him to paint portraits for them. But most of all, he thought of his work for the king of Spain. He was the king's First Painter, his most important painter. Would he ever be able to paint again? Would he lose his job? How would he support his wife and son?

Francisco did get better. That is, he could move and talk again. But he could never hear from that time on. His deafness didn't stop him from painting, though. He didn't even lose his job as the king's First Painter. But after his deafness, the way he painted did change. His paintings began to show more and more of the foolishness and the suffering of the people of Spain, his beloved country. When war broke out between Spain and France, Francisco did not paint pictures of soldiers and generals as heroes. Instead he showed the horror of war, and how war makes people suffer. When he was an old man, he became tired of life in Madrid and moved to the country. There he painted pictures on the walls of his house. People call them his "black paintings," because they are filled with strange creatures and nightmarish scenes, grotesque and frightening. It is as if Goya finally believed the world was full of terror.

Francisco Goya lived a long life, even though he suffered some serious illnesses. In all that time, he produced many different kinds of art and became one of the most famous artists Spain has ever had. We are going to view some of his artwork now.

Viewing the Art

Goya was a prodigious artist who worked in several different forms, and it would be wonderful to give the children a sampling of this variety. You may wish to eliminate some of his more graphic works, depending on the age of your students. You should surely include some of his portraits. If you have studied Velazquez, compare his portraits of the royal family to Goya's, especially Goya's *Family of Charles IV*, a work that is almost scurrilous. The queen who dominates this picture dominated the king in actual life as well. She is shown as an angry woman. (Notice that she even seems to scowl or sneer.) King Charles appears fat and dull-looking, hardly a figure of royal competence. The royal children actually appear scared. Ferdinand, the one in blue on the left will become the future king. Notice that like Velazquez, Goya has placed himself in the back on the left in this royal portrait. View Goya's portrait of his wife, Josefa, and his son Xavier—the only one of his many children to survive. Goya loved children and painted many portraits of them, both alone and with their families. Show some of these, especially the portrait of young Don Manuel Osorio Manrique de Zuniga. The children may also enjoy some of his self-portraits.

Goya's cartoons for the tapestry works show the Spanish people in celebration and diversionary games. Enjoy a sampling of these. Show some of Goya's etchings, *Los Caprichos*, or *The Caprices*, in which he satirizes social foibles such as the idleness of the rich. *The Sleep of Reason* is actually a self-portrait. If you have studied Rembrandt, compare his etchings with Goya's. Finally, view whatever war paintings, such as *The Third of May, 1808*, and black paintings you are comfortable with. What is Goya saying in these works? Is he glorifying war?

Journal Writing

What do the children think of Goya's work? What do they like or dislike about it and why? Of the different subjects and styles—portraits, etchings, etc.—which do the children like best and why? They may wish to concentrate on a single work, especially one that is enigmatic, and discuss their own interpretation of it.

Drama/Art Activity: Playing Goya

Children particularly enjoy enacting scenes from Goya's life. Divide the class into groups. Either give each group a scene to dramatize or have them decide on one themselves. Some possibilities are:

• Goya posing the king and his family for portraits
• Goya becoming ill and going deaf
• Goya painting scenes on the walls of his house

Curriculum Connections

Social Studies

- Study the history and customs of the people living at the time of any of the artists in this section.

- Locate the different artists' countries of origin on a map.

- Study the clothing of the different times and places and draw some of it for a fashion bulletin board. (See Dhanens pp. 128–29, for excellent pictures of clothing, especially the very unusual headpieces of van Eyck's day.)

- Study the shipping and trading industries in the Netherlands. With what countries did they trade? What goods were bought and sold? Several wars were fought during the lifetimes of the artists discussed. Investigate those which interest the children.

- What is the Enlightenment?

Science

- One of Rembrandt's paintings shows the medical profession at work. Compare medicine in his time with ours, with medical practices 100 years before him in van Eyck's time, more than 100 years later in Goya's time. Read about the work of William Harvey who in 1627 explained how blood circulates in the body.

- Read about the development of the microscope, which was first used in Holland. Relate this to the lens in the camera obscura of Vermeer. How does a lens work?

- Research Goya's illness. What was it? Is there a cure for it today?

- All objects absorb light, some more than others. Experiment with objects of various kinds: frosted glass, cellophane, clear glass, a piece of paper, etc. Shine the beam of light from a flashlight on each of the objects. Which absorb so much light that no light gets through? Which allow some light to shine through? Which allow the most light to shine through? Why did Vermeer position the people in his paintings so that light from a window shone on them?

Music

- Listen to some Baroque music, a style prevalent during this time. Find some art works that seem to fit this ornate musical style.

- Talk about Beethoven, a German composer who was a contemporary of Goya and also suffered from deafness. Find a Beethoven piece that seems to fit one of Goya's more somber paintings.

• Play some of Mozart's music. How is it like Beethoven's? How is it different?

Literature

• Read biographies of people who made an impact during the time these artists lived. Some you might want to consider: Descartes, Voltaire, Louis XIV.

• Van Eyck's *Wedding Portrait* contains symbols of marriage and domestic life. What is a symbol? Give some present-day examples of "things that stand for other things." Did any of the other painters use symbols in their work?

References

Bihalji-Merin, Oto. *Goya Then and Now.* Photography by Max Seidel. New York: Harcourt Brace, 1981 o.p. Goya's life and works. Magnificent large photographs and many details for viewing.

Bonafoux, Pascal. *Rembrandt: Master of the Portrait.* Transl. by Alexandra Campbell. New York: Harry N. Abrams, 1995. Discussion and large reproductions of Rembrandt's portraits.

———. *Rembrandt: Self-Portrait.* New York: Rizzoli, 1985 o.p. Reproductions of all the self-portraits accompanied by commentary.

Brown, Christopher, Jan Kelch and Pieter van Thiel. *Rembrandt: the Master & His Workshop.* New Haven, CT: Yale University Press, 1991. Separates genuine Rembrandts from copies of his style. Many reproductions suitable for group viewing.

Brusati, Celeste. *Johannes Vermeer.* New York: Rizzoli, 1993. Brief discussion of Vermeer's life and work followed by large reproductions of fifteen of his works.

Dhanens, Elisabeth. *Hubert and Jan van Eyck.* New York: Alpine Fine Arts Collection, 1980 o.p. A large book with exquisite reproductions of van Eyck's works. There are many separate detail reproductions. Excellent for group viewing.

Guillaud, Jacqueline and Maurice. *Goya: The Phantasmal Vision.* Paris-New York: Crown, 1988. Focuses on the "black paintings" Goya did on the walls of his home. Large reproductions.

Koningsberger, Hans. *The World of Vermeer.* New York: Time-Life Books, 1967 o.p. Vermeer's life and work seen in the context of his milieu.

Lopez-Rey, Jose. *Velazquez: The Complete Paintings.* San Francisco, CA: Alan Wofsy Fine Arts, 1988. Big book containing large reproductions of the artist's paintings.

Munz, Ludwig, and Bob Haak. *Rembrandt.* New York: Harry N. Abrams, 1984. Examines Rembrandt's life and work. Some large reproductions.

Philip, Lotte Brand. *The Ghent Altarpiece and the Art of Jan van Eyck.* Princeton, NJ: Princeton

University Press, 1971 o.p. A lengthy discussion of the Ghent altarpiece. Includes bibliography and black-and-white reproductions.

Pollack, Peter. *The Picture History of Photography*. New York: Harry N. Abrams, 1977. Recounts the history of photography from its earliest beginnings to the present day. Discussion of the camera obscura.

Sanchez, Alfonso E., and Eleanor A. Sayre. *Goya and the Spirit of Enlightenment*. Boston: Museum of Fine Arts, 1989. A catalogue of paintings that demonstrates the influence of the Enlightenment on Goya's work. Large reproductions for viewing.

Schickel, Richard. *The World of Goya*. New York: Time-Life Books, 1968 o.p. Goya's life seen in relation to his times. Large reproductions for viewing.

Schwartz, Gary, ed. *The Complete Etchings of Rembrandt*. New York: Dover Publications, 1994. Rembrandt's etchings reproduced in original size. A key volume for this artist given the suggested art activity.

————. *Rembrandt: His Life, His Paintings*. New York: Viking, 1985 o.p. Examines documents in Amsterdam archives in light of what they tell us about his work.

Serullaz, Maurice. *Velazquez*. New York: Harry N. Abrams, 1987. The painter's life and work. Large color reproductions.

Tomlinson, Janis. *Francisco Goya y Lucientes*. London: Phaidon Press, 1994. Goya's life and works. Absolutely beautiful reproductions for viewing.

Wallace, Robert. *The World of Rembrandt*. New York: Time-Life Books, 1968 o.p. Presents Rembrandt in the context of the world in which he lived. Many reproductions suitable for group viewing.

Wheelock, Arthur K., Jr., et al. *Johannes Vermeer*. Washington, D.C.: National Gallery of Art, 1995. A marvelous book that discusses Vermeer's life and work. Color reproductions.

Whinney, Margaret. *Early Flemish Painting*. New York: Frederick A. Praeger, 1968 o.p. History of the fifteenth century and chapters on Flemish painters, including the van Eycks. Black-and-white reproductions.

Wright, Christopher. *Rembrandt and His Art*. Northbrook, IL: Book Value International, 1981 o.p. A discussion of many of Rembrandt's art works. Large pictures.

Children's Books

Alcorn, Johnny. *Rembrandt's Beret*. Illus. by Stephen Alcorn. New York: Tambourine, 1991. A painter tells his granddaughter about the time some paintings came alive in a museum and how Rembrandt painted his portrait.

Aliki. *The King's Day*. New York: Thomas Y. Crowell, 1989. Very readable picture biography of King Louis XIV of France.

Bonafoux, Pascal. *A Weekend with Rembrandt*. New York: Rizzoli, 1991. Rembrandt speaks to the reader about his life and work. Includes a list of museums in which Rembrandt's art is to be found.

Geisert, Arthur. *The Etcher's Studio*. Boston: Houghton Miflin, 1997. While this story is not gripping, the author provides a wonderful step-by-step explanation of the technique of etching. A perfect picture book to read when discussing Rembrandt's work.

Hastings, Selina, retel. *Reynard the Fox.* Illus. by Graham Percy. New York: Tambourine, 1990. A Dutch folktale about a fox who is so tricky even King Lion cannot match wits with him.

Hodges, Margaret, adapt. *Don Quixote and Sancho Panza.* Illus. by Stephen Marchesi. New York: Scribner's, 1992. An absolutely beautiful picture-book version of selected incidents from the lives of the famous Spanish knight and his squire.

Jacobsen, Karen. *The Netherlands.* Chicago, IL: Children's Press, 1992. A simple presentation of the Netherlands, including its history, important people, and present-day life and customs. Includes glossary.

Johnson, Jane. *The Princess and the Painter.* New York: Farrar, Straus & Giroux, 1994. A picture-book story about Infanta Margarita, the main subject of Diego Velazquez's masterpiece, *Las Meninas.* A wonderful picture of court life in fifteenth-century Spain.

Locker, Thomas. *The Boy Who Held Back the Sea.* New York: Dial, 1987. In this old Dutch tale, a young boy saves his village by plugging a hole in the dike. Locker's beautiful oil paintings are done in the style of the old Dutch masters.

————. *The Young Artist.* New York: Dial, 1989. In this picture book, a young apprentice in the Netherlands is ordered to paint a portrait of the nobles at court when he would really rather do landscapes.

Muhlberger, Richard. *What Makes a Goya a Goya?* New York: Viking, 1994. The author discusses twelve major works by Goya and what makes them different from any other artist's work.

————. *What Makes a Rembrandt a Rembrandt?* New York: Viking, 1993. The author discusses what makes Rembrandt's work different from that of other artists.

Pescio, Claudio. *Rembrandt and Seventeenth-Century Holland.* Illus. by Sergio. New York: Peter Bedrick Books, 1996. Twenty-nine double-page spreads containing a great deal of information on the artist and his times.

Rodari, Florian. *A Weekend with Velazquez.* Transl. by Ann K. Beneduce. New York: Rizzoli, 1993. The reader is invited to spend a weekend with the artist to learn about his life and work. Full-color reproductions.

Schwartz, Gary. *First Impressions: Rembrandt.* New York: Harry N. Abrams, 1992. A wonderful biography that examines the most significant events in Rembrandt's life.

Spier, Peter. *Father, May I Come?* New York: Doubleday, 1993. Two ships are rescued off Holland, one 300 years ago, the other in the present. Readers learn something about Dutch life and the ever-present sea.

Stanley, Diane. *The Gentleman and the Kitchen Maid.* Illus. by Dennis Nolan. New York: Dial, 1994. A young girl visits an art museum and makes up a story about a kitchen maid and a young gentleman from two paintings by Dutch masters. This picture book can encourage children to imagine the lives of the people in paintings they enjoy.

Sturgis, Alexander. *Introducing Rembrandt.* New York: Little, Brown, 1994. A wonderful life of the artist for children, including a brief history of Holland at the time, and the art materials available to Rembrandt.

Venezia, Mike. *Goya*. Chicago: Children's Press, 1991. Excellent simple biography suitable for very young children.

———. *Rembrandt*. Chicago: Children's Press, 1988. A very simple biography suitable for very young children.

Wright, Patricia. *Goya*. New York: Dorling Kindersley, 1993. Brief text for each two-page spread covers Goya's life in chronological order. Photos of Goya's and other artists' works.

Audiovisual Materials

The Age of Rembrandt: Dutch Painting of the Seventeenth Century. A selection of works by leading artists in Holland. (Audiocassette and 18 slides. Available from the National Gallery of Art.)

The Age of van Eyck. Presents van Eyck and his contemporaries in an interactive format. (CD-ROM. Available from the Metropolitan Museum of Art.)

The Age of Vermeer. Presents Vermeer and his contemporaries in an interactive format. (CD-ROM. Available from the Metropolitan Museum of Art.)

Goya. Life of Goya as seen through his works. Excellent views of Goya's art. Narrated by Ricardo Montalban. (Videocassette; 54 mins. Available from Kartes Video Communications.)

Goya. Focuses on Goya's portraits and prints. (16mm film; 7 mins. Available from the National Gallery of Art.)

Goya 1989. Selections from a musical on the life of the artist. While some pieces deal with his love life and may be unsuitable, several are excellent glimpses into his life and work. You may wish to play some songs while the children do their journal writing. (Audiocassette or CD. Available from CBS Records.)

In Search of Rembrandt. Rembrandt as seen through his work. (16mm film; 58 mins. Available from the National Gallery of Art.)

Paintings of the Great Spanish Masters. Paintings by several masters, including Velazquez and Goya. Narration in English or Spanish. (Audiocassette and 50 slides. Available from the National Gallery of Art.)

Two Faces of the Seventeenth Century. Explores in detail a Rembrandt self-portrait in light of his other self-portraits and Velazquez's portrait of Juan de Pareja. (Videocassette; 28 mins. Available from Home Vision.)

Velazquez: Painter of Painters. (Videocassette. Available from Home Vision.)

Other Materials

Light. A Discovery Box accompanied by a 32-page book. Contains a convex lens, prism, and a magnifying glass for experimenting with light. (Available from Scholastic Publishers).

Part V
Impressionism and Post-Impressionism

12 The Impressionists

Whether for good or bad, for long or for short [Impressionism]
is the active influence in the art of today.
It has resulted in an added brilliance of light and color that is refreshing . . .
—KATZ AND DARS, *The Impressionists in Context*

Background Information

Impressionist paintings are among the most popular works of art today. The Musée d'Orsay in Paris is a museum devoted exclusively to Impressionist artists, and it is almost always crowded with visitors. Because we find such art works so accessible and pleasing, it is sometimes difficult to believe that when the Impressionist style first came on the scene in Paris in the late nineteenth century, it represented a radical departure from the art in vogue at the time and was greeted with hostility.

In 1862, four unknown painters—Claude Monet, Frederic Bazille, Auguste Renoir, and Alfred Sisley—met while studying with the Swiss artist Charles Gleyre. Their penchant for painting outdoors, an uncommon pursuit at the time, drew them together. Gradually, other painters of like mind, among them Paul Cézanne, the two friends Edouard Manet and Edgar Degas, Camille Pissarro, and Berthe Morisot joined the group. Each grappled with ways to "capture nature as she is, which is to say solely by means of colored vibrations" (Jules Laforgue quoted in Katz and Dars, p. 62). Their works were refused by the all-powerful Salon, the main exhibitor of art works in Paris, and the artists, who later came to be known as "Impressionists" after a Monet painting entitled *Impression: Sunrise*, were forced in 1863 to hold their own exhibit, the Salon des Refusés, to bring their works before the public. Art critics, who were used to the polished, careful attention to details evident in pieces produced by artists trained in the French Academy system, scorned this exhibition of Impressionist works. In these paintings, they saw only "blotches, strokes and scrapes of compacted pigment, which viewed from a 'safe' distance would then coalesce into meaningful shapes" (Katz and Dars, p. 21).

160

Impressionism, a revolution in the art world between traditionalism and modernity, came on the Paris scene amidst a number of other revolutions: revolutions among the people to protest foreign invasions and poor economic conditions; revolutions in government as kingdoms gave way to republics and the lives of ordinary people assumed a new importance; revolutions in industry with the advent of new inventions and factory machinery; revolutions in architecture as Paris was modernized and narrow medieval streets made way for wide boulevards. Two developments that had great effects on the Impressionists, most of whom championed painting outdoors where they could see first-hand the ever-changing effect of light on objects, were the invention of tin tubes for storing oil paint and the expansion of the railroad. Tubes enabled artists to take their paint, now in stable, nonperishable form, beyond their studio walls and to capture immediately on canvas the scenes before them. And railroads made it easy to leave the city to paint in the countryside. The first official Impressionist exhibition was held in 1874 and several others followed, but they were not financial successes. By 1886, most members of the group had embarked on their own, hoping to have their works accepted by the Salon and reap some monetary gain.

Although the Impressionist period lasted a mere ten years, its impact was felt throughout Europe and even as far as the New World, where it found a more accepting public and attracted such American painters as Mary Cassatt and James McNeill Whistler. While it would seem at first glance that Impressionist painting is a simple affair of broad brush strokes and shimmering, luminous color, it is much more complex than that, and many pictures took weeks to complete. Many Impressionists were influenced by Japanese prints, which were becoming popular in France at the time. Such Japanese touches as asymmetrical compositions and cutting figures off at the edges of a painting, and Japanese designs in wallpaper and other objects, are evident in Impressionist works. Individual Impressionist painters were not swallowed up into one style, but each tried to present his or her own vision of the world. Together, they created a new way of seeing, a new reverence for color and light, a new emphasis on scenes of everyday life so prevalent among Dutch painters a century earlier, and ushered in the art of the modern world.

LESSON 1: Edgar Degas (1834–1917)

❏ The Story

Over a hundred years ago as the artist Edgar Degas emerged from a Paris shop, he saw a woman and a young girl hurrying in the direction of the Opéra, a concert hall where the ballet performed for admiring audiences. The girl held pink ballet shoes by their ribbons, and they bounced against her side as she almost ran to keep up with her mother. The woman looked over at her daughter. "Now remember to stand straight and answer politely. No fidgeting. When they ask you to dance for them, remember everything Madame has taught you." That was all Degas could hear, for the two scurried past him and up the Opéra steps. At the top, the woman paused and looked down at the child. "Gracious, pull up those sagging stockings," she said. Then the mother pushed the stray hairs that had escaped their hairpins off the girl's face, adjusted the girl's dress, and finally led her into the building.

"Poor child," thought Degas. "That mother obviously wants her daughter to be accepted into the ballet school. She will have to perform for Jules Perrot, the ballet master, and endure his cane pounding the floor and his harsh criticisms. I wonder if the girl really wants such a life, or whether it's the mother's idea entirely."

All the way home Degas pondered the matter. He had often attended the ballet and enjoyed it immensely. He loved the way the dancers moved gracefully across the stage and leaped into the air. He had even taken his sketchpad along and tried to capture on paper what he saw during performances. But noticing how obviously tense that young girl looked made Degas think about the lives of the ballet dancers when they were not on the stage. What were the hours of rehearsal like? What about their fatigue? Their stagefright?

The very next day Degas went to see Monsieur Perrot and asked permission to attend rehearsals. Almost every day after that the artist spent time visiting the dance classes at the Opéra. Sketchbook in hand he drew the dancers not only as they practiced their dance positions at the barre but also as they slumped down to rest, chatted among themselves, or worked on their costumes. He saw nervous girls and their mothers waiting in the hall for auditions. He saw girls tying their shoes or the bows on their costumes. The dance master and the dancers got so used to him they hardly looked up when he came in.

Edgar Degas painted many, many pictures of ballet dancers, and they are among the best known of his works today. When he did not go to the Opéra, girls posed for him in his studio. One fourteen-year-old named Marie became the subject of several wonderful sculptures. Degas even put real clothing on a sculpture of Marie, for he was always trying out new and surprising ideas. In fact, he joined a group of painters who were trying methods no other painters had used before. These artists were called "Impressionists," named because they were more interested in painting their impressions of a scene than painting the scene exactly as it was in real life. They used bold colors and quick brush strokes—perfect for Degas, who was trying to capture the movement and grace of ballerinas.

One day his friend Edouard Manet came to visit Degas in his studio. "Why, Edgar, what have you done here?" asked Edouard as he held up a painting. "This appears to be done with oil, but I know it isn't."

"I've colored this ballerina with pastel chalks, then sprinkled boiling water on the colors, and now I'm using my brushes to brush the color in. So it's not pastels and not oil, but it gives the appearance of oil without all the layers of paint. What do you think?" asked Degas.

"I like it, Edgar. Visiting you is always a surprise. I never know what I will find."

Edgar worked on and on for years, always trying new things. He did etchings like Rembrandt. He became interested in photography, for the camera had just been invented. He went to the race track where he sketched the horses and jockeys. He painted portraits of his family and other people he liked. "What will Degas come up with next?" asked the Parisians.

Edgar Degas painted until a few years before his death at the age of eighty-three. You would think that he died a happy man, but he did not. You see, he was never really satisfied with his work. Why, he once said, "If you'd given me a hat full of diamonds, it wouldn't have made me as happy as destroying this work and starting all over again" (Loumaye, p. 57). When we look at his art, you'll be able to see just how well he succeeded at making it perfect.

Viewing the Art

(If this is the children's first introduction to Impressionist painting, give them some background on the Impressionist movement and how revolutionary this type of art was when it first appeared on the Paris scene. In order for the students to appreciate how different and shocking Parisians found Impressionist works, it is helpful to show them the paintings of some artists working around the same time whose works were more conventional. In the mid-nineteenth century, two of the most powerful figures in French art were Jean-Auguste-Dominique Ingres and Eugène Delacroix. Delacroix championed warm color and romantic passion, while Ingres's works harkened back to the cool lines and subjects of classical art. Although the Impressionists embraced Delacroix's bright colors, they moved dramatically away from the clearly delineated lines and the subject matter found in both Delacroix and Ingres. It was a break the French art world could not easily accept. *Delacroix in Morocco* (see References) contains large color prints you can show the children for comparison, for example, *Women of Algiers*, *Arab Saddling His Horse*, and *The Sultan of Morocco and His Entourage*. Show some of Ingres's classical paintings. Among those you might choose are: *Antiochus and Stratonice*; *Mademoiselle Rivière*; and *Luigi Cherubini and the Muse of Lyric Poetry*.

In conjunction with viewing Degas's work, you may wish to read from *Degas: The Painted Gesture* (see References). In this book, eight children attend a weekly art workshop at the Musée d'Orsay in Paris where they discover Degas's work. They even act out scenes depicted by Degas, and your own students may want to do the same.

It would be wonderful to include at least three areas of Degas's work: the portraits, the ballet dancers (including some sculptures), and the racehorses. When viewing the portraits, point out that Degas often painted family members in groups rather than individually. Show the portrait of the Bellelli family, Degas's Italian relatives. What do the children think is going on in the picture? Why are the mother and daughters wearing black? Why is one girl turning aside? Why is the father separated from them in the picture?

While viewing *The Cotton Market, New Orleans*, talk about Degas's brothers running a cotton-exporting business in America. Imagine the difficulty of placing fourteen people in a picture so they could all be seen! In *The Orchestra of the Opéra*, Degas placed his friend, the bassoon player, in front, in the center of the picture, even though bassoonists would not really have had that position in an orchestra. Why does Degas do this? Show some self-portraits. What kind of a man does Degas appear to be? The children might also enjoy Degas's portrait of Manet and his wife. Point out that Manet colored over a portion of the picture because he didn't like it.

There are numerous paintings of ballerinas and racehorses to choose from. Point out that Degas worked with these themes because he loved both music and racing and because they gave him an excellent opportunity to draw figures in motion. What are some of the activities going on in *The Dance Class* and *The Dance Class at the Opéra*? Remind the children of Jules Perrot, the dance master, from the story. Be certain to show the sculpture of Marie, the young ballet dancer. You may also wish to read *Marie in Fourth Position* (see References), a fictional story about the girl who served as a model for Degas. *The Carriage at the Races* is actually a portrait of the family in the carriage. In whatever pictures you select, discuss how Degas created the impression of motion. Also point out the looser brush strokes which place his works with that of the Impressionists rather than with the more traditional artists who came before them.

Journal Writing

Degas captured not only the movement of ballerinas across the stage but also their emotions: their anticipation of a performance, their fatigue, their joy in the dance. Invite the children to choose one such picture previously viewed and write about it. What emotions are being expressed in the dancers' faces and bodies? How does Degas show movement in the picture? What is the story of that particular picture?

Art/Drama Activity: Pastels and Poetry

Materials
- Pastel paper
- Enough boxes of pastels for children to share
- Brushes
- Water
- Fixative (optional)

Have children do pictures of ballet dancers or racehorses (or, if this is too difficult, a scene from everyday life—but not a landscape) and color them with pastels. Then, dipping their brushes lightly in water, have them imitate Degas's technique. Finally, spray the finished pictures with fixative if you wish.

An interesting activity is to have the children choose horse and dance poetry to go with some of Degas's pictures and do choral recitations while displaying the artwork. This is particularly effective if you use any of the slide programs listed below. See the children's books for poetry selections.

LESSON 2: Claude Monet (1840–1926)

(It is most effective to do this lesson in the spring when you can actually plant a garden as a follow-up to the Art/Drama activity. Or if you cannot plant a garden outdoors, try planting under grow-lights indoors.)

❑ The Story

Young Claude Monet, who lived in Le Havre, France, was smiling to himself as he walked along, for he was on his way to Monsieur Gravier's shop to display some very funny drawings. He had made pictures of his teachers and even some important people in the town, but each picture exaggerated something about the person such as an extra-big nose or a very long cigar. "Surely these pictures will bring me many francs," Claude thought to himself.

When he arrived at the shop, another artist was already there having frames made for his pictures. "Good morning, Claude," said the painter. "What do you have there?" Claude showed him the drawings. "You draw well, but why waste your considerable talent on such foolishness? Come paint outdoors with me. Learn about light and color. Work on landscapes. That's what you should be doing."

"Outdoors! What a silly idea," replied Claude. "Why would I ever want to freeze myself in the cold wind by the water or roast myself in the hot afternoon sun, or drown myself in pouring rain? You must be mad! Besides, I am earning good money with my drawings. Of what use to me are colors and paint? You see, Monsieur Gravier sold four of my drawings just this week and is coming from behind the counter now to give me my money." And Claude put the money in his pocket and left.

But three weeks later, the painter, whose name was Eugene Boudin, came to visit. Eugene had a pack on his back and an easel in his hand. "Come on, Claude. Let's go outdoors together and do some painting. I promise you, you won't regret it."

"But I've already told you I'm quite content as I am."

"That's only because you don't know what you're missing! Come with me just this once, and if you're not convinced it is right for you, I will never bother you again," said Eugene.

"Oh, all right, I'll come just for today. At least then you will leave me alone." So Claude, grumbling, put paper, pencils, and paints in a knapsack, snatched up an easel, and hiked with Boudin into the countryside. They set up their easels, and Claude started to sketch the scene in front of him.

"No, no," said Eugene. "Don't draw. Paint what you see quickly before the light changes. Watch me."

So Monet put down his pencils and stood looking over Eugene's shoulder. Suddenly, he saw what Eugene meant. Painting right on the spot was so different from sketching and then finishing a picture in a studio indoors! It was as if the painter were an eye to help people see nature as it is, but also a heart to help them feel the beauty of the scene. "I want to do this for the rest of my life," declared Claude.

Claude's father was not happy with his son's decision and did not want to give him money to study in Paris. But his aunt talked Monsieur Monet into giving Claude an allowance. When Claude began his studies, however, he realized that he did not agree with his teachers. They were talking about painting indoors, using dark colors and making sure that the strokes made with the paintbrush were invisible. Even though leaving his teachers meant no money from his father, Claude went off on his own to paint from nature. He even built himself a boat so he could travel up and down the River Seine, painting.

Painting outdoors wasn't easy. Once he had to tie his easel to a rock to keep it from blowing away. Another time, he even had to tie himself down for protection from the wind! His beard became filled with icicles in the freezing cold. He hurt his leg badly. He developed rheumatism in his hands from painting in terrible weather. And even after all that hardship, the public hated his paintings because they were not what people were used to. The judges at the Salon, the most important art exhibition in Paris, refused to hang most of his pictures, and Claude, his wife, and two sons were often so poor they were in danger of starving. They had to move often to escape landlords who kept asking for the rent money.

There were other artists in Paris who thought as Claude did, and Monet gathered them into a special group that art critics called "Impressionists" after one of Claude's paintings named *Impression: Sunrise*. These painters held their own exhibitions, lent each other money, and encouraged each other through the difficult years. Edgar Degas, Auguste Renoir, and Mary Cassatt were members of this group. Eventually, people got used to Impressionist paintings, and Claude began to sell his work and to become famous. In time he had enough money to buy his own home. He bought a farm in Giverny, about forty miles from Paris, where he settled with his own two boys and six stepchildren. There he planted a beautiful garden, with a pond filled with water lilies and a Japanese bridge. For the rest of his life, he painted the flowers and scenes in his garden. And for the last ten years of his life, he painted huge pictures of the water lilies. He gave these pictures to France when he died at the age of eighty-six.

Claude Monet was one of the first Impressionist painters. He suffered poverty and hardship to paint the way he believed was right, and he gave the world some of its most beautiful landscape paintings. He once said, "My work belongs to the public, and people can say what they like about it; I've done what I could."

Viewing the Art

If at all possible, try to see a Monet painting firsthand in a museum. Have the children look at it close up. They will see what appears as mere globs of paint on a canvas. But when they step back, they can see that these globs are actually figures or parts of a scene. If you cannot visit a museum, try this exercise using a book. Venezia's *Monet* (see References) offers a similar experience.

Monet painted hundreds of seascapes, for having grown up in the harbor city of Le Havre, he loved the water. Show the children as many of these pictures of the sea as you can. Some you might choose are *Waterloo Bridge: Sun through the Mist, Zaandam*; *The Thames below Westminster*; *The Bridge at Argenteuil*; *The Seine at Lavacourt*; and *The Seine at Vetheuil*. The children may also enjoy seeing Manet's picture of Monet in his boat on the Seine.

Monet loved to paint in series so that he could capture the effect of sunlight on an object at different times of the day. Show the students some works from his haystacks series: *Haystacks*; *Haystacks in the Snow: Overcast Day*; *Haystack, Sunset*; and *Haystacks: Snow Effect*. Among the paintings in the Rouen Cathedral series you might choose: *Rouen Cathedral*; *Rouen Cathedral: The Portal and the Tower of Saint-Romain, Full Sunlight—Harmony in Blue and Gold*; *Rouen Cathedral in Full Sunlight*; *Rouen Cathedral: The Portal Seen from the Front—Harmony in Brown*; *Western Portal of Rouen Cathedral—Harmony in Blue*; and *Rouen Cathedral, West Facade, Sunlight*. Before you do, however, it would be wonderful for the class to share Monet's experience of changing light.

Take the class outdoors at different times during the day to view a familiar object on the playground—a slide, a tree, a plant, etc. How does it look in the morning? At noon? In the afternoon? Now view Monet's series paintings. How are they different? When do the children suppose each was painted? Finally, concentrate on some of the Giverny paintings: *Garden at Giverny*; *The Flowering Arches: Giverny*; *The Japanese Footbridge*; *The Water-Lily Pond*; and, of course, the numerous paintings of water lilies. *Monet at Giverny* (see References) has wonderful photographs of Monet and his family at Giverny. The children may enjoy seeing them as they view the paintings Monet did there.

Journal Writing

Review with the children the different characteristics of Impressionist painting: luminous colors; painting from nature, often outdoors; using color to define form, including shadows; using quick strokes rather than fine details to capture the essence of the subject, etc. Invite them to choose one of Monet's paintings and write about how he used some of these techniques in creating the work.

Art/Drama Activity: Monet's Garden

Read *Linnea in Monet's Garden* (see References) with the children. As you read, talk about Linnea's experiences: her preparation for the trip, the places she visited, etc. Display a large map of France and invite the children to trace Linnea's journey by placing small cut-out drawings on the map to represent the museums she visited, including, of course, Monet's house and garden at Giverny. (Remind the children that Monet's house is now a museum which was restored through money raised by Americans and that it can be visited even today.) Follow-up by recreating Monet's house and garden on a mural.

Materials
- Large roll of paper
- Poster paints
- Books with pictures in color of Monet's house and garden to use as reference

Divide the children into groups to paint different scenes from Giverny on a mural. For example, one group can work on the house, another on the bridge and lily pond, another on the flowers surrounding the house, etc. When the mural is completed, display it in the classroom or hall.

LESSON 3: Mary Cassatt (1844–1926)

❑ The Story

If you were a young girl growing up in a well-off family in the United States in the 1850s, you could look forward to getting married, raising children, and taking care of a house. Or you could get married, raise children, and take care of a house. Or, if you really wanted to, you could get married, raise children, and take care of a house!

I suppose you can guess that girls didn't have the opportunities back then that they have now. A girl couldn't consider being a doctor or a lawyer or having almost any other profession. Most women remained at home taking care of their families for their whole lives. So when a young American teenager named Mary Cassatt finally worked up the courage to tell her father that she wanted to be an artist, he said, "I would rather see you dead!"

Mary's father was not a cruel man. He loved all his children and was kind to them. But he had no hopes that his daughter could actually earn a living as an artist in a world that thought only men could do such things well.

But do you think her father's anger stopped Mary? Not at all! She just kept begging and begging even more until he finally gave in and agreed to send her to one of the finest art schools in the country at the time, the Pennsylvania Academy of Fine Arts. The family lived not far away, in Philadelphia, and Mr. Cassatt did not want his daughter to travel any distance, especially since the Civil War between the North and the South over slavery had just begun.

Mary was so excited she could hardly believe it, but when she began her studies, she was in for some disappointments. Unlike men, women were not allowed to paint live models, and women were not taken seriously as artists. They were not even allowed into the same classes as the men.

"How can I ever learn to paint the human body if I can't see live models?"

Mary complained. "They bring us cows to paint! I must go to Europe. Our country is so young there are not very many paintings to study in our museums. I must get to the Louvre in Paris."

Well, you can imagine that Mary's parents did not want to hear this. They had been hoping that she would get painting out of her system and settle down and get married like other young girls. But when they saw that she would not change her mind, they helped her get settled in Paris. Mary loved Paris, even though women were not even accepted into art schools there! Artists were everywhere, and Mary studied with them and on her own. Her greatest teachers were the dead artists whose paintings she copied in the Louvre.

Finally, one of Mary's pictures was accepted by the judges of the Salon, the most important art exhibit in the city! "What an incredible honor," she thought. But there were some artists who were angry because these judges criticized their work and would not display it. These painters, called Impressionists, used brighter colors and broader brush strokes than people were used to and painted pictures of the everyday things around them. Mary especially liked the work of Edgar Degas, and he admired hers as well—although he hated to admit that a woman could really paint! When he saw her painting in the Salon, he said, "At last, a woman who feels as I do." Degas asked Mary to enter some paintings in a special Impressionist exhibit, and she agreed. They became good friends and shared ideas with one another until Degas died forty years later.

Mary learned many things from Degas and the Impressionists. She brightened her colors and blurred details. She used pastels the way Degas did. She went into the countryside to paint the people she found there. But she also experimented on her own. She never married, but she loved her nieces and nephews and painted many pictures of them. She also did many paintings of mothers and children. These pictures do not look posed but rather show a special, tender moment between a mother and child. Mary made prints and copied some ideas from the Japanese after she visited an exhibition of Japanese prints in Paris. One of her prints was of a woman washing herself. "Look at how you've gotten the whole shape of the woman's back with just a few simple lines. You really can draw, and I admire good drawing so much!" said Edgar Degas when she showed it to him.

Mary Cassatt actually became famous in her own lifetime. Her pictures were sold in Europe, and some were even bought by Americans. She also helped her American friends choose good Impressionist paintings for their collections. Even though her parents and all her brothers and sisters died before she did, they lived long enough to see her success and were very proud of her. "Imagine, my daughter—a woman—and a successful painter!" her father said with pride. Today, Americans are proud of Mary Cassatt, too. She was brave enough to begin a career in painting at a time when women were supposed to remain at home, and she proved that she had great talent. Her paintings are admired throughout the world, and many consider her one of our greatest American artists.

Viewing the Art

Mary Cassatt's paintings of mothers and children are very appealing to young children, so be sure to spend a good deal of time on them. *Little Girl in a Blue Armchair, Two Children at the Seashore, Baby's First Caress, The Bath, Young Mother Sewing, Sleepy Baby, The Boating Party, Patty Cake,* and *Child in a Straw Hat* are some good choices. Note how natural and unposed the children look. Can the students tell any stories that might go with the pictures? They will probably also enjoy meeting members of Cassatt's family through her paintings. Include *Mrs. Cassatt Reading to Her Grandchildren; Lydia Working at a Tapestry Frame;* and *Alexander J. Cassatt and His Son, Robert*. In the latter painting, notice how Cassatt shows the close relationship of father and son by painting their clothing almost as if it is one garment. View some prints as well, especially *Woman Bathing, The Letter,* and *Mother's Kiss*.

Journal Writing

Mary Cassatt went against the customs of her day and struggled to become an artist. What thoughts does her story inspire in the children? Do they have aspirations that may be difficult to achieve? What are they, and what steps can they take to accomplish their goals?

Art/Drama Activity: Mothers and Children

Materials
- Paper
- Paintbrushes
- Paints, especially colors used by Cassatt

Invite the children to imagine some everyday scenes involving mothers and children. Brainstorm together and make a list of such activities: eating, getting dressed, playing with toys, reading, etc. Perhaps they can come up with some not treated by Cassatt. If any of the children have younger siblings at home, invite them to share some ideas. Or perhaps the class can visit a daycare center or nursery in the school or near by. Have the children create a gallery of pictures of mothers and children in imitation of Cassatt's work. Are there lullabies or other such songs that may go with some of their or Cassatt's paintings? The children may wish to donate their paintings to the daycare or nursery they have visited.

Note: Curriculum Connections and References follow chapter 13.

13 The Post-Impressionists

It was necessary to throw oneself heart and soul into the struggle,
to fight against all schools without exception,
not by disparaging them but by something different.
To learn afresh, then, though you know, learn again.
To overcome all fears, no matter what ridicule might be the result.
—PAUL GAUGUIN

Background Information

According to art historian H.W. Janson, it is possible to ascribe the term "Post-Impressionist" to any artist of significance working after 1880, the date that marks the end of the brief but far-reaching Impressionist era. More specifically, the term applies to those artists who once numbered themselves among the Impressionists and then moved outside the tenets of the Impressionist movement. That is certainly the case with the artists whose lives and work make up this chapter. Two of them, Cézanne and Seurat, brought Impressionism back to a more classical form. Van Gogh and Toulouse-Lautrec, on the other hand, moved forward to a new and even looser form. In both cases, form had become important.

Early in his career, Paul Cézanne linked himself to the Impressionists, and especially to Camille Pissarro, his mentor, who taught him to paint directly from nature and to use brighter colors. Although he exhibited his work with them, it became clear early on to Cézanne that he was more interested in revealing the solid shapes of things than the Impressionists were, and he struggled throughout his life to give form on canvas to the world around him.

Vincent Van Gogh learned about the wonders of color when he stayed with his brother Theo in Paris and met the Impressionist painters working there. He admired their work and joined them for a time, but for him, Impressionism did not allow enough artistic freedom to express emotions. Van Gogh's later works, with their vibrant color and energetic movement, reflect his surging emotion and troubled spirit.

Georges Seurat used the bright colors advocated by the Impressionists, and even some of the subjects favored by them. But rather than give a brief "impression," he followed a painstaking system of juxtaposing dots of colors in such a way that they fused into coherent forms when viewed from a distance. He would spend a year or more on one painting, perfecting this exacting technique called "Pointillism." Although his theory does not quite work in practice—one can still discern individual dots—Seurat's colors do seem to vibrate and dance off the canvas.

Henri de Toulouse-Lautrec studied the work of the Impressionists as a young art student in Paris. His favorite was Degas, who taught him to capture the small moments of everyday life: a ballet dancer tying her shoe, a woman seated in a cafe, ladies scrubbing in a laundry, jockeys awaiting a race. Lautrec, ever the keen observer, realized after a while that unlike the Impressionists, who strove to record their emotional reactions to a scene, he wished to record facts—exactly what he saw before him. Soon he developed his own style: outlining his figures, using longer, more sweeping strokes, and larger, more brilliant areas of color.

The Impressionists, who were among the first to move away from the accepted and expected forms of classical art and historical painting, paved the way for those who came after them. They forged a pioneering spirit in the art world that was taken up by the Post-Impressionists and continues to this day.

LESSON 1: Paul Cézanne (1839–1906)

❑ The Story

Paul Cézanne was hard at work on a painting in his studio. He was so absorbed that he didn't hear a loud knock on his door. The visitor knocked again and finally heard a gruff "Come in." Paul didn't even look up to see who it was. He just kept on working. All around him on the floor were many completed paintings.

"Paul, what are these paintings doing on the floor? They'll get ruined," said his friend. "And someone told me that when he was painting out in the countryside last week, he saw some of your paintings left behind shrubs and trees. So much work left in the wind and rain—left to thieves, left to be trampled under foot. What is going on?"

"That is what they deserve!" murmured Paul. "They don't please me. Every morning I get up early, and I work until the natural light fades in the evening. And still I do not achieve my goals. I'm not interested in merely showing how I feel about what I see or how light changes the way things look, like your Impressionist friends. I want to show what doesn't change: the shapes of things! I want to be like an architect who puts pieces together to create a building. The rocks and trees, houses, and even the fruit in that bowl are *solid* shapes. The apples have *weight*. Here, feel!" An apple came flying through the air. "I build my pictures, and the brush strokes are my building blocks."

"So that is why some of the fruits in your still lifes appear bigger than we know they are in real life, and why sometimes objects seem to lean to one side. You're really building a construction that pleases you the way a sculptor would shape a piece of clay. You're trying to see these objects in a new way."

"Yes," replied Cézanne. "I paint standing back as far as I can from the canvas so I can see the whole and place things where I think they should be to create balance. Still I don't get it right!"

"But you are succeeding, Paul. Some of us go to the art dealers who have your pictures. We study them and talk about them. Why, just the other day, Gauguin told us that if we really wanted to learn, we should look at your pictures!"

"But they must please ME," said Paul. "I work for months on a picture. I do it over and over again. It must please ME. And so I keep on."

"But you must stop sometime. Come to dinner with us. Relax. Forget your troubles. You will return to your work refreshed. There's nothing like the company of friends to cheer up a person!"

"No, I am best left alone," growled Cézanne. "I don't behave well among people. I lose my temper and say things I shouldn't. Go, and leave me in peace."

Cézanne continued to work, more and more often alone. He didn't even live with his wife and son most of the time, though he loved and supported them. After his father's death, he moved into the family home in Provence, in the south of France, and continued to paint. Slowly his fame spread, and artists from around the world came to study with him. He ignored most of them and worked alone. And he died just as he wished—painting! One day he walked into the countryside to paint. He was caught in a rainstorm on the way home and collapsed in the road. He lay there for hours before someone found him and brought him home. The doctor told him to remain in bed, but he continued to go to his studio to paint. He died a week later of pneumonia at the age of sixty-seven.

Paul Cézanne left over a thousand paintings. You can imagine how many there would have been if he had not destroyed so many! Today these paintings hang in museums all over the world and are worth millions of dollars. Some people call him the "Father of Modern Art," for he tried to find in his paintings the *essence* of his subject.

Viewing the Art

While many of the Impressionists strove constantly to reveal the passing effects of nature, Cézanne was intent on showing nature's enduring forms and colors and the relationships between them (Murphy, p. 7). There is no motion in the artist's paintings, but they are alive with energy. When viewing Cézanne's work, concentrate on his mature style for which he is best known. Call attention to the shapes and the colors he used to achieve solid forms. Notice the horizontal and vertical lines in such pictures as *Orchard in Pontoise, Mont Sainte-Victoire Seen from Bellevue, View of Gardanne,* and *The Bay from L'Estaque.* View more landscapes. Do the children see the parallel brush strokes? The shapes?

Cézanne achieved depth in his pictures in ways that differed from the Renaissance painters and other predecessors. His objects overlap one another, giving the impression that the first is in front of the second. He used reds and oranges to bring objects forward and cold colors like blues and greens to move objects back. Can the children find the artist using these techniques in *Still Life with a Basket of Apples, Still Life with Apples and Oranges, Still Life with Water Jug, Still Life with Bread and Eggs,* and *Mont Sainte-Victoire Seen from Bibemus Quarry?* Then look at Cézanne's use of colors in *The Bather,* where it is not the same. Notice the shades of black on the left in the cloud formations and the white surrounding the bather's body. What effect do the children think these colors have on the depiction of space in the picture?

Point out that people have gone to visit the places in France that Cézanne painted, and have reported that the scenes are often more detailed than the ones we see in the artist's work. He did not hesitate to move buildings or trees, to represent a whole grove of trees by a single one, or to use colors such as green in a sky or blue in a tree trunk. The result contains the essential components of a scene. Look for some of these same characteristics in Cézanne's still lifes. Some fruits are larger than they appear in real life. Fruit bowl bases are off-center, as in *Still Life with Compotier.* Table tops slant up or down. The horizon line of a table is visible behind objects and re-emerges at a different point, as in *Still Life with Green Melon.* Colors are not what we see in nature. Yet the whole achieves the effect Cézanne intended. Invite the children to point out some of these characteristics in the pictures they are viewing.

Finally, enjoy some of Cézanne's paintings of people, especially, *Portrait of Victor Chocquet (seated); The Card Players;* some portraits of his wife Hortense and son, Paul; and those of himself. Note their lack of emotion and individuality and unexpected coloring. Again, Cézanne was more interested in form rather than spirit or personality.

Journal Writing

Paul Cézanne was a difficult man who kept to himself. Do you think this helped or harmed his work? Why? Invite the children to write about one of the still lifes they viewed. What things did they notice about it? Were there any unexpected things in the picture? If you studied the Impressionists, which one is Cézanne most like—Degas, Monet, or Cassatt. Why?

Art/Drama Activity: Composing Still Lifes

Materials

- Large reproductions of several of Cézanne's still lifes. Slides are ideal.
- Three sets of similar materials for composing a still life. Some possibilities are cloth, basket, fruits and vegetables, pitcher, bowl, and figurines.
- Paper
- Paints

Study several Cézanne still lifes together. Talk about the ways Cézanne placed his objects. Cover an object in a picture and look at the picture again. Does the absence of that object destroy the balance in the picture? After the students understand that Cézanne placed his objects to achieve certain effects, divide them into three groups. Give each group a set of objects that are similar in number and kind. Send them to three different parts of the room to compose a still life. Each group should discuss the reasons for placing objects in certain positions. After allowing sufficient time for this activity, invite the three groups to visit each other's work. What are the similarities? Differences? Effects achieved? You can stop the session here or, if there is time, invite the children to paint the still life they have created.

Another worthwhile activity, if you are comfortable with nudes, is to show the children a large reproduction of Cézanne's masterpiece, *The Large Bathers*. Supply tracing paper and invite them to trace the outline of the figures. They will readily notice that the whole piece is triangular in shape. The children may enjoy searching for shapes in other Cézanne paintings and creating pictures of their own using such geometric shapes as spheres, triangles, cylinders, etc.

LESSON 2: Vincent Van Gogh (1853–1890)

❑ The Story

Joseph Roulin wiped his forehead with his large handkerchief as he walked slowly up the street. His almost-empty mail sack swung from his shoulder. Only two more stops and his mail route would be finished. Then he could sit in the cafe, have a glass of wine, and gossip with his friends. And he had plenty to tell them!

"Ah, my friends," he called as he entered the cafe, glad to be out of the hot summer sun. For even though it was late afternoon, summers in his little town of Arles in the south of France were hot indeed. "A fine day, eh? What is the latest news?" asked Joseph.

"Joseph," said a neighbor at one of the tables. "From the twinkle in your eyes, I can tell YOU are the one with some news. Let's hear it."

"You know the new painter in town, the one who lives in the yellow house on the corner—Vincent Van Gogh? He's asked to paint my portrait. Imagine, me, a postman, in a real painting. We're to begin tomorrow."

"Better be careful, Joseph," said one of his listeners. "I've heard so many strange stories about Monsieur Van Gogh. Do you remember that other painter who came to stay with him—Gauguin, I think his name was? The two of them used to go tramping into the countryside together to paint. But when he came in here in the evening, all Gauguin would do was complain. He just couldn't get along with Van Gogh. Gauguin certainly didn't last long. He left before he even had a chance to get settled."

"True," said another. "Van Gogh is a bit strange. The other evening I saw him sitting in front of his easel wearing a crown of lighted candles on his head! He said it was so he could keep painting all night long. I watched him for a while. There he was dipping his brush over and over again into his paints and putting layers of paint on his canvas. He almost seemed angry at the painting!"

The men talked on and on until it was time for them to go home to dinner. "Good luck, Joseph," they called as they each went their separate ways. "Don't let him put globs of paint on you the way he layers paint on his canvases!" Their laughter echoed down the street.

Joseph did pose for Van Gogh the next day. In fact, he posed several times, and so did his wife. Vincent Van Gogh painted several pictures of them, and of many other people in Arles: people working in the fields, men and women posing in a chair like Joseph did, and even people at the cafe. You can see his wonderful pictures of Joseph Rolin sitting proudly in his blue postman's uniform with its shiny gold buttons. But he looks a little uncomfortable, too, maybe because he wasn't used to so much attention.

For months Vincent painted and painted, excited by the brilliant sun and the bright colors in the sunny French town. Vincent often wrote to his brother Theo, an art dealer living in Paris, and told him about the work he was doing. He even put drawings in the letters. Vincent sent Theo pictures to sell in his shop, too—many, many pictures. Even when Vincent had to go to a hospital to rest his troubled mind, he painted over one hundred pictures there. He just never stopped.

Vincent worked as an artist for ten years, in Holland, in Paris, and in Arles. In that short time he did over two thousand paintings and drawings. But only one of Vincent's pictures was sold during the painter's lifetime, and not for very much money either.

Theo saved his brother's artwork and his letters even after Vincent's death and never stopped talking about him. Little by little people began to find out about Vincent's work, and to admire it. When Theo's son grew up, he gave all his uncle's paintings to the Dutch government, for Vincent and his brothers and sisters had been born in Holland. The Dutch government built a special museum for them, and thousands of people visit that museum every year. Not so long ago, one of Vincent Van Gogh's paintings was sold for sixty million dollars! Imagine it: The poor painter who could only sell one painting in his lifetime is now one of the most famous and best-loved artists who ever lived!

Viewing the Art

It is difficult to obtain the full impact of Vincent Van Gogh's work from reproductions in books—to see the tangible layers of paint and the brilliant colors. If at all possible, try to obtain one of the films listed below. If you do use books, begin by showing Van Gogh's early pictures, especially *The Potato Eaters*. Do the children notice the dark palette? The somber subject matter? Concentrate on the paintings done in Arles. The children will enjoy seeing the building where Van Gogh lived, his simple room, his and Paul Gauguin's chairs.

Introduce some of the citizenry of Arles through their portraits: Ada Ginoux, Roulin the Postman. Talk about the weather in Arles, the intense heat and brilliant sun. When you show paintings of the countryside, be certain to include many that feature Vincent's favorite color, yellow, and focus especially on the beautiful *Harvest at La Crau*. Have the children notice the yellows and the artist's strokes, which are like dashes. (If you study Seurat, it is interesting to compare Van Gogh's dashes and Seurat's dots.) Discuss the swirls of motion in *Starry Night* and *Cypresses*. Show some of the beautiful sunflower paintings with which Vincent decorated his little house. Van Gogh did many self-portraits. Notice the intensity in the eyes, the unusual colors. Discuss the differences among the portraits. The children may be curious about the portrait of Vincent with the bandaged ear. Explain that when he was feeling especially depressed, he cut off part of his ear and almost died.

Journal Writing

Have the children write about Vincent and his brother Theo. How did that relationship affect Vincent's work? Do they have a close relationship with a sibling or a friend? How does that relationship affect their lives? Invite the children to choose one picture they especially like and write what they think that picture tells us about Van Gogh.

If you use the song "Vincent" by Don McLean, older children might wish to write a response to it.

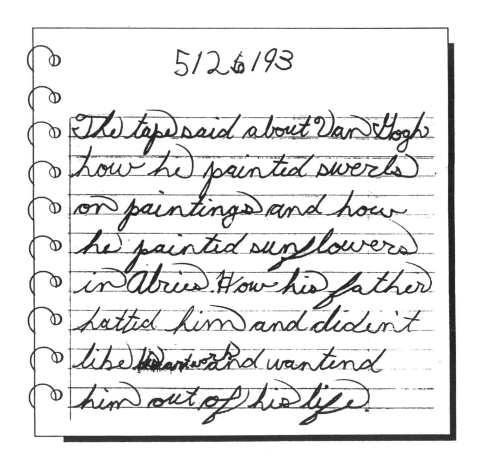

Art/Drama Activity: Brilliant Yellows

Materials

- Paints, especially yellow
- Paper
- Paintbrushes

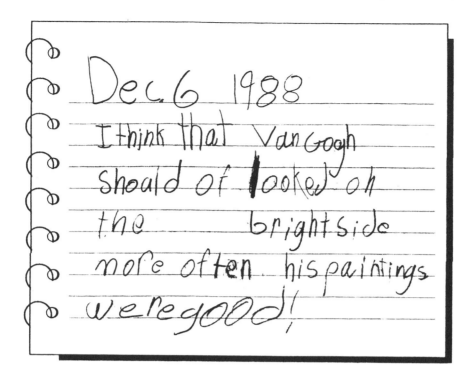

Dec 6 1988
I think that Van Gogh
Should of looked on
the brightside
more often his paintings
were good!

If possible, go out into the schoolyard or on a walk when the sun is at its hottest. How does its brilliance affect what the children see—trees, grass, playground equipment? When you return to the classroom, recall with the children that Vincent Van Gogh loved the color yellow, especially the brilliant yellow of the sun or the bright light of the stars. Talk about different shades of yellow and mix paints with the children to make a few. Add white to yellow to make a pale, creamy color. Add a few drops of red to make a more fiery yellow. Then invite the children to paint a picture of something they saw outside, or a scene they recall when they were outside on a hot day, using shades of yellow.

The children might want to make their own "composition in yellow"—a still life (featuring, perhaps, sunflowers), a scene from their bedroom, a landscape. Recall that when Van Gogh painted his bedroom, he made even the pillows on his bed yellow, though they probably weren't in real life.

LESSON 3: Georges Seurat (1859–1891)

❏ The Story

"**G**eorges, come away from that book. You've been at it long enough! Aman-Jean and I are going to the exhibit of new painters—you know, the ones the critics call Impressionists. Since the Salon won't take their paintings, they are having their own exhibition. Take a break and come along!"

"In a minute, Ernest. But look at this with me first."

"Oh, you and your scientists! You read one scientific book after the other. You're supposed to be studying art, my friend. Why waste your time on science?"

"But, Ernest, I believe science can teach us so much about art. Look at this color wheel here in the book. The writer says that when you put colors next to each other, they pick up one another's colors and look different from the way they are on a page by themselves. Isn't that fascinating? Here, take a look for yourself."

"So? I still don't know what this has to do with our art studies."

"Don't you see, if I put the right colors near each other on my canvas, they can mix together. I tried mixing them myself on my palette, but all I got was black. But if I put the separate colors near each other in my picture, they will mix together in the eyes of the people looking at the picture. I'm going to try that next."

"The viewer's eyes mix the colors? That sounds crazy to me, but if it will satisfy you, try it. For now, though, come with us to the exhibition."

Georges did go to the exhibition, and he liked the Impressionists' work. In fact, he put some of his own paintings in other Impressionist shows. But he didn't want to follow their ideas exactly. He didn't want to capture just a moment or a certain light on objects outdoors. He wanted to plan and compose his paintings. For two whole years he concentrated on practicing his drawing. Then he worked on using color. He even destroyed some pictures he didn't like! His first big painting was a picture of young people swimming, for he loved the water. He made many drawings to get ready to paint this picture and was very proud of it when it was finally finished. But many people thought it was too different from what they were used to.

Georges didn't change his ideas, though. He kept working and working at them. In fact, he made his work even more different by using small dots of paint, instead of short strokes like the Impressionists. By using dots, he thought his colors would seem to dance or vibrate on the canvas when people looked at his pictures and their eyes mixed the colors together.

Georges was a very quiet man who worked steadily from early morning until late at night, painstakingly putting small dots of color on huge canvases. He knew so much about colors that he could actually paint in the evening in artificial light, while some of his friends could only paint in natural light. They would visit him and try to get him to stop working, but he stayed up on his ladder.

"I know how to get him off that ladder," whispered Aman-Jean to Ernest one evening. "I'll pretend I don't understand what he's trying to do with those dots of his. Then he'll come down and start arguing and explaining. Once we get him off the ladder, we'll each grab an arm and take him to the cafe for a bite to eat." Sure enough, Ernest's plan worked, because Georges believed so strongly in what he was doing that he was always ready to defend himself.

Georges Seurat only painted for about twelve years, but he actually became famous in that short time. The picture that made all of Paris start talking about him was a huge painting of groups of people out enjoying themselves on an island on a Sunday afternoon. Georges made over sixty practice drawings and paintings to get ready for *A Sunday Afternoon on the Island of La Grande Jatte*, and he worked on it for two years! Five years later, when he was hanging pictures in a drafty building for an exhibition, Georges caught a chill and developed a throat infection. He died a week later. He was only thirty-one years old. But even though his life was a short one, he gave us some wonderful pictures and a new understanding of how colors work together.

Viewing the Art

Begin by showing some of Seurat's small paintings and drawings before he developed his pointillism technique. There are several pictures of peasants working which the children might enjoy. Note the similarities to the work of the Impressionists. Look at *Bathing at Asnières*. What are some of the things Seurat has done to let us know it is a very hot day? Spend a considerable amount of time on *A Sunday Afternoon on the Island of La Grande Jatte*. Show the children some of Seurat's preliminary drawings and paintings. Talk about pointillism and its effects. Note all the vertical lines. How many different activities can the children discover in the painting? How many colors can they see in the grass, the trees, the water, the clothing? Do they notice that Seurat painted his own frame around the picture? Note the more somber tones in the indoor scene called *The Side Show*. Can the children point out all the horizontal and vertical lines? There is not much movement here in contrast to *The Circus*, Seurat's last painting. He hung it for exhibition shortly before his death. What do the children think he intended to add? Note the predominance of blue. If possible, show the children Seurat's final study for *The Circus* (a reproduction appears in Madeleine-Perdrillat's *Seurat*, p. 193) so they can see how he laid out his colors.

Journal Writing

Invite the children to write about the effect Seurat's pointillism technique has on them. Do they like it? Why or why not? Can they explain what he was trying to accomplish? Some children may wish to write about *A Sunday Afternoon on the Island of La Grande Jatte*. What is their favorite part of the picture? Why?

Art/Drama Activity: Pointillism

Materials

- A color wheel
- Paint

- Paintbrushes
- Paper

Children enjoy imitating Seurat's pointillism to create artwork of their own. If they are old enough for a discussion of the color wheel, talk first about how colors work. Point out complementary colors, that is, those colors that are opposite each other on the color wheel, such as red/green, purple/yellow, blue/orange. When the children apply their dots to paper, encourage them to place colors next to each other that will blend in the viewer's eye to create new colors.

LESSON 4: Henri de Toulouse-Lautrec (1864–1901)

(If possible, try to plan this lesson around the time of a special school or community event so the children can make posters to publicize it. This real-life activity will be quite meaningful to them.)

❏ The Story

Four-year-old Henri, dressed in his finest outfit, sat in the coach between his parents, the count and countess de Toulouse-Lautrec, on the way to his baby cousin's christening. When the ceremony began, he shifted from foot to foot in the cold church, anxious for it to be over so the celebrating could begin. Finally, the adults lined up to sign the registry, signaling that it was time to go. Henri pulled on his father's trousers.

"Papa, I want to sign the book, too."

"But Henri, you can't even write your name yet! It's impossible."

"Then I can draw a cow in the book. Pick me up so I can reach, Papa." Imagine, a four-year-old who could already draw animals quite well. But that wasn't so surprising, for his father and many of his relatives could draw. And they were happy to see Henri pass his time that way. But he was not expected to make drawing and painting his career. No, he was expected to become a fine horseman, to hunt, and to care for his father's large estate.

As Henri grew older, he learned to ride so well it seemed as though he were almost part of the horse. He hunted with his father and his uncles and had a fine time. But his mother worried about him because he was small for his age and not very strong. When he was about thirteen, he slipped and fell and broke a thigh bone. The doctors set the broken bone, but perhaps because their methods then weren't as good as they are now, or because Henri's bones were not very strong, his leg never healed properly. He walked with a cane for a year.

Then one day while the family was gathered in the living room, the doctor came to visit. "Hurry, Henri, get up and greet the doctor," said Henri's father. When Henri rushed to get out of his low chair, he dropped his cane and he fell, breaking the other leg! From that time on, Henri's legs simply stopped growing, while the upper part of his body continued to grow into manhood. You can imagine how strange he looked—a person with a regular-size head, arms, and chest, and very short legs. He had to walk with canes the rest of his life, and he could never ride horses again or take charge of the family property.

What happened to Henri was very sad, but actually, some good did come out of it. He had plenty of time to devote to his art, and a few years later, his wealthy parents gave him a generous allowance so he could go to Paris to study. Henri was very smart, and he worked hard at his drawing until he got so good he set up a studio and began his career as an artist.

Henri knew some of the Impressionists in Paris and liked their work, especially Degas's. But he didn't want to follow their ideas exactly. He wasn't interested in painting pretty pictures, but pictures that told the truth about people. He wanted to use outlines for his figures, and longer strokes of his brush. Every night Henri went into the well-known Paris nightclubs with his sketchbook and chalks and drew what he saw. He drew the singers and dancers and the people in the crowd. Then he would take his drawings back to his studio and turn them into paintings. The owners and the people who came to the nightclubs got used to seeing Henri drawing at his special table every night. They liked the little man who was always full of jokes and liked to have a good time. Soon the owners began to ask him to make posters advertising their nightclubs. They could have the posters printed and hung up around the city to bring in business. Many of Henri's posters were so excellent they made the nightclubs famous. Even today we know about the Moulin Rouge in Paris because of Henri's art.

But you can imagine that being in a nightclub every night got Henri used to drinking, and in a few years he became an alcoholic. His mother was so worried about his health that she hired a man to stay with him at all times to stop him from drinking. Like many people who have a problem with alcohol, Henri was sneaky. He figured out a way to fool the man. He bought a special cane that was hollow inside, and every day before the man arrived, Henri unscrewed the top, filled the cane with whiskey, and screwed the top back on (Bouret, p. 236). Then in the nightclub, when the man's back was turned, Henri drank from his cane! But as his mother feared, all that drinking made Henri sicker and sicker. Soon he could not even paint well. He suffered a stroke and died when he was only thirty-seven. Although he had been working as an artist for less than twenty years, he left over one thousand paintings, more than five thousand drawings, and over three hundred prints and posters!

Viewing the Art

There are many photographs of Toulouse-Lautrec available, so begin by showing the children some of them. They will surely be curious about what he looked like. The children might also enjoy his painting of his mother, the countess de Toulouse-Lautrec, and his portrait of Vincent Van Gogh, if they have studied Van Gogh. Show some of the nightclub paintings and portraits. A few you might select are: *At the Moulin de la Galette*; *At the Moulin Rouge: The Dance*; *La Goulue Entering the Moulin Rouge*; *At the Moulin Rouge*; *Jane Avril Leaving the Moulin Rouge*; *At the Moulin Rouge: The Clownesse Cha-u-kao*; and *Marcelle Lender Doing the Bolero in Chilperic*. Note the outlined figures, the swirling garments of the dancers, the expressions on the faces of the patrons, the fashions of the day. Can the children find the artist in any of the pictures?

The Impressionists used natural light outdoors. Toulouse-Lautrec worked with artificial indoor light, often theatrical. How did he show this light in his pictures? Show some of the posters, especially his most famous, *Jane Avril*. Note how a line that comes out of the musical instrument encircles Jane and returns to the instrument. As you view the posters, cover the words. Notice how off-balance they seem without the writing. Lautrec's genius was that the print in his best posters was an integral part of the whole, not something added on.

Journal Writing

Invite the children to pick a character from one of the artist's paintings or posters. What can they tell about the personality of the person from the piece of art? Would Toulouse-Lautrec have pursued his art if he had not been crippled? Why or why not?

Art/Drama Activity: Poster-making

Materials
- Large poster paper
- Markers, especially black for outlining and lettering

- Reprints of Toulouse-Lautrec's posters to use as guides
- Paints
- Paintbrushes

Invite the children to make posters about an event that will take place in the school or community. They may work individually or in groups. Have them plan the poster beforehand. What illustration will best describe the event? What lettering will they need, and where will it go on the poster so it becomes a real part of the picture, and so the poster is well-balanced? What colors will they use to attract the attention of viewers? When the posters are completed, hang them in the lobby or halls of the school if they describe a school event. Otherwise, obtain permission to hang them in appropriate places in the community. Remind the children to remove the posters when the event they advertise is over.

Additional Activities

Children love to dramatize events in the colorful lives of these artists. Some possibilities for dramatization are:

- Edouard Manet visiting Degas in his messy studio
- The Impressionists banding together to form their own exhibit after their work is repeatedly dismissed by the Salon
- Mary Cassatt's father refusing to allow her to study art
- Meeting of Degas and Cassatt
- Boudin convincing Monet to paint outdoors
- Monet setting up his garden
- Cézanne, the loner, who concentrates only on his work
- Van Gogh and Gauguin in Arles
- Seurat discovering the way colors work on each other
- Toulouse-Lautrec drinking from his cane

On a large map of France and one of Holland, draw in the birthplaces of different artists and where they worked.

Write a newspaper that might have been published in the time of the Impressionists. Assume the role of critics and write about some of the Impressionist paintings. Some children can assume the role of detractors while others see something promising in this new kind of art.

Present a slide show of Impressionist and Post-Impressionist works accompanied by poetry readings. Selected poetry titles follow in the children's book references.

Curriculum Connections

Social Studies

- Study the history of France at the time of the Impressionist movement: the Franco-Prussian War, the change from monarchy to republic, etc.
- Study the old Paris and the new reconstruction of the city by Georges-Eugene Haussmann.
- Make a timeline of Impressionist painters and Post-Impressionist painters.
- Study the Industrial Revolution and its effect on French society.
- Study the fashions of the time; design hats for Parisian women of the nineteenth century.
- Find out about the popular cafés in Paris at the time of the Impressionists. Which ones appear in Impressionist paintings?
- Peruse some of the books listed in the References to find quotes from some newspapers of the time. What did critics say about Impressionist paintings?
- Mary Cassatt was active in the Women's Suffrage Movement. Research the movement in the United States. Who were some of its leaders? What were some of the things they did to try to get women the vote?
- World War I took place during the lifetimes of some artists in this section. Find out what caused this war, what countries were involved, the names of important generals, etc.

Science

- Study the inventions of the era: the camera, the steam engine, the electric light, the car, the airplane.
- Find out what kinds of flowers actually grew in Monet's garden. Plant those that will grow in your area. Design a layout for maximum beauty.

Literature

- Read biographies of important people of this era.
- Find poems that go with some of the artists' works.

• Read the poem "Thoroughbred" by Edgar Degas (See *Degas* by Gordon and Forge, p. 73).

Music

• Find out which great composers lived during the time of these artists.

• Explore the relationship between the art and the music of this era.

• Find musical pieces that go with Impressionist paintings.

References

Adriani, Gotz. *Cézanne: Paintings*. Transl. by Russell Stockman. New York: Harry N. Abrams, 1995. A gorgeous book featuring Cézanne's life and detailed discussions of each of the large color reproductions.

————. *Toulouse-Lautrec: Complete Graphic Works*. New York: Thames and Hudson, 1988. Breathtaking, large reproductions of Lautrec's work.

Bade, Patrick. *Degas: The Masterworks*. New York: Portland House, 1991. Life of the artist and detailed discussion of his major works. Large pictures for viewing.

Barnes, Rachel, ed. *Degas by Degas*. New York: Alfred A. Knopf, 1990. Some of Degas's paintings are presented with comments by the artist.

————. *Monet by Monet*. New York: Alfred A. Knopf, 1990. Some of Monet's paintings are presented along with comments by the artist.

Cachin, Francoise, et al. *Cézanne*. Philadelphia, PA: Philadelphia Museum of Art, 1996. More than 240 large color plates and 262 black-and-white reproductions with commentaries. Produced in conjunction with the Cézanne exhibit at the museum.

Castleman, Rive, and Wolfgang Wittrock, eds. *Henri de Toulouse-Lautrec*. Boston: Little, Brown, 1985. Brief biography along with examination of his graphic work.

Cogeval, Guy. *Post-Impressionists*. Transl. by Dan Simon and Carol Volk. New York: Fabard Press, 1988. Discusses individual artists and schools of the Post-Impressionist period.

Cooper, Douglas. *Henri de Toulouse-Lautrec*. New York: Harry N. Abrams, 1983. A brief biography followed by large reproductions accompanied by notes.

Courthion, Pierre. *Georges Seurat*. New York: Harry N. Abrams, 1988. Seurat's life followed by discussion of forty of his best-known works. Color reproductions.

Dunlop, Ian. *Degas*. New York: Harper & Row, 1979. Degas's life and works. Large reproductions for viewing.

Effeny, Alison. *Cassatt: The Masterworks*. New York: Portland House, 1991. Cassatt's life and detailed discussions of many of her works. Large reproductions.

Feaver, William. *Van Gogh*. New York: Portland House, 1990 o.p. Discussion of Van Gogh's major works.

Forge, Andrew. *Monet*. New York: Harry N. Abrams, 1995. Presents thirty-seven Monet paintings held by the Art Institute of Chicago. Thirty-three reproductions in full color with color details.

Freches-Thory, Claire, et al. *Toulouse-Lautrec*. New Haven, CT: Yale University Press, 1992. Several essays discuss Lautrec's career and artistic activities. Large reproductions for viewing.

Gordon, Robert, and Andrew Forge. *Degas*. Transl. by Richard Howard. New York: Harry N. Abrams, 1988. A beautiful book including Degas's life and large reproductions for viewing.

Herbert, Robert L., et al. *Georges Seurat*. New York: Metropolitan Museum of Art, 1991. An overview of Seurat and his work presented on the centenary of his death. Large reproductions.

House, John. *Monet: Nature into Art*. New Haven, CT: Yale University Press, 1986. Explores Monet's evolution as an artist. Large reproductions.

Institut du Monde Arabe and Flammarion. *Delacroix in Morocco*. Transl. by Tamara Blondel. Paris; New York: Flammarion, 1994. Commentary and reproductions in color of Delacroix's paintings during a trip to Morocco.

Janson, H.W. *History of Art*. 5th ed. Englewood Cliffs, NJ: Prentice Hall, 1995. A survey of the major art periods.

Joyes, Claire. *Monet at Giverny*. New York: Two Continents Publishing Group, 1976 o.p. Monet's life at Giverny recreated through interviews with people who knew him. Wonderful photographs.

Katz, Robert, and Celestine Dars. *The Impressionists in Context*. New York: Crescent Books, 1991. A history of Impressionism and the life and works of major Impressionist artists. Large reproductions for viewing.

Kelder, Diane. *The Great Book of Post-Impressionism*. New York: Abbeville Press, 1986. A huge book that begins with the work of the Impressionists and shows how those who came after them adapted their ideas into new styles. Hundreds of large reproductions.

Kendall, Richard, ed. *Degas by Himself*. Boston: Little, Brown, 1987. Presents the artist through his works and writings from his journals and letters.

Loyrette, Henri. *Degas: The Man and His Art*. Transl. by Park Paris. New York: Harry N. Abrams, 1995. An examination of the artist's life and work. Large reproductions.

Madeleine-Perdrillat, Alain. *Seurat*. New York: Rizzoli, 1990 o.p. Seurat's life and works. A large book containing wonderful reproductions.

Mathews, Nancy Mowll. *Mary Cassatt*. New York: Rizzoli, 1992 o.p. Brief life of the artist and large reproductions of thirteen of her works.

O'Connor, Patrick. *Nightlife of Paris: The Art of Toulouse-Lautrec*. New York: Universe, 1992. Large reproductions accompanied by notes reveal Lautrec's view of Paris at night.

Pissarro, Joachim. *Monet's Cathedral*. New York: Alfred A. Knopf, 1990. Large reproductions of the complete Rouen Cathedral series, including the time of day they were painted.

Rewald, John. *Cézanne*. New York: Harry N. Abrams, 1986. Cézanne's life and work. Beautiful large reproductions.

————. *The History of Impressionism*. 4th ed. New York: Harry N. Abrams, 1990. The history of the movement set in the context of the times.

————. *Seurat*. New York: Harry N. Abrams, 1990. Seurat's life and works; 115 color reproductions.

Rewald, John, Irene Gordon, and Frances Weitzenhoffer, eds. *Studies in Post-Impressionism*. New York: Harry N. Abrams, 1986. Chapters on different Post-Impressionists, including some of those in this chapter.

Schapiro, Meyer. *Cézanne*. New York: Harry N. Abrams, 1988. Brief life of the artist followed by detailed discussions of many of his works. Large reproductions.

Smith, Paul. *Interpreting Cézanne*. New York: Stewart, Tabori & Chang. 1996. Published in conjunction with the 1996 Cézanne exhibit in Philadelphia, this work seeks to find the right way to see the artist's work.

Spate, Virginia. *Claude Monet: Life and Work*. New York: Rizzoli, 1992. The artist's life as seen through his work. Many large reproductions.

Stein, Susan Alyson, ed. *Van Gogh: A Retrospective*. New York: Hugh Lauter Levin Associates, 1986 o.p. Van Gogh's life and work examined through his letters and writings of others about him. Large reproductions.

Sutton, Denys, and G. M. Sugana. *The Complete Paintings of Toulouse-Lautrec*. New York: Penguin, 1987 o.p. An outline of the artist's critical history and large reproductions of all his paintings.

Sutton, Denys. *Degas: His Life and Work*. New York: Abbeville Press, 1991. Degas's life and works. Large reproductions for viewing.

Tucker, Paul Hayes. *Claude Monet: Life and Art*. New Haven, CT: Yale University Press, 1995. Monet's life as seen through his work.

Vigne, Georges. *Ingres*. Transl. by John Goodman. New York: Abbeville Press, 1995. Discussion of the artist's work accompanied by reproductions.

Weckler, Charles. *Impressions of Giverny: Monet's World*. New York: Harry N. Abrams, 1990. Incredible photographs using the grain structure of colored film show the interior of the house and the gardens at Giverny. A must!

Witzling, Mara R. *Mary Cassatt: A Private World*. New York: Universe, 1991 o.p. Thirty-two of Cassatt's drawings, prints, and paintings are discussed. Full-page reproductions.

Zemel, Carol. *Vincent Van Gogh*. New York: Rizzoli, 1993. Brief life of the artist and large reproductions of fourteen of his paintings.

Children's Books

Anholt, Laurence. *Degas and the Little Dancer*. Hauppauge, NY: Barron's Educational Series, 1996. Story about Degas and his statue of the young ballet dancer.

Armstrong, Carole. *My Van Gogh Art Museum*. New York: Philomel, 1996. An exploration of Van Gogh's life and art, including twenty-five peelable, reusable sticker reproductions of the artist's most popular paintings and clues about where to place them in the book. *My Monet Art Museum* by the same author is also available.

Bjork, Christina. *Linnea in Monet's Garden*. Illus. by Lena Anderson. New York: Farrar,

Straus, & Giroux, 1987. Linnea and her neighbor Mr. Bloom go to France to view Monet's works and his home at Giverny. See related videocassette.

Blizzard, Gladys S. *Come Look with Me*. Charlottesville, VA: Thomasson-Grant, 1992. Designed to help children appreciate landscapes. Van Gogh's *Starry Night* is included.

Cain, Michael. *Mary Cassatt*. New York: Chelsea House, 1989. A detailed life of the artist with a few color prints of her works.

Dionetti, Michelle. *Painting the Wind*. Illus. by Kevin Hawkes. Boston: Little, Brown, 1996. This picture-book story of Vincent Van Gogh focuses on the artist in Arles, where his neighbors complain about his strange behavior. But a little girl, captivated by his brilliant paintings, becomes his friend.

Esbensen, Barbara Juster. *Dance with Me*. Illus. by Megan Lloyd. New York: HarperCollins, 1995. A collection of poems showing dance in nature.

Hubbell, Patricia. *A Grass Green Gallop*. Illus. by Ronald Himler. New York: Atheneum, 1990 o.p. A collection of poems celebrating various kinds of horses.

Littlesugar, Amy. *Marie in Fourth Position*. Illus. by Ian Schoenherr. New York: Philomel, 1996. A picture-book story of the little girl who inspired Edgar Degas's wonderful sculpture called *The Little Dancer*.

Loumaye, Jacqueline. *Degas: The Painted Gesture*. New York: Chelsea House, 1992. A group of young students make a study of Degas's work.

———. *Van Gogh: The Touch of Yellow*. New York: Chelsea House, 1993. Two children and their uncle try to determine whether a painting is an authentic Van Gogh by traveling to the sites of his pictures and viewing his works in museums.

Muhlberger, Richard. *What Makes a Cassatt a Cassatt?* New York: Viking, 1994. A discussion of twelve Cassatt works and what makes them unique.

———. *What Makes a Degas a Degas?* New York: Viking, 1993. A lively and interesting discussion of the various aspects of Degas's art.

———. *What Makes a Monet a Monet?* New York: Viking, 1993. Discusses twelve paintings and the unique techniques used by Monet in creating his art.

———. *What Makes a Van Gogh a Van Gogh?* New York: Viking, 1993. Discusses twelve paintings and the characteristics that make them uniquely Van Gogh's.

Newlands, Anne. *Meet Edgar Degas*. New York: J. B. Lippincott, 1988 o.p. Degas's life and art told in a first-person narrative.

Raboff, Ernest. *Henri de Toulouse-Lautrec*. New York: HarperCollins, 1988. Brief biographical sketch and fifteen color reproductions.

Sagner-Duchting, Karin. *Monet at Giverny*. Transl. by John Brownjohn. New York: te Neuels Publishing, 1994. Introduction to the artist's contribution to Impressionism and an analysis of his haystacks and water lilies series.

Sellier, Marie. *Cézanne from A to Z*. New York: Peter Bedrick Books, 1996. Information on the artist arranged in alphabetical order.

Skira-Venturi, Rosabianca. *A Weekend with Degas*. New York: Rizzoli, 1991. The reader is invited to spend a weekend with the artist to listen to him talk about his life and work.

———. *A Weekend with Van Gogh*. Transl. by Ann K. Beneduce. New York: Rizzoli, 1994. The reader is invited to spend a weekend with Van Gogh to learn about his life and work. Reproductions and list of museums.

Springer, Nancy. *Music of Their Hooves.* Illus. by Sandy Rabinowitz. Honesdale, PA: Wordsong/Boyds Mills Press, 1994. A collection of poems about horses and their owners' feelings about them. Some excellent poems to accompany Degas's pictures of racehorses.

Turner, Robyn Montana. *Mary Cassatt.* Boston: Little, Brown, 1992. A very readable biography of the artist with a few colored prints.

Venezia, Mike. *Monet.* Chicago: Children's Press, 1990. A very simple life of Monet for young children. Cartoon illustrations.

———. *Van Gogh.* Chicago: Children's Press, 1988. A very simple life of Van Gogh for young children. Cartoon illustrations.

Waldron, Ann. *Claude Monet.* New York: Harry N. Abrams, 1991. A detailed but readable biography of the artist with reproductions of his work.

Yamaka, Sara. *The Gift of Driscoll Lipscomb.* Illus. by Joung Un Kim. New York: Simon & Schuster, 1995. A painter gives a young girl the gift of colors in this picture book celebration of color.

Welton, Jude. *Impressionism.* New York: Dorling Kindersley, 1993. The history and characteristics of Impressionism and a presentation of many Impressionist artists. Includes index and glossary.

Audiovisual Materials

A Is for Art; C Is for Cézanne. Interacts with 33 works from the Philadelphia Museum of Art. Children can organize their own museum, put together puzzles and gather images they've colored themselves. (CD-ROM for Mac and Windows. Available from the Metropolitan Museum of Art.)

Cassatt. (16mm film; 5 mins. Available from the National Gallery of Art.)

Cézanne. (16mm film; 5 mins. Available from the National Gallery of Art.)

Day in the Country: Impressionism and the French Landscape. Features the work of Monet, Pissarro, Sisley, Manet, Gauguin, Cézanne, Renoir, Van Gogh, and others. (Videocassette; 30 mins. Available from Library Video Company.)

Degas. (16mm film; 6 mins. Available from the National Gallery of Art.)

Degas: The Dancers. Discusses the artist's style and technique and fascination with the dance. (Audiocassette and 18 slides. Available from the National Gallery of Art.)

Edgar Degas: The Unquiet Spirit. (Videocassette. Available from Video Opera House.)

French Impressionism and Post-Impressionism. Presents the art and history of nineteenth-century French painting, with emphasis on the Impressionist movement. (Twenty slides, 12 study prints, 3-piece timeline. Available from the National Gallery of Art.)

Georges Seurat: Point, Counterpoint. Fast forward to *The Bathers* and continue viewing from that point on. (Videocassette; 75 mins. Available from Home Vision.)

Impressionism. Works by Manet, Renoir, Monet, Van Gogh, Cézanne and others. (Audiocassette and 75 slides. Available from the National Gallery of Art.)

Le Louvre: The Palace and Its Paintings. Shows the museum's architecture and its paintings. (CD-ROM for Mac and Windows. Available from Library Video Company.)

Linnea in Monet's Garden. An animated version of the delightful book listed in children's book references. (Videocassette; 30 mins. Available from the Metropolitan Museum of Art.)

Mary Cassatt: Impressionist from Philadelphia. (Videocassette. Available from Video Opera House.)

Monet. (16mm film; 4 mins. Available from the National Gallery of Art.)

Monet: Legacy of Light. (Videocassette. Available from Video Opera House.)

Paul Cézanne: Portrait of My World. Cézanne himself guides viewers, giving his personal reflections on his life and works. Also features other artists of the period. (CD-ROM, 1996. Available from Library Video Company.)

Paul Cézanne: The Man and the Mountain. (Videocassette. Available from Home Vision.)

Toulouse-Lautrec. Produced in conjunction with the exhibit at the Royal Academy in London. Historical photos and shots of Montmartre. (Videocassette; 60 mins., 1988. Available from Home Vision.)

Van Gogh: A Museum for Vincent. Features the collection of Van Gogh paintings in the famous Rijksmuseum in Amsterdam. (Videocassette; 32 mins. Available from Library Video Company.)

Van Gogh: Starry Night. Focusing on Van Gogh's painting of the same name, this CD presents a lecture by art history professor Albert Boime, over 200 images, seven sidebars, and Van Gogh's correspondence. (CD-ROM for Mac and Windows. Available from Forest Technologies.)

"Vincent." A song by Don McClean. Older students may enjoy this tribute to Vincent Van Gogh in which McClean sings about the artist's talent and his troubled spirit. View the painting *Starry Night* as you listen. (CD. Available on Don McClean's album, *American Pie*, from EMI Records Group North America.)

Other Materials

Chronicle Books has a series of art activity packs for children. Each pack contains:

- A booklet on the artist's life and some reproductions
- An artist's notebook which provides some drawing activities for the child based on the artist's work
- A large poster for the child to color

At this printing, the following are available: Monet, Cézanne, Van Gogh.
Contact: Chronicle Books, 275 Fifth Street, San Francisco, CA 94103.

Part VI
The Art
of America

14 Arts of Native America

The parents said, "This has been the struggle of our People. We have suffered
but we have endured. Listen," they said, and they sang the songs.
"Listen," they said, "and they told the stories.
"Listen," they said, "this is the way our People live."
—SIMON ORTIZ, *The People Shall Continue*

Background Information

There is some uncertainty about when the first humans came to North America.
Some scientists say they may have come as early as 50,000 years ago, following
herds of animals across a broad land mass stretching between Asia and Alaska.
Surely they were here 10,000 years ago, for their artifacts tell us a good deal about
their lives and customs. A huge glacier covered North America over thousands
of years, alternately advancing and retreating until the Ice Age came to an end
about 9000 B.C. Then the land bridge was submerged under water that we now
call the Bering Strait, and the peoples who had come over to the North American
side were here to stay.

Scientists call these early Americans "Paleo-Indians." Some thrived in the
harsh climate of the north and remained there. Their descendants are the present-day Inuit living in Canada and Alaska. Others, ever on the hunt for food,
spread, over millennia, across the continent, traveling southward even into Mexico and eastward to the woodlands of New England and the marshes of present-
day Florida. Adapting to the environments in these vastly different regions, these
peoples formed tribes and devised ways to survive and prosper.

The "Indians" received their name by accident, for Christopher Columbus,
arriving in waters off America in 1492, believed he had discovered a route to
India and named the people he found on the land "Indians." This became a
general term for native peoples, but it is more common now to call those on this
continent "Native Americans." Columbus and other Europeans who came to
these shores considered the people they found here to be inferior, primitive savages who needed to be civilized by their superior European selves. In reality,

196

however, Native Americans had by the fifteenth century created highly complex civilizations, languages, customs, and spiritualities; invented many things we use today such as hammocks and snowshoes; built structures that rival the pyramids of Egypt; and developed crops such as corn and squash. Their contributions were and continue to be numerous and invaluable, but we shall concentrate here on only one—their highly sophisticated and beautiful art. Although most Native Americans made baskets and pottery, there are specific arts that were intimately bound to the different environments in which the tribes lived.

Even after the land bridge was submerged, some people left Asia and came to the new continent by sled over the polar caps. They never traveled south into warmer climes but remained in the frozen lands stretching from Alaska to Greenland. Known to Europeans as "Eskimos," which means "eaters of raw meat" in their language, they prefer their own name for themselves, "Inuit," which means "real people." Life in this frozen land was harsh and difficult. Some Inuit lived along the coast and hunted whales, seals, and walrus. These animals provided all they needed for sustenance: food, clothing, and oil for light and heat. They also provided materials for artwork: ivory and bones from which the people carved beautiful figures, many of them made to please animals and entice them to offer themselves up to the hunt. Other Inuit were nomads following herds of caribou and musk ox across the tundra.

The tribes of Native Americans who lived along the Northwest coast of the continent derived their livelihood from the abundance of the sea and the surrounding woods. The waters teemed with salmon, and the forests provided big game and magnificent cedars from which the people built canoes, houses, and items for daily living. Because the climate was generally mild and life relatively easy, these Native Americans had ample time to create works of art, and they used the abundance of cedar trees to carve replicas of the animals that gave them life. These status-conscious peoples gave away their possessions in potlatch (gift-exchanging) celebrations to broadcast their wealth, and proudly carved and painted their family histories into huge poles, known today as totem poles, which they displayed outside their homes.

When white people arrived in California in the eighteenth century, there were over 130,000 Native Americans already living there, speaking over seventy different languages (Griffin-Pierce, p. 137). Food gathering for these peoples was easy because of the favorable climate, the abundance of woodlands, and the proximity to water. The Native Americans of California, especially those in the center of the region, made some of the finest baskets in the world. In addition to beautiful baskets, those in the north, where wood was plentiful, made wood carvings, houses, and canoes, while those in the south made pottery.

The Native Americans living in the Great Basin, that region stretching between the Sierra Nevada mountain range in California and the Rocky Mountains in Colorado, had to adapt to a harsh land. They faced an arid, blistering hot desert in summer and sub-zero temperatures in winter, traveling from place to place hunting and gathering food as best they could. Since these peoples spent much of their time gathering food, they had little left over to produce art. There was some basket- and pottery-making, and rabbit fur was woven into warm blankets for protection against the winter cold.

The southwest area of North America includes the present-day states of Arizona and New Mexico, southern Utah, and southwestern Colorado. It is in this area that we find evidence, such as rock paintings and ancient tools, of the oldest continuous inhabitants of the continent. The Native American peoples of the Southwest include three main groups: the Pueblo, which include the Anasazi and the Zuni; the Navajo and their close relatives, the Apache; and the desert tribes including the Pima, the Papago, and the Mojave (Glubok, 1971, p. 3). The ancient Pueblo built large two- to four-storied apartment dwellings out of stones and clay on natural stone shelves on the sides of steep mountains. They dug large round rooms called kivas into the ground and used them for special gatherings and ceremonies. These people were farmers who climbed hundreds of feet daily to reach their fields.

When drought drove them out of their cliff dwellings in the thirteenth century, they moved further south, where they continued to farm and built small villages with homes made of clay. Although there was not much time for art, the Pueblo made pottery. Their descendants, the Hopi, are known for their beautiful baskets and pottery. Most of the Hopi ceremonies were conducted for the good of the community, and Hopi artists created Kachina masks, which their priests wore in special dances to obtain much-needed rain. They also made Kachina dolls to teach their children about the sacred Kachina cult. The Yuman peoples, who lived in lands made fertile by the Colorado River, farmed corn, beans, pumpkins, and melons. Other less fortunate Yuman groups had to depend on hunting and gathering and moved constantly to follow their food sources. The Pimans lived in the inhospitable desert, where farming was impossible, and they also hunted and gathered wild plants. These peoples made beautiful baskets and some pottery. The Navajo and Apache tribes were relative newcomers to the region, arriving from Canada in the fourteenth century. The Navajo lived in round domed houses called hogans. They farmed the land and did some hunting and gathering as well. Later they became sheep- and goat-herders. Navajo women are noted for their exquisitely designed blankets, while medicine men made special sand paintings for ceremonies to cure individuals from their ills. In the late nineteenth century, the Navajo also began producing silver and turquoise jewelry.

The Great Plains comprise the land from Canada south to Texas and from the Rocky Mountains east to the Mississippi River. It is a vast, flat landscape, buffeted by extremes of heat and cold. The Native Americans who lived on the plains were of two groups. Those, such as the Omaha and the Osage, who lived near the Mississippi, were farmers who supplemented their diet with the buffalo that roamed the plains by the hundreds of thousands. They lived in dome-shaped lodges made of earth. The others, like the Sioux and the Cheyenne, were nomads who followed the buffalo herds and gathered wild plants. They lived in tipis made of poles and animal hides that the women could take down and set up easily when the tribe moved. When Europeans brought the horse to America, the lives of the Plains tribes changed dramatically, for they could hunt more easily and travel greater distances. Much of the art of the Plains tribes involved the buffalo. They made elaborately decorated clothing of buffalo skins embellished with colorful beads and other rawhide articles such as containers and robes. The Plains peoples also used feathers to create elaborate headpieces for battle or ceremonial dances.

The northeastern region of America extended from the Atlantic Ocean to the Mississippi. This land of lush forests was home to the Iroquois and Algonquin tribes. The Iroquois lived in longhouses made of wood and covered with tree bark. These structures housed several families, and many longhouses formed a settlement. The people lived off the fruits of the forest, using the animals and plants for food, shelter, and clothing. They also did some farming. The Algonquins who lived among the birch forests farther north made dome-shaped wigwams and, while they did some farming, relied heavily on the animals and plants of the forest for their needs. The Northeast Native Americans also used materials from the forest for their art. They made birch bark canoes and used other woods to make masks and implements. The animals supplied hides from which the people made clothing beautifully decorated with beads introduced by the Europeans. They also made beads from seashells.

Tribes such as the Cherokee, the Creek, and the Seminole inhabited the fertile lands of the Southeast, bordering the Atlantic Ocean and the Gulf of Mexico. The people prospered in this land with a long growing season, forests filled with game and plants, and waters teeming with fish. Sequoyah, a Cherokee, was the only person in history to create a written language on his own. The Cherokee also had their own schools and a written constitution. The peoples of the southeast made pottery, wooden masks, baskets, and beautiful patchwork clothing.

All of the Native American tribes suffered once Europeans came to the continent. White settlers' ever-increasing thirst for land pushed native peoples further and further from their homes. The now infamous Trail of Tears migration, when the Cherokee were forced to move to western lands, resulted in the deaths of thousands of people. Tribes were decimated through hunger, war, and illnesses brought by the Europeans. Still they endured, and their descendants are here to pass on to us the rich heritage and wonderful arts of their ancestors. While the art of any of the tribes would make a delightful and worthwhile study, space will permit us to linger only on pottery and wood carving here. Nevertheless, there are many books in the bibliography that will enable you to create additional lessons about other ancient Native American arts and even some contemporary artists should you wish to do so.

LESSON 1: Woodcarvers of the Northwest Coast

❏ The Story

Hundreds of years ago, a young boy named Swift Runner lived on the northwestern coast of what is now the United States with his parents and his relatives' families in a very large wooden house. The ancestors of these families were among the first people to come to our continent. Each family had its own space in the house, depending on how wealthy it was. The people did not have money as we do, but they showed their wealth in the number of canoes, blankets, shells, baskets, fancy wooden bowls, or other possessions they had.

It was almost winter. The salmon had been caught and dried for food. The women had made robes of cedar bark and bearskin. There would be storytelling and dancing in the long, cold evenings ahead. But this year was even more special. Everyone in Swift Runner's village was very excited, for their chief was building a beautiful new cedar house for himself and his relatives, and he would give a huge potlatch party when it was ready. Chiefs and people from neighboring villages would be invited, and Swift Runner would be able to play with friends he had not seen all year.

For months, the best carver in the clan had been making a huge entrance pole for the chief's house. The whole village had followed the carver into the forest when he went to choose the special red cedar tree for the pole. It was perfectly straight, with hardly any bottom branches, and over seventy feet tall. It took many hours for the men to bring it down, and the strength of all the men in the village to carry it out of the forest. Now the carving was almost complete. Swift Runner had often watched the artist at work. He saw him carve the human watchman with his tall hat at the top of the pole so there would be someone to guard the families inside and warn them of danger. He saw the animal figures on the pole take shape slowly under the carver's skilled hands. All of these creatures told the story of the chief's ancestors and his tribe.

Finally, the big day arrived. People who had been traveling from early morning were pulling their canoes up onto the land, and crowds began to stream toward the chief's new home.

"Hold still," said Swift Runner's mother as she helped him put on his ceremonial clothes. "You will get ready much faster if you just calm down."

"But, Mother, the potlatch is about to begin. Hurry!" And before she could stop him, he ran to find his friends who were gathered in front of the chief's immense new pole, their heads thrown back to see to its very top. How beautiful it was against the blue sky!

"Welcome, welcome," said the chief, as he handed the head of each household a gift. Everyone received something until the chief had nothing more to give. Then the eating began. Swift Runner had never seen so much food. Everyone ate as much as he or she could so they would not offend their host. The party went on and on far into the night. Storytellers told about how the people first came to be, about how the salmon came to fill the waters and the bear to live in the forests. Swift Runner had heard the stories before, but he never tired of them. They were the stories of his people. Someday he would tell them to his children, and they to their children. He would have his own special pole carved and give a potlatch party for the villages. But for now, it was enough to listen until he could no longer keep his eyes open and his parents carried him home.

Viewing the Art

Explain to the children that wood was a main resource for artwork among the peoples of the Pacific Northwest because they lived in the midst of an immense cedar forest. This wood was a perfect material since it was soft and easy to carve, yet resistant to weather and insects. Show the children as many examples of totem poles as you can. Explain that these poles often told a family's history. Point out the guardian figures at the top, the pointed hats, the animal figures. What colors did the Native Americans use to paint them? How did they make these colors? What animals do you see? You may wish to read Hoyt-Goldsmith's *Totem Pole* or Jensen's *Carving a Totem Pole* (see References) before or after you look at totem poles with the children. If you wish, you could show the children other art created by Northwest Coast peoples. Their wonderful, cone-shaped hats with wide brims to keep off the rain are very special. There are also marvelous figures, masks, bowls, and other implements carved from wood.

Journal Writing

Each figure on a totem pole told the story of the person's family or the tribe. They all had special meaning. In preparation for the art activity to follow, invite the children to think about their own family stories. What figures would symbol-ize special family events or ancestors, such as great-grandparents? Have the chil-dren make a list of such figures and symbols and what they stand for.

Art/Drama Activity: Making a Totem Pole

Materials

- A piece of balsa wood about 7 inches long and 3 inches wide for each student
- Extra small pieces of balsa wood
- Craft knives
- Paints, especially red and black
- Paintbrushes
- Clay

If the children are too young to use craft knives, they can just draw figures on the wood without carving them. Or you can use two or three individual small cereal boxes taped together and covered with brown paper. Open extra cereal boxes flat so the children can cut shapes such as arms or hats and glue them on their totem poles where appropriate.

Using the information from their journal writing, invite the children to make totem poles for their families. The poles should contain figures that tell their family stories. They should first draw the figures onto the wood or cardboard. They can then cut the shapes into the material as you wish. Additional features such as arms can be glued on. Paint the pole and anchor it in a small piece of clay. Display the mounted totem poles in the classroom.

LESSON 2: Pottery Makers of the Southwest

❏ The Story

Sweet Corn lived hundreds of years ago with many families in a pueblo, a home made of clay mixed with straw, in a place that is now Arizona. She was a happy young girl, full of energy and fun. Sweet Corn earned her name well, for she loved to work in the corn, digging up the earth to plant the tiny kernels and watching to keep the hungry crows away from the precious crop.

But this day she was not running among the rows of corn. She was not practicing her pottery-making either. Every afternoon until a week ago she had been working hard with her aunt to learn to make pots and bowls of clay just the way her ancestors had before her. But then her aunt had become ill and could not help her with the clay. Sweet Corn and her mother brought her bowls of corn soup to make her strong. They put cool cloths on her forehead to help her endure the blistering heat of the day. The men had even performed special Kachina dances to bring cooling rains and health to those in the tribe who were ill, but Sweet Corn's aunt continued to grow weaker. And yesterday she had died. Already Sweet Corn missed her. So she was sitting quietly behind the pueblo filling her mind with memories of her aunt, of the hours they worked together grinding corn and working the clay. She was thinking of her aunt's beautiful clay pots—of the one that had been chosen for a special ceremony, of the ones that had been traded to other tribes, of the ones that the family used for carrying water and storing corn meal. Her mother was going to choose one of her aunt's best pots for the burial rite. Sweet Corn wondered which one it would be.

The next day, everyone in the tribe gathered to help Sweet Corn's aunt go to the Spirit World. They carried her body to the burial grounds, where a grave had already been dug. The priests did special dances while the people sang burial chants. Then Sweet Corn's mother presented one of her aunt's bowls to the chief priest. He held it high for all the people to admire. Then he took a small tool, cracked a hole in the middle of the bowl, and placed the bowl right over the dead woman's face. "This woman made this bowl while she was among us," he said. "Now she will take it with her into the next world. Spirit of the woman, see, I have carved a hole for you to leave her and go out into the Spirit World. Be happy there forever."

Sweet Corn listened carefully to the priest's words. They made her feel better, because she knew her aunt would continue to live and be happy in the next life. She joined in the final chanting with a happier heart.

The next day Sweet Corn gathered some clay all by herself. She mixed it with water to soften it and added sand as she had seen her aunt do many times. When it was soft enough for her to work with her hands, she rolled the clay into long ropes and began to coil the clay ropes around and around, building up the sides into a bowl of her very own. She worked quietly, remembering her aunt's careful instructions. Soon the clay began to take shape. Sweet Corn looked down at her work. "Aunt," she said, "you are now in the Spirit World, but in a way you are with me, too. I can remember your words and use your instructions to make bowls. I can continue your work so that our people will always have pots for their food and their ceremonies. Thank you, aunt, for passing your art on to me for the good of our people." And Sweet Corn slept with contentment that night.

Viewing the Art

Show the children as many examples of pottery made by southwestern tribes as you can. Many of the books listed below have exquisite reproductions. Notice the designs. Some are geometric, while others have animal or even human figures. Most have a cream-colored background with designs painted in red, black, and sometimes white. Some are red. The children may also enjoy seeing some Kachina dolls.

Journal Writing

Native Americans believed that art was for the good of the people, not just an individual talent to profit a single person. What do the children think of this concept? Can they think of ways in which they or others can use a talent for the good of the group? Can they think of other artwork made for all people (e.g., Mexican murals, cave paintings, Renaissance architecture)? How are these things the same? Different?

Art/Drama Activity: Pottery

Materials

- Self hardening clay (white or cream if possible, otherwise red)
- Reproductions of Native American pottery designs for the children to copy
- Red, black, white paint
- Paintbrushes
- Fine sandpaper

Have the children make clay bowls. Begin by working the clay so that it is soft and malleable. Then roll it into long strips. Coil the strips around a few times until the base is as large as desired, then begin building up the sides. When the sides are completed, try smoothing out the piece as much as possible so that the coils no longer show. Allow to dry and harden for several days. Sand gently and then paint designs.

Encourage the children to work quietly and contemplatively as the Indian potters probably did. You may wish to read aloud Byrd Baylor's beautiful book, *When Clay Sings* (see References), as they work.

Additional Activities

- Have a Native American feast, complete with dancing and authentic foods. See *A Native American Feast* (by Penner) for information and recipes.

- Learn and play some Native American games. See *The Games the Indians Played* by Lavine.
- Make some Native American clothing. Wear it to the feast.
- Share some Native American literature at the feast: folktales and/or poetry.
- Visit a museum to view Native American art work.
- Learn some words in any of the Native American languages.
- Research the different groups of people mentioned in the background information. Illustrate your findings on a large mural, being sure to include types of houses, dress, ways of obtaining food, kind of art, etc.
- Make replicas of different types of Native American homes: longhouses, tipis, hogans, pueblos, etc.

Note: Curriculum Connections and References follow chapter 17.

15 Colonial Historical Painting

I have (God be praised) passed through the many dangers of the seas
and am now at my studies with Mr. West who gives me encouragement
to persue my plan of painting and promises me all the instruction he
is capable of giving.
—CHARLES WILLSON PEALE to John Beale Bordley, London, 1767

Background Information

The colonial period in America was, for most of the Europeans newly settled there, a time of intense hardship and industry. Obtaining food and shelter was the first order of business. Land needed to be cleared, crops put in, houses built. But eventually life improved, and cities and towns began to spring up. By the eighteenth century, many Americans became well established in trades. They were able to build bigger and better homes, and looked to decorate them. Architects copied the Georgian style popular in England, and the furniture within the houses they built was made by American craftsmen who copied such English masters as Chippendale and Hepplewhite.

Because the Puritans of New England were a sober group, they disdained ostentatious decoration, but they cherished portraits of family members. Since many people died young and children often did not survive beyond infancy, these portraits served as reminders of loved ones no longer present and as a record of family history. Dutch colonists, as they had in their homeland, favored portraits, still lifes, and paintings of ordinary folk engaged in their daily activities. Coming from a land in which the sea played such an important part, they loved seascapes as well. However, because they were working so hard to conquer the wilderness, they, and other newcomers to America as well, had no desire to grace their homes with landscapes.

While wealthy plantation owners in the southern colonies were able to import their art from England, those in the north looked mainly to local talent. The country was too young for established schools of art, so for many years, there were no trained American artists. Some European artists came to the New World to earn their living, and they were kept busy painting portraits and other works for people eager to duplicate the amenities they had left behind. But many portraits were painted by sign painters or decorators who used stencils to emulate English wallpaper patterns. These self-taught artists, both men and women, traveled from town to town offering their skills to interested families. Most of their delightful pictures were unsigned, and many, especially those that were not portraits, have not survived. But enough have to give us a wonderful glimpse of life in eighteenth- and nineteenth-century America.

As the nation grew and prospered, Americans became more and more self-sufficient. American-born artists began to engage in formal study and to rise in prominence like their European counterparts. Eventually, Americans would establish art schools to rival those in the Old World, but in the nation's infancy, artists had to travel to Europe to study. Even in the tumultuous years of the American Revolution there were those who managed such travels—men like John Singleton Copley, Gilbert Stuart, Benjamin West, and Charles Willson Peale—who have given us portraits of all the great leaders of their day. Their work and pioneering spirit paved the way for artists who would come after them to record the people, the landscape, and the ideas of this immense and diverse country.

LESSON 1: Benjamin West (1738–1820)

❑ The Story

"**F**ather is dead, Benjamin," said his brother, Raphael. "At last his sufferings are over. We must tell the people of England that their great painter is gone." Slowly the two young men closed their father's eyes and pulled the sheets up over his face. Then they quietly left the room to notify the authorities of the death of their father, the great painter Benjamin West. For days all of England mourned. Many lined the streets for his funeral. Then Raphael and Benjamin Jr. began the sad business of packing up hundreds of their father's paintings. They planned to travel to the United States to convince the representatives in Congress to set up a museum in Philadelphia, where their father was born, and to put his pictures there so Americans could enjoy the work of their first great American-born painter.

As they worked, they began to talk about their father. "How did he ever become an artist?" asked young Benjamin. "He grew up in a little village in Pennsylvania where there were no pictures at all. The people there were Quakers and didn't believe in decorating their houses with art."

"But remember," answered Raphael, "Grandfather's friend showed Father a picture when he came to visit, and from that moment on, Father wanted to paint pictures of his own. It was hard, because he had no materials—not even a brush—and his parents didn't believe in painting pictures!"

"Well, I'm glad they didn't stop him," said Benjamin. "They didn't even punish him when they found out he had cut fur off his cat's tail to make a paintbrush! Poor cat! I'll bet he didn't like the idea one bit!"

"No, I guess not," said his brother. "But once Father had a brush, and the Indians living in the woods nearby taught him how to use plants and tree bark to make colors, there was no stopping him. He just painted picture after picture." For days the brothers continued to prepare and crate their father's pictures and to talk about his long career as an artist.

A few weeks later, the two men boarded a ship for America. It was the year 1820, and the new country had already fought a war with England for independence and another war in 1812 to remain free of England's control. So when Raphael and Benjamin appeared before the representatives in Congress, some of the members were not happy that Benjamin West had spent his whole adult life in England, the country that had so recently been an enemy. "Why should we build a museum to honor a man who left us for England?" they asked.

"But, sirs," replied Raphael. "Our father had to leave because there were no art schools at all in America where he could study. Even as a teenager he was painting fine portraits, but he wanted to become even better. He needed to learn from the work of the great masters, so he went to Italy and then to England. The English people loved his work so much that they begged him to stay. The king of England made him his special painter, and the Royal Academy of Art made him its president. Many English nobles asked him to paint pictures for them. The years just passed, and he never had a chance to return home. But he never stopped loving America. He always asked for news of his country, especially during the Revolutionary War, which saddened him greatly. And when other American artists came to England to study, he always helped them. I can remember our house always full of struggling artists taking lessons from father. And he never even charged them for his services!"

Then one of the representatives stood up. "What these two young men say is true. My nephew went to England to learn from West, and he wrote back glowing reports of how much help he received, how inspired he was by the old man's continuing to paint huge pictures and try new things even though he was ill and in pain. Surely, an artist who was so loved and honored by Englishmen can find some honor in his native country!"

"Yes, sir," said another congressman. "What you say is true, but where is our new nation going to get money for a museum at this time? We have just built an Academy of Art in Philadelphia so our young men can study art in their own country. Let us display some of West's works there in the state where he was born."

And so it was agreed. Benjamin West's sons gave the United States government some of their father's pictures for display in the art school. And today many of the pictures of this great artist do hang in museums in Philadelphia and other American cities. When we look at some of his work, we will see how he changed the way painting was done in his day and why he is considered one of the great artists of colonial times.

Viewing the Art

Begin by showing some of West's early work before he received any formal training, such as the portraits of Jane Morris and *The Death of Socrates*, so that the children can see the growth in his skill as an artist. Contrast these with such portraits as *The Cricketers, John Allen, Mrs. West and Raphael West* (does this last remind the children of any Italian madonna paintings?), done after West's trip to Italy. Show some of West's early historical paintings. Some you might select are *Venus and Cupid, Paetus and Arria, Venus Lamenting the Death of Adonis, The Departure of Regulus from Rome*, and *Leonidas and Cleombrutus*. Spend considerable time on West's *The Death of General Wolfe*. When West's work, depicting Wolfe in his uniform, was unveiled, Sir Joshua Reynolds, one of the most important British painters of the day, felt that showing General Wolfe in his boots and leggings rather than in Greek or Roman clothing as was the custom, would erode respect for the national hero. Reynolds's opinion caused a great controversy. Point out that although two painters, Edward Penny and George Romney, had painted General Wolfe in his British uniform several years before, their paintings were not as large or important as West's. The king of England was so shocked by the painting that even though Benjamin West was his court painter, he refused to buy it. Later, though, when the painting was accepted as a masterpiece, he asked for a copy of it. Wolfe was a British general who died fighting Americans. What details in the painting signal that Wolfe is a British officer? What parts of the picture indicate the connection with America? Show other historical and Biblical paintings as you wish, especially the two huge paintings West completed in his later years: *Christ Healing the Sick* and *Death on the Pale Horse*. The children would also probably enjoy seeing West's self-portraits.

Journal Writing

If the children had been a member of the Congress asked to set up a museum in West's honor, would they have voted to do so? Why or why not?

Art/Drama Activity: Posing and Painting History

Materials

- Large roll of paper for a mural
- Pencils
- Paints
- Paintbrushes
- Pictures of people of eighteenth- and early nineteenth-century America so children can have an idea of clothing styles
- Polaroid camera and film, if possible

Brainstorm with the children about some of the things that were going on in our country during the time Benjamin West was growing up and during his stay in England. Some suggestions are: the Boston Tea Party, in which Americans dumped tea overboard in Boston harbor to protest the British tax on tea; American and British troops fighting the American Revolution; Washington crossing the Delaware; writing the Declaration of Independence; Washington being made the first president; treaties and other interaction with Native Americans, etc. Invite the children to assume roles and pose some of these scenes so that they can get an idea of how figures can be arranged to tell a story. If you have a camera, take a picture of each group's pose. Otherwise, ask the children to keep their poses in mind because they will have to draw them in a short while.

Remind the children that historical paintings tell the story of events that happened in the past. Have the children pretend that they have gone to England to study with Benjamin West and have learned how to do historical paintings. Invite them to paint pictures of some of the historical events already discussed and posed as a story of what was going on during Benjamin West's lifetime. Each group of children should paint the scene it posed, using the Polaroid picture or their memory of the scene as a reference. Assign each group a space on the mural and invite them to first draw and then paint their scene. Display the completed mural in the classroom or hallway.

LESSON 2: Charles Willson Peale (1741–1827)

❏ The Story

"Sir, this letter is from your friend, Chief Justice Allen. I hope his recommendation will encourage you to help me learn to improve my painting."

"Charles," replied Benjamin West, "you are an American. That is enough for me. Of course I will help you. How I miss my country! I've been in England for seven long years, as you know. But I've made such a reputation here that I cannot leave now. Would you believe that I could not even get home to marry my fiancée? I had to bring her here instead! Welcome to my studio. I will teach you what I know."

And that's how young Charles Willson Peale, a boy born in Maryland, came to stay with Benjamin West, a boy born in Pennsylvania, who now was a talented young artist living in England. Charles studied with Benjamin for a long time. When he didn't have enough money to buy his own food, Benjamin invited him to eat with his large family. But then news of trouble in America reached England. The American colonists were unhappy with the British who ruled them. They didn't like the taxes the British placed on them, and they wanted to be free to make their own laws. It seemed war would break out any time.

"Benjamin, I must leave as soon as possible," said Charles. "I love art and know I still have much to learn. But I love my country more. I must go home and fight in General Washington's army."

"I shall miss you, Charles," said Benjamin. "Who will fix things around here when they break? Who will make my children laugh with his jokes and tricks? But you have learned a good deal. You're a fine artist, and I know you will do well. Write to me whenever you can and let us remain friends."

When Charles arrived home, he did serve in Washington's army, but he brought his paints along, too, and painted portraits of the people around him every chance he got. When the war ended, he continued painting, and his portraits were very popular, for he did something that was unusual for his time: He put hints in his pictures of how his subjects made their living. He put a book and quill pen in his portrait of a lawyer, a guitar in a picture of a musician, navigating instruments in a portrait of a boatman.

Yes, people bought Charles's portraits, but he was restless. There was so much more he wanted to do. The country was just beginning. The people needed to learn so many things. They needed schools, museums, and art galleries just like the people in Europe had. When Charles saw something that needed to be done, he didn't ask someone else to do it. He did it himself. So before long, he began working on starting a natural history museum and art gallery in Philadelphia. He talked the leaders of Philadelphia into giving him room for his project, and they agreed to let him use the top floor of a building that was empty. He had animals in the yard outside for people to see and enjoy. And he had stuffed animals inside—animals some people had never seen before. And not only that, he painted special scenery that showed people where the animal lived when it was in the wild. One time, he even went on a dinosaur dig and brought back the bones of a huge mastodon. He put the bones together and displayed the animal skeleton in his museum. He painted pictures of all the leaders of the country—men like George Washington, who became his close friend; Thomas Jefferson; Benjamin Franklin; and many others—and displayed those pictures in the museum, too. Every single man who helped form the new government of the United States had his picture painted by Charles Willson Peale.

You would think that with all the work he did, Charles would be too busy to have a family. But he actually got married three times, for two of his wives died, and he had sixteen children! He named most of them after famous European artists. Not all his children lived, but many did, and several became good artists like their father.

Charles was so busy that the years flew by. Before he knew it, he was in his eighties. But did he sit quietly and relax? Did he let his children take over for him? Of course not. He wanted to keep trying new things. He experimented with new kinds of painting, with using light and shadow. He kept inventing things, too. One day, a group of men asked him to paint a portrait of himself for his museum. Charles thought about it for a long time. He wanted that portrait to tell people the story of his life. We're going to look at it shortly.

Viewing the Art

Show some of Peale's portraits, especially those of George Washington and other leaders the children might know about. It is quite interesting to compare the seven portraits of Washington done by Peale. When Washington sat for his portrait in 1795, both Charles and his son Rembrandt painted his picture. It is fascinating to compare the two. Charles's is idealized, showing a strong, determined "Father of His Country," while Rembrandt's shows Washington as the old, retired man he was. Peale did several portraits of his family members that might interest the children. Show *James Peale Painting a Miniature* (his brother); *Mrs. Charles Willson Peale* (Hannah Moore); *Rachel Weeping* (Rachel is one of Peale's wives, and the child is their daughter Margaret, who died in infancy); *The Peale Family*; and *The Staircase Group: Raphaelle and Titian Ramsay Peale*. When showing the latter, tell how Peale displayed this painting framed by an actual doorway with some steps in front of it. It was so realistic that a visiting George Washington actually greeted the boys. If you wish, read them the delightful picture-book *The Joke's on George* by Tunnell (see References).

Peale also did several self-portraits the children might enjoy. The one referred to in the story, *The Artist in His Studio*, tells us much about Mr. Peale. Look carefully and see how much you can notice about Peale's life. Some things the children should see are the museum itself, the palette to represent his painting, the bird exhibits, the mastodon jaw and mounted skeleton, the taxidermy tools, the portraits of famous leaders. Show also *The Exhumation of the Mastodon* and point out that the device being used to haul water out of the pit was invented by Peale. The story of the mastodon project is recounted in the picture book *Mister Peale's Mammoth* by Sam and Beryl Epstein (see References).

Journal Writing

Have the children write about Peale's different portraits of George Washington. How are they alike? Different? What do they say about the character of the man? What do the children feel is Peale's greatest contribution? Why?

October 2, 1991

Charles Peal had 17 children.
He killed animals, preserved
them and stufed them.
For our play we could
have a boy pretned
he his Gorge
Washington and say
"How do you do boys"
I could, I'm not saying
I will but I could
dress up like his wife
and bring my baby
doll and she could
be one of his daughters.

Ruth

Drama/Art Activity: Portrait Gallery

Materials

- Paper
- Pencils
- Paints, markers, or colored pencils

Pair the children. Begin by having each partner write what he or she knows is special about the other. Perhaps someone is a good soccer player, plays the piano, runs fast, loves to read, etc. Then invite the children to do each other's portrait, including in the picture some symbol indicating that person's special characteristic: a sheet of music or a piano in the piano player's picture, for example. Make a gallery display of these portraits in imitation of Charles Willson Peale's gallery.

Note: Curriculum Connections and References follow chapter 17.

16 Anonymous American Primitives

There will always be nonacademic art so long as there are artists
willing and able to create their own styles in accordance
with their own instincts.
—JANE KALLIR, *The Folk Art Tradition*

Background Information

Since it took a while after the American Revolution for artists to begin plying
their craft and for their subjects to have the means or the leisure to consider
home decoration, the high point of American primitive, or folk, art was between
the end of the eighteenth century (about 1790) until the 1870s, when the photograph became practical and popular. We discuss folk art here as a bridge between
the two centuries. "Primitive" or "folk" are not disparaging terms but ways to
distinguish art that is done by untrained, natural artists. While such art was
for many years considered inferior, critics now generally recognize that it has a
delightfully fresh quality, and the extant pictures are highly prized. Since folk
artists were not trained in the principles of perspective or anatomy, they made
little attempt to adhere strictly to reality in their pictures. Their figures are
rounded, the clothing giving little evidence of being draped over real flesh and
bone. In fact, many even painted the torsos or clothing at home in the winter
months when traveling was difficult, and then added faces when they could travel
to a sitter's home. It is this abstract quality of primitive paintings that makes
them valuable and charming.

Primitive or folk painters were often engaged in other work as well. They
formed the ranks of the farmers, house or sign painters, carpenters, doctors, and
housewives of the developing nation. They traveled from house to house, offering
their services and charging very little. Many of them did not even bother to sign
their works. In order to give you a larger body of work from which to choose, we
will treat the genre as a whole here, rather than isolate a single artist. And we
will concentrate on portraits of children, since these will resonate very especially
with those you teach. The story that follows, then, is about no particular person,
but rather an account of how these folk paintings may have come to be.

❏ The Story

"**M**other, I see him, I see his wagon coming down the road," cried little Sarah as she jumped up and down. "May I run down and show him the way to our house?"

"No, child," said Sarah's mother, wiping her hands on her apron. She had been baking all morning. Her hair was damp from the heat of the fire, and wisps of it escaped her cap and hung along the sides of her face. "The road is muddy from the rains. He will be here soon enough."

Sarah stood by the doorway, hopping from foot to foot in her impatience. At last the wagon pulled up in front of the house and a slim man jumped out, picked up a satchel, and came to the door. Before he had a chance to knock, Sarah's mother opened it and invited him in. "Good day, madam. I've come to do your walls as we arranged last fall. I've brought my stencils with me and can set to work immediately. When I'm finished, your parlor will look as though it is papered in one of the finest European patterns—and without the expense!"

"Wonderful. My husband has brought in the ladder from the barn. It's set up for you in the parlor. And be sure you stop for some refreshments mid-afternoon. I've just baked some cakes."

"I'll look forward to it, madam," said the man as he began to remove his jacket and roll up his shirt sleeves.

"May I watch?" asked Sarah, looking for a hint of approval on her mother's face.

"I don't think so, my dear," her mother responded. "You'll be in the way, and you may get paint on that new dress you insisted on wearing today."

"Madam, I never splatter," said the painter. "And I'll make sure the little lady stays on the opposite side of the room. She'll be no bother at all. I'd rather like the company."

"Well, if you're sure."

Hardly able to hide her excitement, Sarah followed the stranger into the parlor and settled herself in a chair a good distance from where he began spreading out cloths on which to mix his paints. Then she watched in fascination as her mother's parlor walls slowly filled with dainty flowers. Why, it was beginning to look as grand as the big houses they saw in the city when they went in her father's wagon for supplies. She chattered away about her friend Mary, who lived only a short wagon-ride away, and about her doll, Agnes, and about how soon she would be old enough to go to the school house and do her lessons. The amused painter managed an occasional "M-m-m. . . ."

Finally Sarah's mother called them into the warm kitchen for tea and cakes. As they were eating, the man said, "You have a delightful daughter, madam. So full of life and expression. I surely would love to paint her picture."

"You paint portraits as well as designs on walls?"

"Oh yes, madam. In fact, I've done several of your neighbors, and they were quite pleased with the results. A picture of your loved one hanging in the parlor will really make it special. In fact, I could do the two of you—a mother and child portrait. Very touching."

"Well, it would be a wonderful thing to have. We've already lost two children, and no likeness of them to keep their dear faces in our memory. But we haven't much money," Sarah's mother said sadly.

"Oh, madam, I wouldn't charge much. Since you've hired me to do the parlor, I could do the portrait as well for very little more."

"Please say yes, Mother," begged Sarah. "And I could hold Agnes. You will put Agnes in the picture, too, won't you, sir?"

"If it's Agnes you want, then Agnes you shall have," he said, smiling. "She'll help you sit still for me."

And so the woman arranged to have the painter come back the following week, when she would have on her Sunday dress, to do a portrait of herself and her daughter. It was hard for Sarah to sit still for so long, but she managed. The painter worked as quickly as he could, until at last he produced the finished picture. Sarah could hardly believe her eyes. There she was, and Mother and little Agnes sitting comfortably in her lap. Her mother was pleased, too. She paid the painter and proudly placed the portrait on the mantle for her husband to see when he came in from the fields. "I'll be off then, madam," said the painter. "But I'll be back this way again next year. Perhaps your husband will want to sit for me then." Sarah watched him pack his paints and saw him out the front door. She didn't stop waving until his wagon was a small speck in the distance.

In the first hundred years of our country's existence, there were many painters like the one in our story—men and women, too—who traveled from house to house painting portraits. These artists never went to school to study art. What they knew, they taught themselves. I did not give the painter a name in this story because most of these portrait painters never signed their pictures. We have some of their wonderful paintings, but we don't know who they were. When we look at their work, we will learn a great deal about what life was like in our country, especially for the children, over a hundred years ago.

Viewing the Art

As you view these works, point out to the children that the men and women who did them are called primitive or folk artists because they lacked formal training. They painted what they knew to be true about people rather than what they actually saw. They were interested in the overall pleasing design of the picture rather than accurate perspective or accurate anatomy. While viewing these pictures, invite the children to comment on all the things they learn about the children in them who lived so long ago. *Small Folk: A Celebration of Childhood in America* by Brant and Cushman (see References) is perfect for this purpose. However, there are a number of other books on primitives listed that will serve you well. Keep a list of the playthings, pets, and other artifacts the children mention during their enjoyment of the portraits. If you use *Small Folk*, show other artworks in addition to the portraits, for example, carved playthings. This will enable the class to see children's work tools, furniture, and toys. They will need this information later during the art activity.

Journal Writing

Invite the children to create a life for one of their favorite children in the pictures. Does the child come from a wealthy or middle-class family? How do they know this? How does the child spend his or her time?

Art/Drama Activity: Museum Advertising

Materials

- Paper
- Colored pencils
- Pictures for reference

Have the children pretend that they are working for an advertising firm. Their job is to create advertising for art magazines announcing the opening of a new museum dedicated to the children of the eighteenth and nineteenth centuries. Each child should write a brief ad about some of the things in the museum. To accompany the text, they can draw a child in the dress of the times; draw some toys that might be on display in the museum; draw some tools or work instruments that might be on display.

Note: Curriculum Connections and References follow chapter 17.

17 Painters of a Changing Nation

America, America, God shed His grace on thee,
And crown thy good with brotherhood,
From sea to shining sea.
—KATHERINE LEE BATES, "America the Beautiful," 1893

Background Information

Americans in the nineteenth century turned their focus inward on themselves and their growing nation. Another war with England in 1812 convinced them that isolation from Europe was the best course, and the desire for things from the Old World, even great works of art, fell off. Instead, American artists themselves took up brush and palette and began to depict the land and its inhabitants. A people looking for escape from the drudgery of daily toil welcomed the works of the new Romantic painters, artists like Thomas Cole and the painters of the Hudson River School who rendered the beautiful landscape of the Catskills and the Hudson Valley, shrouded in dreamy mists and clouds. Realists, on the other hand, concentrated not on the land but the people, painting what they saw around them. Among them, Thomas Eakins, the great portraitist, and Winslow Homer, famous for his genre paintings of ordinary people and his poignant pictures of the Civil War, were two of the greatest American painters of the century.

The Louisiana Purchase in 1803 more than doubled the size of the United States so that it stretched to the Rocky Mountains, tempting settlers with the promise of rich new land. John James Audubon, lured by the fascinating wildlife of the vast wilderness, became famous for his exquisite renderings of birds. George Catlin, rightly fearing that the westward migration would put an end to the Indians' free roaming on the plains, rushed to capture on canvas as many of these native peoples as possible before their way of life disappeared forever. Frederic Remington painted and sculpted American cowboys and their beloved horses. And Albert Bierstadt traveled all the way to the Rocky Mountains and brought their awesome grandeur home to New York in sketches that he transformed into dramatic paintings. American painters were not so immersed in their own country that they ignored what was happening across the ocean, however. When the Impressionists began to shake the French art world, forcing artists to see color and light in new ways, some Americans such as Mary Cassatt, James Abbott McNeill Whistler, and John Singer Sargent joined their ranks.

American artists throughout the nineteenth century recorded the growth and diversity of a new nation. With an enthusiasm and thirst for adventure symbolic of the country itself, they worked in the cities and on the frontier, painting what they saw and felt. They founded schools of art, took their place beside the masters of Europe, and prepared the way for the century of freedom and experimentation that was to follow.

LESSON 1: George Catlin (1796–1872)

❑ The Story

All day long Indians lined up outside the tipi where George Catlin was painting portraits. They had seen the portrait Catlin had painted of their chief, and they were so amazed they could hardly believe it. They had never seen such magic before, and now everyone wanted a picture. Each man felt a part of himself was in the picture, so he carried his painting carefully back to his tipi and placed it against the wall. He spent hours looking at it and wondering how the strange white man could do such a marvelous thing.

But not everyone was happy. One of the braves was jealous because the chief said he must be one of the last to have his picture done. So he squatted down where George was painting. "Ha," he said to the man who was posing for his portrait. "You are only half a man!"

"Half a man?" "How dare you insult a brave warrior like me! How can you say that?"

"Come look for yourself, then. This man paints only half of your face. He must think you are only half a man."

Now it was true that George Catlin was painting a profile, or side view, of his subject, so of course only half of his face was showing. But the brave felt he had been insulted. He ran out of the tipi to get his gun and fight the man who had insulted him. But when his wife saw what he was doing, she secretly unloaded his gun so that he would not be harmed, for she loved him a great deal. Her plan didn't work, though, because when the other man raised his gun, her husband could not fire back, and he was shot dead. This caused a great deal of trouble, as many in the tribe wanted revenge for their friend's cruel death.

"Oh, how horrible," moaned a heart-broken George Catlin. "I have walked thousands of miles through dangerous lands to help the Indian, and now I have caused deaths because of my pictures. I want to bring my pictures to Washington, D.C., so that the American people can see that the Indians are not savages. I want them to see the strong, noble faces of the chiefs, the beauty of the women, their colorful clothing and beautiful decorations. I want them to see how talented and special these people are. That is my dream. But now look at what has happened."

But George kept moving, traveling from tribe to tribe. He wanted to complete his work before white settlers drove the Native Americans from their homes forever. "Perhaps if people see my paintings and all the wonderful things I have collected like peace pipes and clothing, they will come to respect Indians as I do and allow them to remain on the land," he thought. For six long years George traveled and painted, and when he finally went back east to his wife, Clara, for good, he set up exhibits of his collection. He tried to convince the government to buy his paintings for the Smithsonian museum in Washington, but Congress kept refusing. Meanwhile, George was running out of money to support his family and was growing desperate.

"I know what I'll do," he told his wife. "I'll tell Congress I'm going to take my collection to Europe and sell it there. I know the American government would never want these paintings of their own American Indians to leave the country." But Congress still did nothing. So George took his collection to Europe and held many exhibitions. Even Queen Victoria of England came and was very impressed.

Yet George didn't make enough money to take care of his wife and four children. First his young wife died, then his youngest child, little George—the pride of his father's heart. George Catlin himself was ill and growing deaf. Still the American government would not listen and buy his collection. An American man finally took it to pay off some of George's debts and stored it in a warehouse. Then George's rich brother-in-law came and took away his three daughters: "My sister and your son have died. I don't want anything to happen to these girls. My wife and I can give them a fine home and education."

So George was left with no family and no collection. Most people thought he was just a fanatic and ignored him. But he didn't stay locked in a room by himself. He actually went on a long trip to South America and painted the people there—even though he was sixty years old and quite ill! At last George was too sick to continue painting and went to New Jersey to be with his three grown daughters. He had not seen them in fifteen years! They took care of him, but could not make him well. He died at the age of seventy-six, saying, "What has happened to my collection?"

When he was alive people did not understand how important George Catlin's work was. Now we know that if it had not been for his bravery, we would be missing a great deal of information about Native Americans. Although some of his collection was destroyed by rats and dampness in the warehouse, much of it has been restored. We will look at some of his paintings now, but you can enjoy the actual pictures if you go to the Smithsonian Institution in Washington, D.C. George Catlin would be pleased to know that his collection is now where he always wanted it to be.

Viewing the Art

From the mid-1800s on, as its use became more widespread, the camera began to assume the role the portrait once had—a momentous change in how we were to preserve our history. Make use of both by showing the 1824 self-portrait of George Catlin as an incredibly handsome young man and contrasting it with the photograph of him in Brussels that is now in the Smithsonian. Talk about how the years of travel, danger, and hardship took their toll. Explain that the Indians never harmed Catlin, as they did other whites, because they sensed his respect and admiration of them. Among the many wonderful pictures from which to choose, the children might particularly enjoy *Wun-nes-tow*, *Kee-o-kuk*, *Ten-squat-a-way*, *La-doo-ke-a*, *Ha-won-je-tah*, *Tah-teck-a-da-hair*, *Tis-se-woo-na-tis*, *Ah-mou-a*, *Tal-lee*, *His-oo-san-chees*, *Os-ce-o-la*, *Mandan Medicine Man*, *Kiowa Girl and Boy*, and *Champion Choctaw Ball-Player*. Show the children the two pictures of *Wi-jun-jon* going to and returning from Washington. Tell the children how saddened Catlin was by the fate of this Indian. (He went to Washington in his distinguished native dress and returned wearing clothing that was not suitable for him and having acquired a taste for whiskey, which led to his downfall.) This picture reveals how Catlin felt about the whites' treatment of Native Americans.

Journal Writing

Because George Catlin painted such precise pictures of Indians, we know many small details of their appearance and dress. Using words instead of drawings, describe another student in the room. For example, note what shirt and pants (or skirt) is worn, the pattern of the material, if there is a belt, belt loops, or pockets and where they are, and so on. Try to paint a picture in words so that someone reading those words could actually draw an accurate picture, from head to foot.

Art/Drama Activity: Make a Book

Materials

- Paper and pencils
- Tempera paints
- Brushes
- Catlin pictures to serve as models

Catlin wrote several books about his adventures in the West and the peoples he met and painted there. Divide the children into groups to work on a similar book of their own. Have each group compose a brief paragraph or two with paintings to go with it based on the artist's work. When each group has finished and the paintings are dry, bind their pages together into a book. Decide on a title and design for the cover. Display the book on a special stand or keep it in the classroom library.

Lesson 2: Winslow Homer (1836–1910)

❏ The Story

Young Winslow Homer sat in his apartment in New York writing a letter to his family in Cambridge, Massachusetts. It was the 1860s, and Civil War was raging between the North and South. Winslow wrote,

> I have finally returned from the war front. While I was there, I drew many pictures on wood for *Harpers* magazine. They paid me well, but I decided to quit, since I have no stomach for war. In fact, even while battles were going on all around me, I preferred to draw the men in their camps rather than the fighting. Their faces and their emotions interest me. Now I am working on my own, and trying my hand at painting, something I know very little about as yet. I am taking a few classes and will try to turn some of my Civil War sketches into oil paintings. These along with some pictures I'm painting of people in the countryside are giving me a good deal of practice. I will submit two of my best pictures for the exhibit at the National Academy of Design. If no one buys them, I shall know that I have no talent for painting and will give it up. I think of you all often. Winslow.

"Give up painting for good?" cried Winslow's favorite brother, Charles, when he read the letter. "We can't let that happen! He has too much talent, and

I know he will continue to get better and better. I must do something to get thoughts of quitting out of his head." Then Charles, who loved the outdoors, went out for a long walk. Breathing the cool, fresh air helped him think. Three hours later, he returned, beaming. "I know exactly what I shall do," he announced. "I will go to New York and buy those paintings myself. Winslow need never know. Will you all promise to keep my secret?" Of course, the family did, and Charles left the next day for New York. He went straight to the academy and bought his brother's paintings, refusing to sign his name or say who he was.

Winslow didn't find out what Charles had done until years later, and he was pretty angry when he did. In fact, he wouldn't even speak to Charles for a few weeks! "Oh, come on, Win," said Charles. "It was for your own good. I know how stubborn you are. Imagine how awful it would have been for you to stop painting. Do you regret all the wonderful work you have done since then? You see, my plan worked!"

Winslow had to admit that his brother was right, for he did become an incredibly good painter. He was so good, in fact, that he became famous in his own lifetime. Reporters called him and wanted interviews for their newspapers and magazines, but Winslow ignored them. "My life is my own business," he said. "What people should be concerned with is just my art." Then he left New York and went to England, where he stayed in a small fishing village and painted pictures of the fishermen and their wives. He began to love the sea more and more, and he realized that for the rest of his life he wanted to paint nature.

When Winslow returned to the United States, he decided to move to Maine, where he could be far away from people. "I do my best work alone," he said. He lived in Maine by himself for twenty-seven years, painting the local people, especially his handyman, and the ocean. His favorite times were when there was a storm at sea. He would put on his yellow rain slicker and stand on the cliff watching in awe as the waves rose and crashed against the rocks. He painted many pictures of these storms. Summers he would go tramping through the woods with Charles, hunting and painting the animals and scenery.

Winslow Homer made wonderful wood-block prints when he was a young man. He could have become rich doing that, but he wanted to try something different, and so he learned to paint with oils. People loved his oil paintings, but he still wasn't satisfied, so he began working with watercolors. Right up until the end of his life, Winslow Homer kept trying to paint better and better pictures. When he became very sick and went blind, Charles went to Maine to take care of him, and Charles and their younger brother, Arthur, were with him when he died. Winslow Homer was always proud that except for a few lessons about using paint, no one ever taught him art. He developed his own methods and style.

Today many people consider him the best American watercolor artist who ever lived.

Viewing the Art

Begin by showing some of Homer's early works: pictures for *Harpers* such as *Skating on the Ladies' Skating Pond in Central Park* and *August in the Country*. Discuss some of the Civil War paintings. Tell the children that Homer's *Prisoners from the Front* made the artist famous when he was still a young man. Talk about the faces of the men in the picture—the defeated Confederate prisoners, the Union officer. What are they thinking and feeling? Is the Union officer cruel? Kind? Proud? Other Civil War pictures you might choose are *In Front of the Guard-House* and *The Sutler's Tent*. The class may especially enjoy some of Homer's paintings of children such as *Nooning*, *Homework*, and *Country School*. Show pictures of the strong women and fishermen Homer painted in England such as *Gale* and *Watching the Tempest*. The children may be interested in knowing that Homer painted *Life Line* in New York by stringing a line on the roof and having two models pose for him. He repeatedly doused them with water until he got the look he wanted. The painting was a huge success. Show some of Homer's famous oil paintings of men and the sea: *The Lookout—All's Well*; *Herring Net*; and *Eight Bells*. Spend considerable time viewing some watercolors, including scenes from the tropics and some woodland animals and scenery, the result of Homer's summer trips with his brother. Tell children the story of the *Fox Hunt*. Homer had friends bring him dead crows that he froze and used as models for the painting as he needed them. But when he pinned the frozen crows in position, they thawed out too quickly and became limp and useless. Frustrated, Homer had to scatter corn to lure live crows to fly near his home so that he could paint them from life. The ducks in *Right and Left* were painted a year before his death, and *Driftwood* was his last picture.

Journal Writing

Winslow Homer rejected the limelight and chose instead to live alone in a remote area in Maine. What do the children think of that decision? What were some advantages of Homer's living apart from people? Disadvantages? How might his work have been different had he stayed in New York? Are there times when they work better alone? With others? When and why do they choose to be alone? If you have studied any of the Impressionists or Post-Impressionists, discuss which artists led similar solitary lives, and why you think they did.

Dec 12/4/95

Winslow Homes
he did painting for a
Magazine, but beafor
he said: I will never
work for some one
again! Then he did
pictures of boats and
children at school. When
he went to France
he learn that they used
more color. He lived
in Maine and his house
it was by the shore
his Mother was a Water-
painter (But was not
famouse) he learned from
his Mother, He beacame
Famouse when he was
old.

Art/Drama Activity: Watercolors

Materials

- Watercolor paper
- Enough sets of watercolors for the children to share
- Brushes
- Water
- Cloths for wiping brushes

In imitation of Winslow Homer, one of the country's greatest watercolorists, have the children make watercolor paintings. Demonstrate how the paints look different depending upon how much or how little water is added to them. It would be most fitting for the children to do nature scenes, so if the weather is fair and your school has some woods or trees near by, take a walk to get some ideas. The children might like to sketch what they see and return to the classroom to turn their sketches into paintings. At the very least, have some reproductions of Homer's nature scenes for them to use as reference.

Additional Activities

Drama. Children enjoy acting out several scenes from the lives of the artists they have studied. Some possibilities:

- Benjamin West makes a paintbrush out of his cat's tail.
- Benjamin West learns how to make paint from the Indians.
- Benjamin West helps American painters who come to England to study. Peale is one of these.
- George Washington is fooled by Charles Willson Peale's painting of his sons.
- Charles Willson Peale goes on a dig for dinosaur bones.
- Charles Willson Peale sets up his natural history museum.
- Untrained painters travel door to door painting portraits.
- George Catlin's painting of an Indian's profile causes trouble in the tribe.
- George Catlin tries to convince Congress to buy his Indian collection.
- Charles buys his brother Winslow's paintings on the sly.
- Winslow Homer tries to paint thawing crows.

Create a gallery of American painters. Paint portraits of the artists studied and include an object in the portrait that says something special about them.

Curriculum Connections

Social Studies

- Make a large map of North America and indicate the places in which the different groups of Native Americans lived. Can the children also locate some of the tribes George Catlin visited?
- Study the different encounters of Native Americans with European Americans (i.e., Thanksgiving, treaties, fur trading, any of the Indian wars, etc.).
- Learn about different Native American customs.
- Learn about the first settlers to come to America. Who were the different groups? Why did they come? Place their settlements on a map.
- Learn about the American Revolution. Why was it fought? Against whom? Which Indians participated? On what side?
- Learn about the Civil War. What were the issues? Some battles? The outcome?
- What were some changes in fashions from the eighteenth through the nineteenth centuries?

Science

- Learn about the contributions Native Americans have made, i.e., crops such as corn, beans, and squash as well as drought- and insect-resistant strains; inventions such as snowshoes.
- Study the history of the horse in this country and its impact on Native American life.
- Learn about Native American calendars.
- Find out about the plants Native Americans used for healing.
- What was medicine like in colonial times? During the nineteenth century?
- Discuss some inventions of the eighteenth and nineteenth centuries such as the telegraph and the steam engine.
- Research some of the animals that appear in Winslow Homer's watercolor paintings.

Literature

- Read biographies of famous Native Americans and others who worked with or fought against them.

- Read biographies of some of the great founders of our country, of Lincoln and the leaders of the Civil War.
- Native Americans are wonderful storytellers. Read Native American folktales. Those listed in the bibliography are only a fraction of what is available.
- Enjoy Native American poetry. Some books are listed in the bibliography.
- Walt Whitman was a great poet of the nineteenth century. Enjoy a few of his poems. Who were some other great writers of the times?
- Find poems to go with Winslow Homer's beautiful seascapes.

Music

- Learn some Native American music and dances using books from the bibliography.
- Make Native American instruments, such as flutes and drums.
- Learn some songs of the American Revolution and the Civil War. Talk about the origins of our national anthem.

References

Brant, Sandra, and Elissa Cullman. *Small Folk: A Celebration of Childhood in America*. New York: E.P. Dutton, 1981 o.p. Information about childhood in early America as well as reproductions of children's portraits and other artifacts.

Broder, Patricia Janis. *American Indian Painting & Sculpture*. New York: Abbeville Press, 1981. Large book containing beautiful reproductions of twentieth-century works.

Brody, J.J., Catherine J. Scott, and Steven A. LeBlanc. *Mimbres Pottery*. New York: Hudson Hills Press, 1983. Reproductions of Southwest Indian pottery.

Cikovsky, Nicolai, Jr., and Franklin Kelly. *Winslow Homer*. Washington, D.C.: National Gallery of Art, 1995. Published in conjunction with the Homer exhibit, this book contains more than 200 works that span Homer's career and commentaries on each.

Cooper, Helen A. *Winslow Homer Watercolors*. New Haven, CT: Yale University Press, 1987. Thorough discussions of the watercolors. Reproductions for viewing.

Feder, Norman. *American Indian Art*. New York: Harry N. Abrams, 1995. Explores various aspects of Indian art such as origins, materials used, ecological aspects. Large reproductions.

Hendricks, Gordon. *The Life and Work of Winslow Homer*. New York: Harry N. Abrams, 1979 o.p. A huge book on the life and work of the artist accompanied by reproductions for viewing.

Hill, Tom, and Richard W. Hill, Sr., eds. *Creation's Journey*. Washington, D.C.: Smithsonian Institution Press, 1994. Art and photographs in the Smithsonian collection and voices of Native Americans shed light on their beliefs and traditions.

Jacka, Lois Essary. *Enduring Traditions: Art of the Navajo*. Photos by Jerry Jacka. Flagstaff, AZ: Northland Publishing, 1994. Large reproductions of modern-day Navajo pottery, jewelry, sculpture, rugs, paintings, sand paintings, and baskets fill this beautiful book.

Jonaitis, Aldona. *From the Land of the Totem Poles*. Photos by Stephen S. Myers. Seattle, WA: University of Washington Press, 1991. Describes in text and pictures the Northwest Coast Indian art collection at the American Museum of Natural History.

Kallir, Jane. *The Folk Art Tradition*. New York: Galerie St. Etienne/Viking, 1981. Discussion of folk art accompanied by reproductions suitable for viewing.

Lipman, Jean, and Tom Armstrong, eds. *American Folk Painters of Three Centuries*. New York: Hudson Hills Press, 1980 o.p. Biographies and some representative works of thirty-seven artists.

Lipman, Jean, et al. *Five-Star Folk Art: One Hundred American Masterpieces*. New York: Harry N. Abrams, 1990. Four centuries of American life represented in paintings, sculpture, furniture, and textiles.

Lipman, Jean, Elizabeth V. Warren, and Robert Bishop. *Young America: A Folk-Art History*. New York: Hudson Hills Press, 1986 o.p. A history of folk art accompanied by large color reproductions.

Penney, David W., and George C. Longfish. *Native American Art*. Southport, CT: Hugh Lauter Levin Associates, 1994. Features Native American works of art from every part of the United States. Large reproductions.

Richardson, Edgar P., Brooke Hindle, and Lillian B. Miller. *Charles Willson Peale and His World*. New York: Harry N. Abrams, 1983. Biography, large color reproductions, and essays by distinguished scholars.

Rosenak, Chuck and Jan. *The People Speak: Navajo Folk Art*. Photos by Lynn Lown. Flagstaff, AZ: Northland Publishing, 1994. Discusses current Navajo folk artists. Large reproductions.

Rumford, Beatrix T., and Carolyn J. Weekley. *Treasures of American Folk Art*. Boston: Little, Brown, 1989 o.p. A history of folk art accompanied by large color reproductions.

Simpson, Marc. *Winslow Homer: Paintings of the Civil War*. San Francisco, CA: Fine Arts Museums of San Francisco, 1988. A study of Homer's Civil War paintings. Large reproductions accompanied by period drawings and cartoons.

Stewart, Hilary. *Totem Poles*. Seattle: University of Washington Press, 1993. Excellent explanation of totem poles created by the Native Americans of the Northwest coast.

Trimble, Stephen. *Talking with the Clay*. Santa Fe, NM: School of American Research Press, 1987. Tells the story of Pueblo pottery from the point of view of contemporary potters.

von Erffa, Helmut, and Allen Staley. *The Paintings of Benjamin West*. New Haven, CT: Yale University Press, 1986. A chronological discussion of many of West's paintings and career, with large color reproductions. Also documents all of West's known works.

Children's Books

Abby Aldrich Rockefeller Folk Art Center Staff and Amy Watson. *The Folk Art Counting Book*. Williamsburg, VA: Colonial Williamsburg Foundation, 1992. A counting book utilizing works from the Abby Aldrich Rockefeller Folk Collection.

Arnold, Caroline. *The Ancient Cliff Dwellers of Mesa Verde*. Photos by Richard Hewett. New York: Clarion, 1992. Describes the Anasazi, who built extensive cliff dwellings and disappeared in the thirteenth century.

Ashabranner, Brent. *A Strange and Distant Shore*. New York: Cobblehill, 1996. When seventy-two Indian chiefs and warriors were imprisoned in 1875 as punishment for raids against frontier settlements, they began to paint pictures to recapture their lost world of freedom on the Plains.

Baker, Betty. *Little Runner of the Longhouse*. Illus. by Arnold Lobel. New York: HarperCollins, 1989. Little Runner and his people prepare for a New Year celebration in this fictional "I Can Read" book.

Baylor, Byrd. *When Clay Sings*. Illus. by Tom Bahti. New York: Aladdin Paperback, 1987. In poetic text the author imagines the history of some pieces of prehistoric Indian pottery.

Beneduce, Ann Keay. *A Weekend with Winslow Homer*. New York: Rizzoli, 1993. The painter invites the reader into his home and talks about his art. List of museums containing Homer works.

Biel, Timothy Levi. *The Civil War*. San Diego, CA: Lucent Books, 1991. Study of the Civil War, including important leaders.

Bowen, Gary. *Stranded at Plimoth Plantation 1626*. New York: HarperCollins, 1994. Diary of a young orphan stranded at Plimoth Plantation in 1626. Carefully researched account of life in the New World accompanied by beautiful woodcuts.

Brenner, Barbara. *If You Were There in 1776*. New York: Bradbury Press, 1994. Puts the reader in the New World in the year 1776. Lively presentation of major leaders and events of that year.

Bruchac, Joseph. *Between Earth & Sky*. Illus. by Thomas Locker. San Diego: Harcourt Brace, 1996. Legends about Native American sacred places. Includes a map locating tribes and a listing of the special places. Beautiful illustrations.

———. *The Boy Who Lived with the Bears*. Illus. by Murv Jacob. New York: HarperCollins, 1995. Six Iroquois folktales.

———. *Children of the Longhouse*. New York: Dial, 1996. In this short novel set in a Mohawk village in the late 1400s, a twin brother and sister, well-loved in the community, make enemies of an older gang. Filled with Mohawk traditions, including a ball game we now know as lacrosse.

———. *Flying with the Eagle, Racing the Great Bear*. New York: BridgeWater Books, 1993. A collection of Native American tales from the Northeast, Southeast, Southwest, and Northwest.

———. *Four Ancestors*. Illus. by S.S. Burrus, Jeffrey Chapman, Murv Jacob, and Duke Sine. New York: BridgeWater Books, 1996. Illustrated by four Native American artists, the tales in this beautiful book explain the wonders of the four elements: earth, air, fire, and water.

Bruchac, Joseph, and Gayle Ross. *The Girl Who Married the Moon*. New York: BridgeWater Books, 1994. A collection of Native American tales from the Northeast, Southeast, Southwest, and Northwest.

Bruchac, Joseph, and Jonathan London. *Thirteen Moons on Turtle's Back*. Illus. by Thomas

Locker. New York: Philomel, 1992. Celebrates the seasons through a collection of poems based on the legends of various Native American tribes.

Bulla, Clyde Robert. *Charlie's House*. Illus. by Theresa Flavin. New York: Alfred A. Knopf, 1993. A poor homeless English boy goes to America as an indentured servant in the early eighteenth century. A wonderful glimpse of the time for primary-age children.

Burby, Liza N. *The Pueblo Indians*. Broomall, PA: Chelsea House, 1994. The history of Pueblo interaction with Europeans. Color essay on Pueblo architecture as well as many black-and-white photos.

Caduto, Michael J., and Joseph Bruchac. *Keepers of the Earth*. Illus. by Carol Wood. Golden, CO: Fulcrum, 1989. Native American legends and ecology activities for children. Audio-cassette available.

————. *Keepers of Life*. Illus. by John K. Fadden et al. Golden, CO: Fulcrum, 1994. Discovering plants through Native American stories and earth activities for children.

Capek, Michael. *Artistic Trickery: The Tradition of Trompe L'Oeil Art*. Minneapolis: Lerner, 1995. Discusses the ways in which artists trick viewers into believing what they have painted is real. Peale's *The Staircase Group* and other accomplishments of the Peale family are included.

Carter, Alden R. *The Civil War*. New York: Franklin Watts, 1992. Examines the Civil War from the first battle to the final surrender.

Clymer, Theodore, sel. *Four Corners of the Sky*. Illus. by Marc Brown. Boston: Little, Brown, 1975 o.p. Native American medicine chants, game songs, and lullabies.

Curry, Jane Louise, retel. *Back in the Beforetime*. New York: Margaret McElderry, 1987. A collection of tales from the California Indians.

Dewey, Jennifer Owings. *Stories on Stone*. Boston: Little, Brown, 1996. This picture book presents some of the rock art found in the southwestern United States and attempts to answer questions about the ancient native peoples who produced it and what they were trying to say.

Doherty, Katherine M., and Craig A. Doherty. *The Zunis*. New York: Franklin Watts, 1993. Examines the history, religion, social structure, and daily life of the Zuni Indians. Illustrations and glossary.

Epstein, Sam and Beryl. *Mister Peale's Mammoth*. New York: Coward, McCann & Geoghegan, 1977 o.p. A picture-book story of Peale's dinosaur dig.

Fichter, George S. *American Indian Music and Musical Instruments*. New York: David McKay Company, 1978 o.p. Describes various kinds of Indian music and instruments and gives instructions for making the instruments.

Fradin, Dennis. *The Thirteen Colonies*. Chicago: Children's Press, 1988. Very simple account of why settlers came to America and life in the Thirteen Colonies.

Freedman, Russell. *Buffalo Hunt*. New York: Holiday House, 1988. Describes the importance of the buffalo to the Plains Indians, methods of hunting, and uses of the animal.

————. *Indian Chiefs*. New York: Holiday House, 1987. Biographies of six western Indian chiefs written by a master biographer.

Glubok, Shirley. *The Art of the Southwest Indians*. New York: Macmillan, 1971 o.p. Very simple presentation of the arts of the southwestern Indians for young children.

Griffin-Pierce, Trudy. *The Encyclopedia of Native America*. New York: Viking, 1995. Very readable history of the different groups of Native Americans in North America, their customs, arts, and interaction with Europeans.

Hakim, Joy. *The First Americans*. New York: Oxford University Press, 1993. Very readable history of Native Americans.

————. *Making Thirteen Colonies*. New York: Oxford University Press, 1993. A delightful history of the United States from colonization to the middle of the eighteenth century.

Haley, Gail E., retel. *Two Bad Boys*. New York: Dutton, 1996. A Cherokee tale about Boy, who is lonely until he finds Wild Boy, a child who claims to be his brother.

Harrell, Beatrice Orcutt, retel. *How Thunder and Lightning Came to Be*. Illus. by Susan L. Roth. New York: Dial, 1995. A Choctaw tale that explains how two birds accidentally create thunder and lightning.

Haslam, Andrew, and Alexandra Parsons. *Make It Work! North American Indians*. New York: Thomson Learning, 1995. Explores different aspects of Indian life such as clothing and suggests related activities.

Hausman, Gerald. *Eagle Boy*. Illus. by Cara and Barry Moser. New York: HarperCollins, 1996. In this Navajo legend, a boy is carried off by eagles and learns their ways.

Henry, Marguerite. *Benjamin West and His Cat Grimalkin*. Illus. by Wesley Dennis. New York: Simon & Schuster, 1985 o.p. The story of young Benjamin West and how he made a brush from his cat's tail.

Hirschfelder, Arlene B., and Beverly R. Singer, sel. *Rising Voices: Writings of Young Native Americans*. New York: Charles Scribner's Sons, 1992. A collection of poems and essays in which young Native Americans speak about themselves. For older children.

Hirschi, Ron. *People of Salmon and Cedar*. Illus. by Deborah Cooper. Photos by Edward S. Curtis. New York: Cobblehill, 1996. Discusses the culture and history of the Northwest Coast Indians.

Hoyt-Goldsmith, Diane. *Pueblo Storyteller*. Photos by Lawrence Migdale. New York: Holiday House, 1991. A young Cochiti girl describes how her grandparents make pottery story dolls in their pueblo.

————. *Potlach: A Tsimshian Celebration*. Illus. by Lawrence Migdale. New York: Holiday House, 1997. The Tsimshian people living in Alaska have a potlach feast to celebrate their heritage. The pictures and story will give students an excellent idea of what a potlach is like and greatly enhance the story told about the Northwest Indians in chapter 14.

————. *Totem Pole*. New York: Holiday House, 1990. A young Indian boy describes how his father makes a totem pole for a neighboring tribe.

Jensen, Vicki. *Carving a Totem Pole*. New York: Henry Holt, 1996. A close-up look at a Nisga'a artist's carving of a doorway pole and how it embodies the culture of a people. Sepia photographs.

Jones, Hettie, sel. *The Trees Stand Shining*. Illus. by Robert Andrew Parker. New York: Dial, 1993. Poems of North American Indians. Suitable for young children.

Lavine, Sigmund A. *The Games the Indians Played*. New York: Dodd, Mead, 1974 o.p. Describes different Indian games.

Littlechild, George. *This Land Is My Land*. Emeryville, CA: Children's Book Press, 1993. The artist, a member of the Plains Cree Nation, explains some of his paintings in this beautiful picture book.

Martin, Rafe. *The Rough-Face Girl*. Illus. by David Shannon. New York: G.P. Putnam, 1992. An Algonquin version of Cinderella.

McDermott, Gerald, retel. *Coyote*. San Diego, CA: Harcourt Brace, 1994. A Zuni tale in which Coyote meets disaster when he insists the crows teach him to fly.

Moore, Reavis. *Native Artists of North America*. Santa Fe, NM: John Muir Publications, 1993. Brief biographies of five contemporary Native American artists.

Morrow, Barbara. *Help for Mr. Peale*. New York: Random House, 1994 o.p. The picture-book story of how Peale and his children moved his extensive museum specimens to larger quarters.

Mott, Evelyn Clarke. *Dancing Rainbows: A Pueblo Boy's Story*. New York: Cobblehill Books, 1996. Photos and text tell the story of a young Tewa Indian boy as he and his grandfather prepare to participate in a special tribal dance.

Ortiz, Simon. *The People Shall Continue*. Illus. by Sharol Graves. San Francisco, CA: Children's Press, 1988, revised. Poetic history of Native Americans for young children.

Panzer, Nora, ed. *Celebrate America in Poetry and Art*. New York: Hyperion, 1994. A gorgeous book of poetry accompanied by art prints that celebrates the two hundred years of America's history.

Penner, Lucille Recht. *A Native American Feast*. New York: Macmillan, 1994 o.p. Authentic Native American recipes including cooking techniques, manners, and customs.

Petersen, David. *Sequoyah: Father of the Cherokee Alphabet*. Chicago: Children's Press, 1991. A simple biography with index and list of important dates.

Philip, Neil, sel. *Earth Always Endures: Native American Poems*. Photos by Edward S. Curtis. New York: Viking, 1996. An anthology of poems written by members of Native American tribes from the woodlands, the plains, the deserts, and the pueblos. Accompanied by magnificent black-and-white photos.

Rockwell, Anne E. *Paintbrush & Peacepipe: The Story of George Catlin*. New York: Atheneum, 1971 o.p. A very readable biography of the artist accompanied by sinopia, or red ochre, pencil drawings by the author.

Ross, Gayle, retel. *How Turtle's Back Was Cracked*. Illus. by Murv Jacob. New York: Dial, 1995. A Cherokee tale that explains the cracks on a turtle's back.

Smith-Baranzini, Marlene, and Howard Egger-Bovet. *U.S. Kids History: Book of the American Indians*. Illus. by T. Taylor Bruce. Boston: Little, Brown, 1994. Explores lives and customs of different Indian tribes with suggestions for related activities.

Sneve, Virginia Driving Hawk. *The Cherokees*. Illus. by Ronald Himler. New York: Holiday House, 1996. A picture book in which the author describes the tribe's history, social life, arts, and situation today.

———. *Dancing Teepees*. Illus. by Stephen Gammell. New York: Holiday House, 1989. A delightful collection of poetry written by Native American children.

Sufrin, Mark. *George Catlin: Painter of the Indian West*. New York: Atheneum, 1991. A complete biography of the artist with bibliography.

Terkel, Susan Neiburg. *Colonial American Medicine.* New York: Franklin Watts, 1993. Describes the illnesses prevalent in colonial America and the sometimes outrageous remedies for them.

Tunnell, Michael O. *The Joke's on George.* Illus. by Kathy Osborn. New York: Tambourine, 1993. A delightful picture-book story of how one of Peale's paintings tricked George Washington.

Van Laan, Nancy. *In a Circle Long Ago.* Illus. by Lisa Desimini. New York: Apple Soup/Knopf, 1995. Twenty-five stories, poems, and songs from over twenty different North American tribes fill this beautiful book.

Waters, Kate. *Samuel Eaton's Day.* Photos by Russ Kendall. New York: Scholastic, 1993. A picture-book account of a day in the life of a Pilgrim boy.

———. *Sarah Morton's Day.* New York: Scholastic, 1989. A picture-book account of a day in the life of a Pilgrim girl.

———. *Tapenum's Day.* New York: Scholastic, 1996. A picture-book story of a young Eastern woodlands boy striving to become a warrior counselor. Photos taken in present-day Plimoth Plantation.

Wheeler, M.J. *First Came the Indians.* Illus. by James Houston. New York: Margaret K. McElderry, 1983. Poetic description of six major American Indian tribes for young children.

Wilson, Janet. *The Ingenious Mr. Peale: Painter, Patriot, and Man of Science.* New York: Atheneum, 1996. This biography examines the many facets of Charles Willson Peale's talent, including his involvement in politics, his painting, his inventions, farming, and even motion pictures. Bibliography.

Audiovisual Materials

American Art for the National Gallery. Features full views and details of over 2,600 works, spanning three centuries and representing nearly all of the National Gallery's American painting and sculpture collections. (Laserdisc. Available from Forest Technologies.)

Ancient Art of the American Woodland Indians. (Audiocassette and 27 slides. Available from the National Gallery of Art.)

Art of the American Indian Frontier: The Collecting of Chandler and Pohrt. Shows the art of the peoples of the Eastern Woodlands and Great Northern Plains. (Twenty slides, 8 study prints, booklet. Available from the National Gallery of Art.)

The Boy Who Lived with the Bears and Other Iroquois Stories. Storyteller Joseph Bruchac performs the tales in this award-winning collection. See the book edition in the References. (Audiocassette. Available from HarperCollins.)

Catlin. (16mm film; 6 mins. Available from the National Gallery of Art.)

The Far North: 2,000 Years of American Eskimo and Indian Art. (Audiocassette and 48 slides. Available from the National Gallery of Art.)

How Rabbit Tricked Otter and Other Cherokee Animal Stories. Drawn from the time when people and animals spoke the same language, this collection of Cherokee animal folktales is performed by storyteller Gayle Ross. Accompanied by traditional flute music. (Audiocassette. Available from HarperCollins.

A Nation of Painters. Untrained artists working from the time of the American Revolution until the Civil War. (16mm film; 7 mins. Available from the National Gallery of Art.)

Morgan's Adventures in Colonial America. Children are transported in time to colonial America where they learn about the Revolutionary War era. Teacher's guide with additional activities and resources. Ages 7–12. (CD-ROM for Mac and Windows, 1996. Available from HarperCollins Interactive).

Survey of American Painting. Includes works by Benjamin West, Winslow Homer, and Mary Cassatt, among others. (Audiocassette and 40 slides. Available from the National Gallery of Art.)

Winslow Homer: The Nature of the Artist. (Videocassette; 29 mins. Available from the National Gallery of Art.)

Other Materials

Art First Nations. Two kits, one for elementary and the other for intermediate students, featuring the art of various native peoples of North America. Each kit contains a teacher's guide with art activities, curriculum extensions and other information, and 20 study prints. (Available from Art Image Publications.)

Native American Kachina Kit. Inspired by the Kachina dolls of the Zuni and Hopi tribes, this kit includes an unpainted plaster figure, paints, feathers, a brush, and an illustrated booklet to enable a child to create a Zuni warrior. (Available from the Metropolitan Museum of Art.)

Raynes, Polly. *Watercolor.* Los Angeles: Price Stern Sloan, 1992. An introduction to the art of watercolor. Includes blank pages on which to work and paints.

Wooden Bead Loom. Everything children need to build and string their own loom and weave glass beads into various articles. (Available from the Metropolitan Museum of Art.)

Part VII
The Art of
Mexico

18 Traditions of a Proud People

LESSON 1: The Ancient Mayans

> Of the moral effect of the monuments themselves,
> standing as they do in the depths of a tropical forest,
> silent and solemn, strange in design, excellent in sculpture,
> rich in ornament, different from the works of any other people . . .
> I shall not pretend to convey any idea.
> —JOHN LLOYD STEPHENS, in *The World of the Ancient Maya*

Background Information

The Mayans are descendants of those ancient peoples who came across the land bridge between Asia and Alaska down through what is now the United States and into Central America and Mexico at least 10,000 years ago. Their agricultural way of life enabled them to settle in one place and establish complex societies. The ancient Mayans built pyramid-shaped temples to rival those in Egypt. Without the benefit of the sophisticated measuring instruments we use today, they devised three calendars: one containing 365 days for calculating the events of daily life; one of 260 days for planning religious ceremonies and the planting of crops; and one based on the phases of the moon.

Considered to be among the most literate of ancient peoples, the Mayans made paper from fig tree bark and devised both a written language using hieroglyphs and a number system based on lines and dots. They developed the concept of zero as a place holder for writing large numbers. The Mayans were able to determine the orbit of Venus and some of the other planets and to predict accurately eclipses of the sun and moon.

Mayan society was established under strict class rules. Each large city had one chief who usually ruled for life and passed his position on to his descendants. Other lesser rulers assisted him in his task. The priests, some of whom were rulers, were the highest class of society. They taught and organized religious ceremonies. Second highest were the wealthy families living privileged lives in comfortable homes close to the center of the city and the temples. There was a warrior class and a farming class as well. Farmers lived in simple huts, worked the land, and gave some of their produce to the wealthy. The people indicated their social status by the manner in which they painted their bodies: black patterns for children; red for married people; red and black for warriors; black and white for slaves captured in war; blue for priests and nobles.

Most of Mayan art had to do with their religious ideas. Mayans believed that the universe was created by a supreme god named Hunah Ku. He created people, too, but several of his first attempts were unsuccessful—until he used corn as his raw material. For Mayans, corn was not only a source of their own existence, but also the staple that sustained them throughout their lives. Yum Kax, the corn god, was thus an important deity. The people devoted much of their art to the honor of their gods, creating sculptures of and temples for the different divinities, almost all of whom were related to nature, and decorations for ceremonies in their honor. Itzamna, god of the sun; Chac, god of rain; Ex Chua, god of warriors and merchants; and Ixchel, goddess of pregnancy, were especially venerated by the people. Mayan ruins and reconstructions are evidence of their sophisticated architectural and engineering skills and the incredible carving and painting done in the name of religious worship. Like the Egyptians, the Mayans sent important people on their journey into the afterlife equipped with jewelry, especially jade, and artifacts the dead would need for the afterlife. They also wove decorative clothing embellished with the feathers of birds who shared their tropical rain forest environment, made lovely baskets, and created ornately painted jars.

Mayan civilization was at its height c. 250–900 A.D. when, for unexplained reasons, it began to decline. Some archaeologists believe that poor farming methods may have resulted in the people's inability to provide adequately for themselves. The arrival of the Spanish in the sixteenth century effectively put an end to the way of life these ancient people had been practicing for centuries. The Spanish burned precious Mayan books, believing them to contain the work of the devil. They brought diseases that killed thousands of Mayans who had no resistance to them. Today there are about two million Mayan people living in Mexico and Central America. While they are mostly Catholic, they still follow some of the ancient customs of their people. However, the glories of ancient Mayan civilization, with its impressive temples and wondrous ceremonies, are gone forever.

❏ The Story

Over a thousand years ago, a young Mayan girl living in what is now Mexico was getting ready for a special ceremony in honor of Yum Kax, the corn god. She and her family would have to hurry, for it was almost dawn. The priests in the temple were going to reveal whether or not the time was right to begin planting. Everyone was preparing for the big event. Her father was arranging his special feathered headdress. The girl watched him place it on his head where it seemed to reach high into the sky, showing how important he was. She watched her mother put on her most decorative garment and place huge earrings in her beautiful ears. Her brother was exercising for the game of *pok-to-pok* in which he would play that afternoon. What a difficult ball game that was! He and his teammates would have to get a hard rubber ball through a high hoop without even using their hands! If her brother's team won, the people watching the game would reward them with jewelry. She decided she would do her part to help him.

"Here," she said. "Let me tie leather cloths on your hips and arms and elbows to protect you from the hard ball." And she gathered up the strips and set to work. When she had finished, her mother helped her put on special earrings and bracelets and the family, ready at last, walked the short distance into the center of the city where the temple to the corn god was located. Her father proudly carried a basket of choice vegetables the family was offering to Yum Kax.

The girl saw people gathering from all parts of the community: poor farmers and powerful warriors, as well as prosperous families like her own. The crowds, carrying their offerings, pressed into place at the foot of the temple stairs. In the darkness it was hard to see the beautiful carvings and statues that decorated the temple, but the girl knew it was a fine and fitting place in which to honor the god of corn. Finally the musicians carrying their big drums, conch shells, and flutes took up their positions, and the dancers, arrayed in their fabulous masks, placed themselves nearby. A quiet descended on the people.

As the sun slowly rose in the sky, everyone looked up to see a priest on the platform of the temple pyramid. The people began to pass up to him their offerings for the corn god and to watch silently as the priest spread out the gifts and prayed to Yum Kax on their behalf. Would the god be pleased? Would he accept their humble offerings and grant a good growing season for the corn that was to sustain their lives?

It seemed to the girl as if everyone were holding their breaths, waiting for an answer. Finally, the priest faced the crowd, raised a conch shell to his lips, and blew into it. The loud blast seemed to vibrate right through the girl's body. "My people," the priest proclaimed, "Yum Kax is pleased with your offerings. He says the time is right for planting. The rains will come in their season, and the corn will grow tall and strong and continue to give life to us all. Let the celebrations begin!"

A cheer rose up from the crowd as they made way for the dancers. The musicians began to play while the dancers leaped and whirled to the beat. The girl's father lifted her high on his shoulders so that she could see the swirling streamers and the prancing feet. At last the dancers, exhausted by their efforts, stopped and moved from the center of the crowd and the *pok-to-pok* teams took their places on the court. The ruler and his nobles sat in their special grandstand to watch while the people milled around. How proud the girl was that her big brother was a player! "May you be swift and sure and lead your team to victory," she whispered to herself as she watched him move on the court. And he did hit the ball many times, but not through the target. For two hours the weary players moved the ball back and forth, but not once did it go through the hoop. Finally, one of her brother's friends gave the ball a powerful hit with his hip and it went sailing through the hoop. The team let out a shriek of victory and went running through the crowd for gifts of jewelry. Her brother ran to their mother and gave her a beautiful jade bracelet, the reward of his achievements. How proud the family was of him!

"Now, my son," said his father, "let us relax and rest after this eventful day. It is time for the feasting." Like everyone else, they set out good food and drink. For the rest of that day and even through the night, the murmur of joyful talk and laughter could be heard. At last the sun rose once more in the sky and the sleepy people went to their homes. Tomorrow they would plant their kernels, tend the tender plants, and watch anxiously for the first ears of corn to appear—the promise of life and health.

Viewing the Art

Begin by showing the children some Mayan architecture, done mostly to honor the gods or to provide palaces for rulers. The temples at Uxmal are especially fine examples. Explain to the children that the Mayans built their pyramids of limestone rocks sometimes hauled over long distances. They built narrower and narrower layers of these bricks, held together with mortar, and then built a temple at the top. About every fifty-two years, they built another temple over the old one, so that archaeologists have uncovered layers and layers of Mayan art.

Compare these pyramids to those of the Egyptians if the children have studied Egyptian art. Mention that the Mayans, too, buried art treasures with people so they would have them in the afterlife. If the children have studied the Greeks, ask how Mayan temples compare to Greek temples. Show the Temple of the

Magician, the largest structure at Uxmal; the nunnery (probably a school for wealthy children); the governor's palace; the ball court. Notice the beautiful carvings, or friezes, over the seven doorways of the nunnery and the corbeled arches that are somewhat like Gothic arches except that they form a straight line instead of a point on the top.

Show some carvings of statues and of hieroglyphs. Many of the carvings are statues of the gods the Mayans honored. Be sure to show a Mayan head that represents what the people considered true beauty: the sloped pointed forehead, the large hooked nose, ears enlarged with the weight of jewelry, crossed eyes. Explain to the children that when babies were born, Mayan mothers pressed their heads between boards to achieve a long slanted forehead and hung a bead from a lock of hair in front of their eyes so that their eyes would become crossed. Mayans also put clay on their noses to make them look larger. Finally, show some mural paintings found inside palaces and tombs and paintings on pottery.

Journal Writing

Invite the children to compare the Mayan idea of beauty with their own. Is one better than the other? Why or why not? Or ask them to consider the Mayan architectural achievements in light of the fact that they had no building machinery such as bulldozers or cranes. Why do they think the Mayan civilization declined?

Art/Drama Activity: Mayan Writing and Celebrations

Materials

- Pens and ink, black pencils, or black tempera paint and thin brushes
- Samples of Mayan hieroglyphs representing the 20-day months and/or the five heavenly bodies: sky, sun, moon, Venus, Earth. (These are in *Art of the Maya* by Henri Stierlin; see References.)
- Large sheets of paper

Have the children pretend to be artisans carving hieroglyphics on a new temple for one of the gods. Explain that since the Spanish who later conquered the Mayans destroyed their books, we have not been able to tell what the hieroglyphs mean. (If the children have studied Egyptian art, recall how the Rosetta Stone helped to decipher Egyptian hieroglyphics.) However, we do know the Mayan hieroglyphs for the months and the heavenly bodies. Invite the children to copy these on their papers. If you have access to a blender, you can even make imitation Mayan paper by pulverizing scraps of construction paper, yarn, bits of fabric, and water; squeezing the water out; and drying the "paper" on a flat surface.

As a drama activity, the children might enjoy enacting a Mayan celebration in honor of the gods. A child can take the role of the leader, others can be dancers, others musicians, others enthusiastic people in the crowd. They can make drums to play and/or use recorders or flutes as well.

LESSON 2: Diego Rivera (1886–1957)

> To be an artist, one must first be a man, vitally
> concerned with all problems of social struggle, unflinching
> in portraying them without concealment or evasion, never
> shirking the truth as he understands it, never withdrawing from life.
> —DIEGO RIVERA

Background Information

In the early 1800s, after more than two hundred years of Spanish rule, Mexicans became inflamed with a desire for independence and, led by Miguel Hidalgo y Costilla, began an eleven-year struggle to that end. Mexican independence was finally declared in 1821, but so many lives had been lost and resources spent in the contest that the fledgling country was riddled with problems. In addition, Mexico engaged in repeated conflicts with the United States over what is now Texas and, in the end, was forced not only to relinquish Texas but also to sell to the United States huge chunks of land stretching to the Pacific for a paltry sum. More internal strife between the ruling conservatives and the liberals, who wanted to enact reforms in educational and job opportunities, rocked the country in the latter half of the century until, in 1877, an army general named Porfirio Diaz seized power. He brought order and control to Mexico at the expense of long sought-for freedoms, and his dictatorship lasted more than thirty years.

Diego Rivera and Frida Kahlo lived at a time when Mexico was seething with unrest as poor workers and landless farmers agitated for revolution. The revolution of 1910 deposed Diaz, but he regained control in 1913. Violence and uprisings continued until 1919, and true democracy only became a reality in 1934.

Although he was studying art in Europe, Rivera returned home and became involved in the revolution for a time. But realizing that his life was in danger and that he could do more for his country through his art, he left for Italy to study the ancient art of fresco painting. For seventeen months he examined the works of the great masters of frescoes and returned to his beloved Mexico once again, this time ready to tell her story on her walls. Previously Mexican art had been "Europeanized," but Rivera and other muralists changed that: drawing on the brilliant colors of the sunny land, they depicted Mexican history for the common man in vast, popular murals.

From the early Mayan and Aztec civilizations, through the Spanish conquest, to the plight of the workers and peasants of his day, Rivera sought in his art the heart of the native peoples. Both Diego Rivera and his wife, the painter Frida Kahlo, were passionate about their native land and championed Mexico in their art. Frida dressed in Mexican Indian garb even in her travels in the United States and supported her husband in his efforts to win rights for the poor. Together they made the world more aware of their country, its struggles, and its triumphs. Today many Mexicans, especially the descendants of the Indians who once thrived in highly literate and organized societies, are still striving for a decent wage and a way up from their abject poverty. Diego Rivera's murals stand as a beacon of hope for them and for everyone who cares about equal justice for all.

❑ The Story

"Frida, Frida, wonderful news has just come in the mail!" artist Diego Rivera shouted to his wife. Frida was busy painting at her easel, but she put her paints aside and went to her husband.

"What are you so excited about?" she asked. Then she saw that Diego was holding a letter in his hand.

"The great John D. Rockefeller of New York City has asked me to paint a mural in the RCA building in Rockefeller Center. It is a great honor and a challenge. But it will mean staying away from our beloved Mexico even longer than we had planned. I've worked on this mural for the auto workers in Detroit for so many months already. I want to go home."

"Of course you must do that mural," replied Frida. "A few more months away from Mexico won't make that much difference." So as soon as Diego finished his work in Detroit, the two artists packed their things once again and left for New York.

After drawing sketches for the mural in the RCA building, Diego had workers set up a huge scaffold, and he began to paint. From early morning until late at night he worked, even eating his meals up on the platform. Newspaper reporters found out about the project and came with their notebooks and cameras to get stories about the famous artist at work. But then one day Diego put the face of Lenin, the Russian Communist leader, into his mural. When the reporters saw that, they wrote about it in their newspapers. The people who passed through the lobby of the RCA building saw Lenin's face, and some of them complained. Many Americans hated the ideas of the Communist politicians and were afraid they wanted to take over the world the way they had taken over the system of government in Russia. But Diego liked Communist beliefs. He felt the Communists wanted to give every person a chance to earn a decent living, and so he put the Communist leader in his mural.

Finally, John D. Rockefeller came to visit Diego. "You must replace Lenin's face with someone else's," he told the painter. "I know that you mean well, but the managers of this building are too angry. They are saying that I'm giving you money to spread dangerous ideas. I can't have my reputation ruined."

Diego was furious. "You knew I was going to do this. I showed you my sketches and you okayed them. Now you're changing your mind. Well, I won't change my mind. Lenin's stays in the mural." Diego began painting more quickly than ever. He wanted to finish the job before something happened. Then one morning when he came to work, he found canvas taped over his mural. Mr. Rockefeller was waiting for him. "Go home, Diego. Go back to Mexico. America is not ready for your ideas. Nothing will happen to your mural. Just go."

Sadly, Diego and Frida packed their things and set out for home. No sooner had they left than a group of workers went into the lobby of the RCA building with sledge hammers and pounded Diego's mural to dust. When he heard the news, Diego was heartbroken. "Frida," he said. "I wonder if it has all been for nothing. I worked so hard to study art so that I could use my talent to make the world a better place. I traveled to Europe and stood out in the rain for hours to study the paintings of the great Paul Cézanne in Paris. I worked on new kinds of art with the great Pablo Picasso. I even went to Italy to study how Michelangelo and Raphael painted frescoes on walls. And now my work has been destroyed."

"Ah, Diego," his wife answered. "That one mural no longer exists—yes— but look at all the others you have done! And the ones you will do in the future. Stay here in Mexico and paint the story of our people on walls all over the country so that all Mexicans, even the ones who cannot read writing, can read your pictures and be proud of their heritage."

And so that is what Diego did. He painted stories of the Mayan and Aztec Indians who first lived in Mexico. He painted pictures of the Spanish conquerors and of the peasants who fought in revolutions to make Mexico free. He painted pictures of farmers in the fields and women weaving baskets. He painted flowers and fiestas. He painted the stories of his people until the day he died. He even left them a museum of ancient Mexican artwork he had been collecting all his life. Today the Mexican people honor Diego Rivera as one of their greatest artists. His murals give them hope for a better future.

Viewing the Art

The children will enjoy seeing some of Rivera's self-portraits as well as his drawings at age three of a train and at age twelve of a woman's head. Diego Rivera's art extends beyond the murals for which he is famous. He ventured into Cubism and Impressionism as well. Canvases such as *Flower Day* and *Zapatista Landscape*—a good introduction to the Mexican Revolution and its leaders—are among his finest works. After showing these, reserve the bulk of your time for the murals, since those are the focus of the art activity to follow. Diego and Frida have something in common with Michelangelo. Both Diego and Michelangelo painted huge expanses, on scaffolds. Like Michelangelo, Frida painted (often) on her back. Emphasize that Rivera's murals tell stories and encourage the children to work together to discern what those stories are. Begin with the artist's murals of the ancient Indian civilizations: *Totonac Civilization, Huastec Civilization, The Papermakers*. Some of the others you may choose to view are *The Dyers, The Sugar Refinery, The Ribbon Dance, Our Bread, Distribution of the Arms, Alliance of the Peasant and the Industrial Worker, Partition of the Land, The Agitators*, and *The History of Mexico*. What is Rivera saying about his country, about the treatment of the poor, about labor? Can the children find Diego and/or his wife in any of the murals?

Journal Writing

Rivera painted his murals to tell stories about people or issues he really cared about. Ask the children to write about something they feel is really important for people to think about. Environmental concerns, getting along with those of different races and backgrounds, or homelessness are just some of the possibilities. Tell the children that after they have written in their journals, they will share their ideas with one another in preparation for painting a mural. The mural will contain those issues most mentioned in their writing.

Art/Drama Activity: Mural Painting

Materials
- A large sheet of paper from a roll
- Tempera paints
- Paintbrushes
- Pencils
- Regular-sized paper (8 1/2″ x 11″)

Begin by discussing the children's journal writing. What issues were mentioned repeatedly? Which issues do the children feel should be depicted on their mural? Will the mural have just one theme, or panels containing different ideas? When the children have decided on the content of the mural, talk about the scenes that need to be painted to illustrate their ideas. Divide the class into the number of groups necessary to paint those scenes. Each group should sketch its scene on small papers first, as Rivera did, and then proceed to sketching and then painting the mural. Display the mural in the hall or school lobby. The children might also want to use it to focus the school or another class on an activity: cleaning up a nearby lot, for example, if it's a mural about the environment.

LESSON 3: Frida Kahlo (1907–1954)

> The only thing I know is that I paint because I need to,
> and I paint always whatever passes through my head,
> without any other consideration.
>
> —FRIDA KAHLO

Background Information. See Diego Rivera.

❑ The Story

"**F**rida," said Alex as they rode home from high school on the bus together, "that was a crazy thing you and your friends did last week—riding down the corridor on a donkey! If you keep that up, they will expel you. Then how will you ever become a doctor?" But Frida didn't have a chance to answer, for at that very moment, a trolley crashed into the bus and she was thrown into the street.

When Alex ran out to her, he saw that she was in terrible condition. Many of her bones seemed to be broken, but worst of all, a hand rail from the trolley was pushed right through her stomach. "Help, get an ambulance!" Alex screamed, as he covered Frida with his jacket. At the hospital the doctors were afraid she would die, for she had broken her spine, collarbone, ribs, pelvis, and right leg—the same leg that had been weakened by polio when Frida was only six. And, of course, there was no telling how much damage the hand rail had done.

Eighteen-year-old Frida did not die, but she had to stay in bed for months, completely encased in plaster casts. How boring it became! Frida was such a bright person, and here she was, stuck in bed and unable to go to school or do things with her friends. Hoping to help, her father, who was a photographer and a painter, suggested, "Frida, why don't you try using my paints?" From that moment on, Frida changed her mind about becoming a doctor. All she wanted to do was paint. Her mother had a special easel made so that Frida could paint in bed, lying down, without moving. "Come, pose for me," she begged all the members of her family. Frida painted and painted, and the months passed. Finally she was able to get up and walk, but throughout her life pain never left her, and her body was always weak.

One day her father came home with some news. "Everybody's talking about Diego Rivera," he said. "He's painting a huge mural about our revolution. The whole town is talking about it." "Hmmm," thought Frida, "I must see this for myself." So the next morning she went to the courtyard where Diego was working. She stood at the foot of his scaffold and watched him all morning. Every day that week she went back. Now Diego liked pretty women, and he was flattered that this beautiful young girl came to see him work. Finally one day he saw that she had a large package under her arm. "What is it you have there?" he called from the scaffold.

"Some of my paintings," Frida replied. "I want you to tell me if they are any good." Diego came down right then, even though he almost never stopped his work for anybody. One by one Frida showed him her pictures. "Yes, these are good," said the artist. "You must keep painting."

Frida could hardly wait to tell her parents. "Momma, Poppa!" she shouted as she burst in the door. "The great Rivera thinks I have talent. Isn't that wonderful news?" From that day on, Frida was more determined than ever to become an artist. And she was determined to get Diego Rivera to pay more attention to her. She continued to watch him work, she even brought him food—until finally, they fell in love and got married. Their marriage never went smoothly, but they loved and helped each other, and respected each other's talent, all their lives. Within a few years, Frida's work had become so famous that an art gallery wanted to exhibit her paintings. Frida was so ill that she couldn't get out of bed, so they dressed her in a beautiful Mexican dress and carried her and her bed to the exhibit. There she was, in the middle of the gallery, greeting all the visitors from her huge four poster bed!

Frida died just a year after that, and Diego was heartbroken. When we look at her paintings now, they tell us the story of her life—about how much she suffered from her injuries and how unhappy she was that she could never have children. But they also tell us that she was a strong-willed independent woman who loved her husband and her country. The Mexican people are proud that she is one of them.

Viewing the Art

Some of Kahlo's paintings contain scenes—such as evisceration or childbirth or death—that may be upsetting to children. Be sure that the books you leave around the room do not have these in them.

Tell the children that many of Frida Kahlo's paintings are self-portraits and that many of them are sad because she had to endure so much suffering in her life. These make interesting viewing, but at the same time, make sure to show some actual photographs of the artist lest the children come away with the impression that she actually had bushy eyebrows and a mustache! There are many fine photographs in Herrera's *Frida Kahlo* (see References).

Show *My Grandparents, My Parents, and I (Family Tree)*. Tell the children that Frida's maternal grandparents were Mexican, so she painted them over the hills of Mexico. Her paternal grandparents were from Germany, so they are suspended over the ocean they crossed from Europe. Frida herself stands in the beloved blue house she grew up in, holding a red ribbon connecting herself to her grandparents. The baby in her mother's womb is probably Frida. Frida puts a camera, symbol of her father's profession, in her portrait of him. *The Bus* is probably a reminder of the horrible accident Frida suffered when she was eighteen. Talk about the variety of people the artist put in this picture. *Frida and Diego Rivera* is a wedding portrait. What do the children notice? (the great difference in their sizes, the palette in Rivera's hand symbolizing his work, Frida's Mexican costume and the bright Mexican colors, the ribbon across the top—a typical Mexican custom).

In *Fulang-Chang and I*, Kahlo gives herself very monkey-like features. Notice her hair and eyebrows. Show more of Frida's self-portraits: *Roots, Self-Portrait Dedicated to Leon Trotsky, Self-Portrait on the Border Line Between Mexico and the United States, The Two Fridas,* and *The Frame.* From what the children know of her life, what do they think the artist is saying about herself in these portraits? Notice the decorative birds and flowers Frida painted on glass as a background for herself in *The Frame.* Frida Kahlo has been called a surrealist painter (that is, a painter whose works embody the fantastic). What surrealist elements have the children noticed in their viewing of her pictures?

Journal Writing

Frida Kahlo continued to paint up until her death, in spite of constant pain and weakness. How do the children think she was able to do this? Have they ever conquered obstacles to accomplish something of which they are proud?

Art/Drama Activity: Self-portraits

Materials

- Mirrors (ask the children to bring in small mirrors from home)
- Paints in bright colors
- Paper
- Paintbrushes

Invite the children to look at themselves in their mirrors and paint self-portraits. They may wish to try this in pencil first. Encourage them to look in the mirror and not at their papers and keep drawing until they have finished. They will probably be surprised and amazed at the results. They can repeat the process once they are ready to use paints, or paint over their drawing. They may wish to add some symbols in their pictures as Kahlo did, or to frame them with special decorations as she did in *The Frame*. They may even wish to include a ribbon across the top.

Curriculum Connections

Social Studies

- Find out more about the beliefs and practices of the Mayans.
- Locate Mayan civilizations on maps of Mexico and Central America.
- Find out what Mayans wore.
- Learn about the tropical environment of the Mayans. What animals and plants flourished there?
- Find out about Mexico and its people. Discuss some of the problems between America and Mexico over immigration.
- Have a feast of Mexican foods (see Rivera, *Frida's Fiestas*, for recipes).

Mathematics

- The Mayans were the first to use zero as a place holder and developed an elaborate number system. Find out what it was (see Pine and Levine, *The Maya Knew*) and write from 1 to 50 in Mayan numerals.

Science

- Find out about Mayan farming methods.
- The Mayans devised three calendars. Study them in class.

- What did the Mayans know about astronomy?
- Read *Quetzal* by Patent (see References) to find out about this bird that is especially loved by the people of Central America and Mexico.

Music

- Learn about Mayan instruments. What does a conch shell look like? Can anyone bring one in?
- Make drums and other Mayan instruments.
- Play some modern Mexican music. What is a mariachi band?

Literature

- Read biographies of the Spanish leaders who conquered the Mayans.
- Find out about Mayan folktales. Read *People of the Corn* by Gerson (see References). Read some Mexican folktales.
- Read some poems and stories in *The Tree Is Older Than You Are* by Nye (see References). The children may especially enjoy "Prayer to the Corn in the Field."

Physical Education

- Learn more about the Mayan game *pok-to-pok*. Try playing it.

References

Arquin, Florence. *Diego Rivera: The Shaping of an Artist, 1889–1921*. Oklahoma: University of Oklahoma Press, 1971 o.p. Diego's early life and study in Europe before embarking on his painting of murals.

Favela, Ramon. *Diego Rivera: The Cubist Years*. Phoenix, AZ: Phoenix Art Museum, 1984 o.p. Presents Rivera's work in Cubism. Large reproductions.

Henderson, John S. *The World of the Ancient Maya*. Ithaca, NY: Cornell University Press, 1983. Traces the rise and development of Mayan civilizations. Illustrations by the author and examples of hieroglyphics.

Herrera, Hayden. *Frida Kahlo*. New York: HarperCollins, 1991. Photos of Frida and Diego and large color reproductions of her work.

Lowe, Sarah M. *The Diary of Frida Kahlo*. New York: Harry N. Abrams, 1995. Kahlo's diary compiled during the last ten years of her life, accompanied by 338 illustrations, 167 in color.

Rivera, Guadalupe, and Marie-Pierre Colle. *Frida's Fiestas*. Photos by Ignacio Urquiza. New York: Clarkson Potter, 1994. A gorgeous book by Rivera's daughter which contains recipes and reminiscences of life with Frida Kahlo.

Rochfort, Desmond. *Mexican Muralists: Orozco, Rivera, Siqueiros*. New York: Universe Publishing, 1994. Traces the lives of the three artists through the revolutionary days and provides color photos of their major murals.

Schele, Linda, and Mary Ellen Miller. *The Blood of Kings: Dynasty and Ritual in Maya Art*. Photos by Justin Kerr. New York: George Braziller, 1986. New information about the rise and fall of the Mayans before the arrival of the Spanish. Large reproductions and information on hieroglyphics.

Stierlin, Henri. *Art of the Maya*. Transl. by Peter Graham. New York: Rizzoli, 1981 o.p. Study of the Mayan civilization and art. Excellent reproductions for viewing, including hieroglyphics.

Children's Books

Baquedano, Elizabeth. *Aztec, Inca & Maya*. Photos by Michel Zabe. New York: Alfred A. Knopf, 1993. Presents the history and beliefs of the Aztecs, Incas, and Mayas.

Braun, Barbara. *A Weekend with Diego Rivera*. New York: Rizzoli, 1994. The author speaks to the reader about his life and work. List of places where Rivera's work can be found.

Brenner, Anita, retel. *The Boy Who Could Do Anything & Other Mexican Folk Tales*. Illus. by Jean Charlot. North Haven, CT: Linnet Books, 1992, reissue. Twenty-six stories from pre-Columbian Indian folklore.

Casagrande, Louis B., and Sylvia A. Johnson. *Focus on Mexico*. Photos by Phillips Bourns. Minneapolis: Lerner, 1986. Examines life in Mexico, past and present.

Cockcroft, James. *Diego Rivera*. New York: Chelsea House, 1991. Examines Rivera's life and work. Photos and color reproductions.

Ehlert, Lois. *Cuckoo/Cucú: A Mexican Folktale/Un Cuento Folklórico Mexicano*. Transl. by Gloria de Aragón Andújar. San Diego: Harcourt Brace, 1977. This Mexican tale, told in both English and Spanish, is the story of lazy Cuckoo, the only one who can save the season's seed crop from fire. The outstanding collage illustrations are inspired by Mexican crafts and folk art.

Gerson, Mary-Joan, retel. *People of the Corn*. Illus. by Carla Golembe. Boston: Little, Brown, 1995. The folk story of how the Mayan gods created the people from corn. Beautifully illustrated.

Goldstein, Ernest. *The Journey of Diego Rivera*. Minneapolis: Lerner, 1996. An analysis of Rivera's murals and paintings. Many full-color reproductions.

Greene, Jacqueline D. *The Maya*. New York: Franklin Watts, 1992. A complete yet readable description of the Mayan civilization for children.

Grifalconi, Ann. *The Bravest Flute*. Boston: Little, Brown, 1994. On New Year's Day, following

Mayan custom, a boy leads a procession over a mountain trail carrying a heavy drum and playing his flute. A beautiful picture book.

Hargrove, Jim. *Diego Rivera: Mexican Muralist*. Chicago: Children's Press, 1990. Examines the life and work of Rivera, complete with many photos.

Jacobsen, Karen. *Mexico*. Chicago: Children's Press, 1984. A very simple book that discusses the history and customs of the Mexican people.

Johnston, Tony. *The Magic Maguey*. Illus. by Elisa Kleven. San Diego: Harcourt Brace, 1996. In this picture book the people in a Mexican village love the beautiful maguey plant that grows on the land of a wealthy man, and they save it from destruction.

McKissack, Patricia C. *The Maya*. Chicago: Children's Press, 1985. A very simple study of the Mayans. Pronunciation guide.

Neimark, Anne E. *Diego Rivera: Artist of the People*. New York: HarperCollins, 1992. An excellent biography of the artist for children. Some reproductions.

Nye, Naomi Shihab, sel. *The Tree Is Older Than You Are*. New York: Simon & Schuster, 1995. Poems and stories from Mexico written in Spanish and English and illustrated by Mexican artists.

O'Dell, Scott. *The Amethyst Ring*. Boston: Houghton Mifflin, 1983. In this novel a Spanish seminarian witnesses the fall of the Mayan and Incan civilizations with the arrival of Cortes and Pizarro.

Patent, Dorothy Hinshaw. *Quetzal*. Illus. by Neil Waldman. New York: William Morrow, 1996. The story of the quetzal, a bird found in Central America and Mexico, and its significance for ancient peoples.

Pine, Tillie S., and Joseph Levine. *The Maya Knew*. Illus. by Ann Grifalconi. New York: McGraw-Hill, 1971 o.p. Describes the things the Maya were able to do, with suggestions for related activities.

Sherrow, Victoria. *The Maya Indians*. New York: Chelsea House, 1994. Discusses the history, culture, and daily activities of the Maya Indians. Includes pictures, chronology, and glossary.

Sills, Leslie. *Inspirations: Stories About Women Artists*. Niles, IL: Albert Whitman & Company, 1989. Lives of four female artists, including Frida Kahlo. Some reproductions.

Sullivan, Charles, sel. *Here Is My Kingdom: Hispanic-American Literature and Art for Young People*. New York: Harry N. Abrams, Inc. 1994. A gorgeous book in which poetry and art are combined.

Turner, Robyn Montana. *Frida Kahlo*. Boston: Little, Brown, 1993. A life of the artist accompanied by some reproductions.

Volkmer, Jane. *Song of the Chirimia/La Musica de la Chirimia*. Minneapolis: Carolrhoda, 1992. A bilingual Mexican tale about the coming of music to the world.

Winter, Jeanette. *Josephina*. San Diego: Harcourt Brace Jovanovich, 1996. Inspired by Josefina Aguilar, a contemporary artist working in Ocotlan, Mexico, this is the story of Josefina and how she forms in clay the many wonderful things she sees around her.

Winter, Jonah. *Diego*. Transl. by Amy Prince. Illus. by Jeanette Winter. New York: Knopf, 1991. A picture book that presents the life of the artist in English and Spanish.

Wisniewski, David. *The Rain Player*. New York: Clarion, 1991. Pik challenges the rain god to a game of *pok-a-tok* to bring rain to his people. Beautiful cut paper illustrations.

Audiovisual Materials

Diego Rivera. (Videocassette. Available from Video Opera House.)

Frida Kahlo. (Videocassette. Available from Video Opera House.)

The Mystery of the Maya. Seeks to answer why the Maya chose such inhospitable areas for their habitation, how they achieved their incredible knowledge, and why they abandoned their cities. Presents Mayan art and architecture. (Videocassette; 25 mins. Available from Wombat Productions, Inc.)

Part VIII
Art of the Twentieth Century

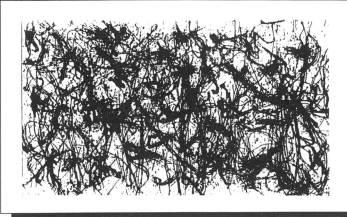

19 Five Modern Masters

Twentieth-century explorations in art have broken many boundaries.
New ideas, followed by new techniques and new materials
have led to new expressions in all the arts and have given us
new insights into ourselves and our world.
—ROSEMARY LAMBERT, *The Twentieth Century*

Background Information

Change has occurred during the twentieth century more rapidly than in all the
centuries that preceded it. Telephone use has become widespread, trains have
gained speed, airplanes have taken to the skies, and spacecraft have traveled to
the moon and distant planets. Inventions such as the radio, movies, television,
and, most recently, computers, have made it possible to communicate almost
instantly with most areas of the world. Because it no longer takes considerable
time for news in the art community to spread, art movements have traveled back
and forth across the Atlantic with alacrity, and this century has spawned more
"isms" than any other. Perhaps, too, because the twentieth century has known
the devastation of two world wars, a worldwide depression that stretched over
many years, and numerous civil wars, artists have struggled more than ever to
express on canvas, in architecture, and in sculpture their own and humanity's
reaction to a world of constant change and turmoil. Due to considerations of
space, only a few of the principal artistic trends of the century are mentioned
here.

The Spanish artist Pablo Picasso initiated one of the first art movements of
the twentieth century, Cubism, in which he abandoned realistic details and tried
to show the different sides of objects simultaneously. Cubism, spawned from African art, had far-reaching effects on other artists as they tried to find new ways to
represent three-dimensional objects in a two-dimensional space. The Fauves, led
by French painter Henri Matisse, expressed themselves by using intense, unexpected colors in their works. Northern Europeans, among them Edvard Munch,
communicated through their swirling lines and colors their inner emotions and

turmoil in a movement called Expressionism. Frequently depicting machines, the Futurists, who had their origins in Italy, tried to deny the past while emphasizing constant motion towards the future through use of repeated lines in their work.

Building on the ideas of the Expressionists, artists such as Kandinsky and Mondrian pioneered abstract painting, a style using line, shape, and color without benefit of representation. While the Dadaists, who took their name from the French word for hobbyhorse, mocked the established art scene by their random placement of objects and by treating commonplace things as works of art, the Surrealists focused on the fantasy world of the unconscious. Max Ernst and Salvador Dali were two prominent artists from this group.

At the turn of the century, when New York City was teeming with new immigrants who often lived in the poorest conditions, a group of painters called The Eight (and referred to pejoratively as The Ash Can School) made these city dwellers the subjects of their representative paintings. Led by Robert Henri, the group included George Luks, William Glackens, John Sloan, and Everett Shinn. Ernest Lawson, Arthur B. Davies, and Maurice Prendergast eventually joined them.

The Second World War in Europe forced many artists to come to the United States, and New York became the new art capital of the world. A host of American artists such as Frank Lloyd Wright, Grant Wood, Andrew Wyeth, Alexander Calder, Georgia O'Keeffe, Jackson Pollock, and Louise Nevelson began to take their places beside the greats of Europe. Andy Warhol used objects of mass culture such as soup cans and soda bottles in surprising ways and gave rise to a new art called Pop Art in the 1960s.

Contemporary twentieth-century artists are using such technologies as photography and, most recently, the computer, to push realism far beyond what we have ever experienced. Performance art is confounding viewers with its insistence on more active involvement. And it is clear that as we enter a new millennium, artists will continue to seek new ways to express their ideas about themselves and the world around them. And it is also clear that their work may initially shock and outrage us much as Giotto and, much later, the Impressionists, surprised their contemporaries.

How are we to judge this new art? What will we say to our students who complain, "It doesn't look like anything. All I see are lines and colors"? Surely, it will not help to compare these works to what we might have been used to in the past. Rather, we should look, not at what they lack, but at what they have to offer. Philip Yenawine, in *How to Look at Modern Art*, offers his own criteria: "Good art sustains my interest over time, perhaps for its original appeal, perhaps for reasons that are new each time I see it" (p. 144).

LESSON 1: Henri Matisse (1869–1954)

❑ The Story

"FRANCE IS AT WAR WITH GERMANY!" screamed the headlines of the Paris newspapers. The once-lively city was plunged into gloom. Citizens, fearing poison gas attacks from the Germans, carried gas masks with them wherever they went and practiced racing to shelters for protection against bombs. "I can't go to the shelters," complained the famous artist, Henri Matisse, who was already over seventy years old. "The damp down there will make my hands cramp so badly that I will never be able to paint again! There is only one thing to do: leave France."

Henri's assistant obtained a special visa for him so that he could leave the country. He had a ticket to South America and his luggage was packed. "Let me stroll along my beloved streets one more time," he told his assistant. "Then we'll leave." Henri put on his coat and hat and set out. He had only gone a few blocks when he met another artist, the famous Pablo Picasso. "Ah, Pablo, how fortunate to see you before I go. I am about to leave for Rio de Janeiro."

"You and everybody else, Henri. Look down that road. Family after family heading for the border like refugees. Well, no one is scaring me away. I'm staying!"

"I had no idea that so many people were leaving," replied Henri. "Why the city will be empty, and if everyone leaves, what will become of France? I guess I will stick it out in my own country, too. You and I, Pablo, doing our art as best we can. Let's stay in touch."

The two artists parted, Henri got his money refunded for the tickets to South America, and instead went to southern France, where he began working once again on his paintings. But each day pains in his stomach got worse and worse until he could hardly hold his brush.

"Father, I'm taking you to the doctor, like it or not," declared Henri's daughter, Marguerite, when she came for a visit. And she did that very afternoon.

"I'm sorry, Mr. Matisse," the doctor said, after he had examined the artist. "It's cancer, and we have to operate right away."

"But my work!" said Henri. "What will become of my work?"

"You will not have to worry about your work if we don't operate," said the doctor. "You'll be dead!"

Well, that wasn't much of a choice for Henri, so of course he let the doctors operate—more than once, in fact, and he recovered. But his stomach muscles were so weak Henri could no longer stand up for very long. He had to spend the rest of his life in bed or in a wheelchair. He no longer had the energy to stand before an easel all day and paint with oil. But did he give up? Not at all! He just found a new way to do his art. Henri had his assistants paint large strips of paper in brilliant colors. Colors were always very important to Henri because they helped him express what he was feeling. Once Henri had his sheets of paper, he would look carefully at objects he loved—birds or leaves or other things in his room. He would think of places he had been, like the beautiful South Pacific where the waves splashed up on the beach. Then he would take his scissors and cut out shapes to represent those objects and have his assistants arrange and rearrange them on a wall or background until the arrangement pleased him.

People heard about Henri's new art, and everyone wanted to see it. Publishers asked him to illustrate books with his cutout shapes. The wealthy Rockefeller family in New York asked him to design a special window. And nuns in a convent asked him to do the artwork in their new chapel. Henri went to the chapel in his wheelchair. He drew simple outline shapes on the walls by using a piece of charcoal fastened to the end of a long stick. And he designed beautiful stained glass windows.

All of his life Henri Matisse tried to find the simplest lines to express himself in his art. Some people think that of all of his work—his wonderful oil paintings, his sculptures, and his drawings—he succeeded best of all as a sick old man working in the nuns' chapel. Henri Matisse died just two years later, but art lovers will always remember his wonderful shapes and colors. Many consider him one of the greatest artists of the twentieth century.

Viewing the Art

It might be helpful to preface the viewing by talking to the children about modern art. If they expect to see purely representational art (though Matisse did not move totally away from the representational—that would come with later artists), they will be disappointed, or feel that this kind of art is inferior. Instead, it's important for them to realize that artists were trying to find new ways to express their feelings and even their fantasies. Just the way Renaissance artists discovered linear perspective and shading to represent three dimensions on a two-dimensional plane, so modern artists experiment with new ways to do the same thing.

Tell the children that as a younger artist, Henri Matisse was the leader of a new art movement called Fauvism. When the French people saw the wild colors Matisse and his artist friends used, they called them *fauves*, or wild beasts. Begin by showing the children two of Matisse's portraits of his wife: *Woman with the Hat* and *Portrait of Mme Matisse/The Green Line*. Note the unexpected colors (multicolored background, green lines in the face). What do these colors achieve?

How do the children react to them? Show other works that reveal Matisse's brilliant use of color. A few choices might be: *The Joy of Life, Interior with a Violin* (Matisse was an accomplished violinist), *The Red Studio, Goldfish, Still Life with a Red Jug*; then discuss them.

Matisse tried to achieve motion and solid forms with the simplest of lines. Show some sculptures and pictures that exemplify this: the sculptures *La Serpentine* and *Large Seated Nude*, and the paintings *Dance I* and *Dance II*, *Red Still Life with Magnolia, The Pewter Jug, The Rumanian Blouse, The Pink Nude* (if you can, show the twenty-two versions of this, to demonstrate how hard Matisse tried to get it just right), and his great mural *Dance*. Tell the children that Matisse was asked to make a mural to fit into several arches. He worked for a long time on it only to find out that the measurements he had been sent were wrong and his paintings were not tall enough. He began the whole project again! Finally show the cutouts, those in the Vence chapel and others: *The Swimming Pool; Parakeet and the Mermaid or Siren; Blue Nude; Polynesia: the Sky; Polynesia: the Sea*; and Matisse's two versions of *The Snail*. His book *Jazz* (see References) has excellent large cutouts for viewing.

Journal Writing

One of Henri Matisse's first teachers told him "You were born to simplify art." Did he fulfill his teacher's prophecy? Why or why not?

Look at one of Henri Matisse's brilliantly colored pictures for as long as you can. How do you react to it? Why?

Art/Drama Activity: Paper Cutouts

Materials

- Large sheets of colored or white paper
- Tempera paints
- Paintbrushes
- Scissors
- Glue

Invite the children to make cutouts in imitation of Henri Matisse. If they can, have them paint white sheets of paper from which to cut their shapes and to use as background. If they do so, advise them to make their paint strokes go in only one direction. The children can make varying shades of a color by adding

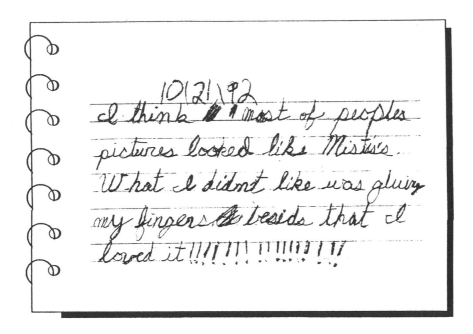

10/21/92

I think ~~I'~~ most of peoples pictures looked like Mistiss. What I didnt like was gluing my fingers ~~to~~ besids that I loved it !!!!!!! !!!!!!! !!

more water to the paint or adding white to the color with which they are working. They may also cut their shapes from colored paper.

As the sheets are drying, have the children experiment with color. What colors make each other vibrate or stand out? What colors look good together? They should also find an object in the room to study at length. What is its essential shape? How does it make them feel? Or they may think of a scene they particularly like. When they are ready, they should cut shapes to represent the object or scene. They may make repeated cutouts if they wish. It is also possible to use the shape that is left in a sheet after the cutout is removed if they cut all in one piece. These are positive and negative shapes. Arrange the shapes on another colored sheet until the desired effect is achieved, and glue them down.

You may wish to use the book *Meet Matisse* by Munthe (see References) in conjunction with this art activity.

LESSON 2: Pablo Picasso (1881–1973)

❏ The Story

"**H**ere, Pablo," said the young boy's father. "See if you can finish drawing this dove for me. I have to rush to school now to teach my class and haven't the time myself."

"Sure, Poppa," the boy answered. "You know I love to draw." Pablo picked up his father's chalks and went to work. When his father returned home later that afternoon, he was amazed at what he saw. "Son, this drawing is better than I could have done myself! Here, take my chalks. From now on you will do the drawing in this family. You are more talented than I am. How would you like to apply to the art school where I teach? The entrance examination is very difficult, but I know you can do it."

"Do you mean it, Poppa? I can leave my school and study art! You know how I hate my studies. I'll never be able to add and subtract well, but drawing— ah, that is my first love."

"Yes, son, I can certainly see that. You are in luck, for it so happens that the admissions office is interviewing prospective students all this week. Come to the school with me tomorrow."

Pablo could hardly sleep all that night. Art school! Could it be that his dreams were coming true? The next morning he dressed carefully and went to the admissions office with his father. "So you want to study at our school?" the director asked.

"Yes, sir, more than anything," replied Pablo.

"Well, your father tells me you have talent, but we must treat you the same way we treat all the other young people who apply here. You must first pass an examination. And it is not an easy one. You will have one month to present me with a drawing of a human figure. At the end of that time I will expect to see you here. If you are late, I shall consider it an automatic failure. All the students I am seeing this week have the same deadline. Do you think you can do that?"

"Oh, yes, sir, and I shall begin right away."

Pablo hurried home and worked all day on his figure and by evening, he had finished. "Finished, Pablo! That is impossible. Such difficult work demands time," said his father when the boy announced at dinner that he had completed the task. But when he saw the drawing, his father had to agree that it couldn't be any better. The next day Pablo brought it to the director.

"Well, I can see you have no real interest in attending this school," the director said. "I'll take a look at what you have there, but it's obvious that anything done in such a hurry must be slipshod and a waste of my time." Pablo, who didn't look very worried, said nothing, but handed his portfolio to the director. The room was silent for a long time as the director studied Pablo's work. Finally, the man spoke. "Are you certain this is your work—completed just since yesterday morning?"

"Yes, sir. My father can verify that if you have any doubts."

"Well, I have never seen anything like it. It is absolutely perfect! We would be honored to have you in our school."

And that's how Pablo Picasso, one of the greatest artists of all time, began his art education. He graduated from that school and went to another, but quit because he found it too boring. He didn't agree with the ideas of his teachers. Pablo was too filled with his own ideas and was anxious to try them out. So he left his family and Spain, his country, and went to Paris, France, the art center of the world. Pablo Picasso kept changing all of his life. In the beginning of his career, he was not very successful. In fact, he was so poor that he had to burn some of his pictures in the fireplace to keep warm! Other times he had to paint his pictures over one another because he had no money to buy new canvas. But little by little people began to buy his paintings. Pablo was able to paint beautiful pictures just the way painters did in the time of the Renaissance, pictures that looked exactly like the objects or people he used as models. And people bought those paintings. Pablo could have said to himself, "Well, I am successful now. I'll just keep painting like this and making money." But he didn't. He wanted to keep trying new things. He wanted to take what he saw in front of him and use his imagination to change it in surprising ways.

He started a whole new style of art called Cubism in which he was able to show all the sides of a thing or person at the same time. Imagine that! At first, people didn't like the new art. But then it began to catch on and artists all over the world began to have the courage to use more imagination in their art, too. Many new kinds of art began to develop. Pablo Picasso became so famous that crowds of people tried to follow him around and visit him in his studio. He had to have many locks on his doors! But he kept on working and trying new things right up until the day he died at the age of ninety-two! Can you believe that just a few years before his death, he did over 300 engravings in one year? He never seemed to get tired.

So fasten your seat belts. We are going to travel through so many different kinds of artwork that you might think it was done by different people. But really, it was done by one incredible man: Pablo Picasso!

Viewing the Art

Begin by showing some of Picasso's representational works, especially his pictures of children, which should be especially appealing. Some choices might be *Child with Dove*, *The Gourmet*, *La Soupe*, and *Paulo on a Donkey*. Explain that perhaps because he was poor and suffering himself, Picasso went through a period when he painted serious subjects in shades of blue. Two examples you might want to show are *Crouching Woman* and *The Old Guitarist*. This was followed by his rose period, during which he painted many circus types. Be sure to show *Family of Saltimbanques*. Picasso created a sensation with his painting *Les Demoiselles D' Avignon*, the beginning of his Cubist period. Spend considerable time on this picture. You might wish to say nothing and have the children talk about what they see. They should notice the two figures on the right as being particularly distorted; the African masks (mention Picasso's love of African art); the many angles instead of rounded forms. What is Picasso saying about women here? Show *Three Women*, which is a less distorted version of the same theme. Other Cubist pictures you might show are *Harlequin*, *Three Musicians*, *Factory at Horta de Ebro*, *Portrait of Daniel-Henry Kahnweiler*, and the *Portrait of Dora Maar*. Show the first collage in the history of painting, Picasso's *Still Life with Cane Chair*. Show other Cubist collages, especially if that is the art activity you will choose later in the lesson.

Some paintings from Picasso's Surrealist period you might show are *The Kiss* and, especially, *Guernica*. Explain that *Guernica* is Pablo's response to the horrors of war. What are some things the children see? What is he saying about war? Finally, have fun with Picasso's sculptures, especially those in which he uses found objects in novel ways. Some examples are *Woman with an Orange*, *Woman Reading*, *Woman with a Pram*, *Bull's Head*, and *Baboon and Young*. What are some of the surprising things Picasso uses in these sculptures? What do the children think of the effect?

Journal Writing

Invite the children to choose one piece of art they have viewed and write about it. What do they like about it? What is surprising about it? What do they think the artist was trying to say with that particular creation?

Art/Drama Activity: Art from Scraps

There are two activities that are particularly effective with a study of Pablo Picasso. Plan to do one or both, depending on the amount of time you wish to spend on the artist. Whatever you decide, it will be necessary to prepare for the activity(ies) in advance by having the children collect objects. If you intend to make a sculpture, discuss with the children what it might be beforehand. They may wish to make an animal or a building. What kinds of objects may be useful for such a project? Another possibility is to have the children assemble their

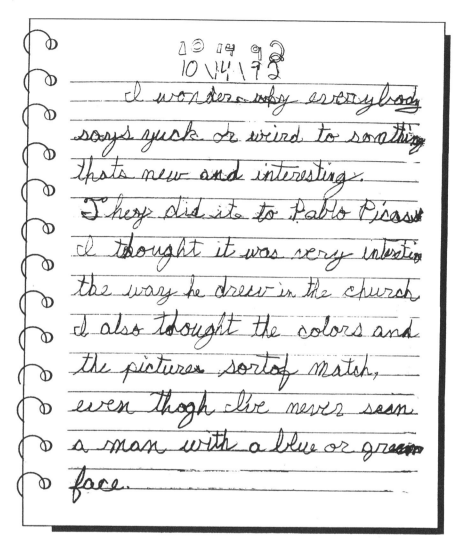

10\14\7_

I wonder why everybody says yuck or weird to something thats new and interesting. They did it to Pablo Picasso I thought it was very interesting the way he drew in the church I also thought the colors and the pictures sortof match, even thogh I've never seen a man with a blue or green face.

objects and determine what figure emerges from arranging them. You may decide to do this as a whole class project forming one sculpture. Or you may divide the children into groups, each group creating its own sculpture.

Activity 1: Sculpture Using Found Objects

Materials

- Objects collected by teacher and students. Suggestions might be old toys, screws, nails, pieces of pipe, parts of appliances, cloth, cardboard, etc.
- Glue

Have the children experiment with arranging their objects until they are pleased with the result. Glue them in place to form a permanent figure.

Activity 2: Collage

Materials

- Objects collected by teacher and students: scraps of paper, cloth, wood, etc.
- Large sheets of paper
- Glue
- Scissors
- Paints
- Paintbrushes
- Colored pencils

You may wish to study some of Picasso's collages again for inspiration. When the children are ready, have them arrange their objects on the paper in whatever way pleases them. They may use paints or pencils in their work as well. Glue everything down.

LESSON 3: Georgia O'Keeffe (1887–1986)

❏ The Story

Georgia O'Keeffe wiped her forehead as she came into her small studio. It had been a busy day of teaching, and she was hot and tired, and yes, she had to admit it, discouraged. Oh, she enjoyed her teaching. It was exciting to help young people develop their talents and put their ideas on canvas as her teachers had once helped her. But being an art teacher was not what she really wanted. She wanted to be an artist. And now she felt herself caught in the trap that everyone had always told her would be set for her—the teaching trap. For in the years of her youth, it was assumed that young ladies could not become famous artists. Only men could do that.

Georgia frowned to herself. Why, it was only recently that women were even allowed to study art and draw from live models like the men were. Well, who cared about that. She'd never much liked painting pictures of people anyway. She wanted to paint objects, especially objects in nature. And her teachers had even admitted she had talent, so why was she stuck here teaching? "Let's see that talent, Georgia," she said to herself. Quickly she began to go through her stacks of finished paintings and stand them up all around the studio. Then, hands on her hips, she slowly circled the room, looking at each painting with a critical eye. After awhile, Georgia stopped her circling and sat down. "That's what's wrong," she thought. "There's no Georgia in any of these paintings. They are simply expressions of what my teachers have told me to do. Look, these represent ideas from my teachers at the Chicago Institute of Art. These are from my teachers at Columbia University in New York. But where am I? Where are my ideas, my own personal style?"

Right then and there Georgia made up her mind to do something very hard. She collected all her pictures and put them in the back of her closet. "I'll never take those out again or try to sell any of them," she said to herself. "From this moment on, I will begin all over again trying to find my own expression. No hiding behind pretty colors; just charcoal. Then we'll see whether I have the talent to be a real painter." Right after her classes were over each day, Georgia worked on her charcoal pictures. She worked long and hard for months until she had done many of them. Then she rolled them all up, put them in a mailing tube, and sent them to her friend, Anita, in New York City. "Anita," she wrote, "these are my latest drawings. They are my attempt to find my own art, not someone else's. Don't show them to anyone, but please tell me what you think of them. I trust your judgment. If you say they are worth something, then I will continue to struggle to become an artist. Otherwise, I shall continue to earn my living teaching."

When Anita looked at Georgia's drawings, she could hardly contain her excitement. "How can Georgia tell me not to show these to anyone? They're too good to hide!" For two weeks Anita did as her friend requested and showed them to no one. Finally, she could stand it no longer; she packed up the drawings and took them to the photographer, Alfred Stieglitz. Both she and Georgia had been to his studio many times and admired his photographs. Stieglitz often helped young artists get started and ran exhibits of their work. He looked at the drawings for a long time without saying anything. Then, finally, he told Anita how much he liked them. "Georgia has great talent," he said. "She must come back to New York and launch her career!"

"Georgia," wrote Anita. "Please forgive me, but I had to show your drawings to Stieglitz. He thinks you have talent and should come back to New York. I hope you're not angry with me." Georgia wasn't angry at all. She was really delighted, and as soon as her teaching term was over, she packed up and went to New York. When she had been back for a few months, she heard people talking about a new exhibit at Stieglitz's studio by a person named O'Keeffe.

"What does he think he's doing?" screamed Georgia to Anita. "He can't just show my pictures without my consent!" Georgia grabbed her coat and hat and went storming off to see Stieglitz. But he soon calmed her down. The people who were coming to see her drawings liked them. He had even sold one for four hundred dollars!

More and more people began to find out about Georgia's unusual paintings. She painted abstract pictures, that is, pictures that didn't represent anything a person could recognize, but that showed her feelings. She painted giant pictures of flowers to get busy New Yorkers to stop and notice the beauty of nature. Soon she and Stieglitz fell in love and got married, and he continued to run exhibits of her pictures. Together they traveled to Lake George, N.Y., every summer where Georgia could paint the beauty of the countryside. And then she began traveling to New Mexico where she painted the rocks and bones and wide open skies over the desert. When her husband died, Georgia moved to New Mexico for good and continued to paint there. Even when her eyesight became poor, she found ways to work with colors to express the feelings she had.

Georgia O'Keeffe fulfilled her dream of becoming a famous artist. The president of the United States gave her one of the country's highest awards, the Medal of Honor. Many other countries and colleges gave her awards, too. She became a very rich woman. But she never really cared much about these things. She continued to wear simple clothing and live very simply in her adobe house in New Mexico. Georgia O'Keeffe continued to paint almost until she died at the age of ninety-eight. By being honest with herself she achieved her dreams.

Viewing the Art

After you have explained what abstract art is, begin by showing some of O'Keeffe's abstract works. You might wish to show them without the titles and get the children to express how the pictures affect them. Then show the titles and continue the discussion, using, if you can, some of O'Keeffe's own words about her pictures from *Georgia O'Keeffe* (see References). The children will especially love her description of the trouble involved in preparing the huge canvas for *Sky Above Clouds IV*. Some good choices for viewing are the different variations of *Evening Star*; *Orange and Red Streak*; *From the Plains I and II*; *Painting No. 21*; *Music—Pink and Blue I*; *At the Rodeo*; *New Mexico*; and *Black and White*. Be sure to show some of O'Keeffe's western pictures, since New Mexico meant so much to her. An excellent book for viewing these pictures is *Georgia O'Keeffe in the West* by Bry and Callaway (see References). Include some of her pictures of bones and note the attention O'Keeffe gives to the holes in the bones as well as to the shapes of the bones themselves. Finally, show some of O'Keeffe's huge flowers. Can the children name any of them? What does the artist achieve by making them so large?

Journal Writing

One of Georgia O'Keeffe's teachers told her that her goal should be to fill a space in a beautiful way. Do the children feel she has accomplished this? Why or why not? Perhaps they could pick one picture to illustrate their point of view.

Art/Drama Activity: Nature Paintings

Materials

- Large pieces of paper
- Pencils
- Paints
- Paintbrushes

Tell the class that they are going to imitate Georgia O'Keeffe by making paintings of something in nature—paintings that are much larger than the thing would actually be in real life. In that way, they can notice every single detail about the object they have chosen: its lines, shape, colors, etc. Then take the class outside and allow each child time to choose an object: a branch, a rock, a blade of grass, a flower (if they can be picked. Otherwise, you might have a bouquet of different kinds of flowers in the classroom for the occasion). When the children return to the classroom, they should spend a considerable amount of time observing the object from all angles. When they are ready, they should draw the object on their papers, being sure to fill the entire space. Finally, they can paint the completed drawing.

LESSON 4: Louise Nevelson (1900?–1988)

(You will need to prepare for this lesson well in advance. Ask each child to bring in a shoebox. The children should also begin collecting objects with interesting shapes: thread spools, empty match boxes, pieces of wood, twigs, corrugated cardboard, etc. that are small enough to be arranged in the box.)

❑ The Story

Louise sat sipping a cup of tea as she looked at her work. The sculptures that filled her studio stared back at her, silent giants in the large room. The rent was due soon, and she had no more jewelry left to sell to pay it. "What do I have to show for all I have sacrificed?" she thought. "I gave up my marriage; I sent my son to Rochester to live with my parents and hardly see him. I even sold my wedding bracelet so that I would have enough money to go to Europe and study art. I have worked night and day on my sculptures trying to create something new. And no one will even give me a chance to exhibit my work."

The more Louise thought about her situation, the angrier she became. Finally, she made up her mind. She contacted all the artists she knew. "Whose art gallery is the most important gallery in New York?" she asked them. No matter who she asked, the same name kept coming up: Karl Nierendorf. "Well, Mr. Nierendorf, you're in for quite a surprise," Louise muttered to herself as she straightened up her studio and arranged her sculptures in the best possible light. Then she put on her most attention-getting outfit and headed straight for Nierendorf's Gallery.

"Mr. Nierendorf, I am Louise Nevelson and I want to exhibit my sculpture in your gallery," she said as soon as she walked in the door. Nierendorf stared at her in disbelief. No one ever told HIM what to do. HE told THEM. After all, he was the most important art dealer in the city! But something about this determined woman made him agree to go to her studio and look at her work. When he did, he was so impressed that he agreed to show her work in one month! Usually, galleries took a full year to arrange for an exhibit. Louise was thrilled and worked day and night to get her pieces ready. She cleaned and repainted them and planned how they would be arranged.

When the big day arrived, Louise was nervous. Her success depended on whether the art critics and the visitors to the gallery liked her work, and she desperately needed to sell some sculptures to pay her bills. Well, the art critics did love Louise's work. They thought it was new and interesting. She was creating abstract art in her sculptures the way some modern painters were on canvas. But she did not sell a single piece! Nor did she sell anything at her next exhibit. However, galleries were beginning to notice her and offering to exhibit her work. Mr. Nierendorf even wanted to show her work again, but he died before he got the chance.

His death saddened Louise so much that for awhile, she could hardly complete any sculptures. But she knew she must go on, and she did, working long hours every day. She even roamed the streets of the city looking for things to put in her sculptures. One evening she was all dressed up for a fancy party when she saw some pieces of wood in somebody's garbage. "I can't let that great wood go to waste," she said. And before her friends could stop her, she went rummaging through the garbage to pick the wood pieces out. She saved scraps of iron, vegetable crates—anything that might be useful. Then Louise created a wonderful new show called *Moon Garden + One*. Everyone loved it so much that the Museum of Modern Art in New York City bought the most important part of the exhibit, a piece called *Sky Cathedral*. From that moment on, Louise Nevelson was famous. It had taken thirty years of hard work and many disappointments! Louise received hundreds of requests to do sculptures for buildings and exhibits. In fact, if you go to New York City, you can see some of her huge sculptures on the sidewalks in front of buildings.

Everyone looked forward to seeing Louise at her exhibits. They never knew what she would be wearing next. She was almost a work of art herself. She wore fancy hats and turbans, long, long dresses and coats made of all sorts of unusual materials, and many pairs of false eyelashes at the same time! She never seemed to lose her energy. All through her seventies she continued to work on huge sculptures, trying new materials like metal and Plexiglas. People thought that surely when she reached eighty, Louise would not be able to continue such hard work, but she did. Louise Nevelson, in fact, worked almost to the end of her life and died of heart failure at the age of eighty-eight. Although she was born in Russia and came to the United States when she was six, we consider her one of our greatest American artists. She received all the highest awards the United States can give, and she proved that women can become just as successful as artists as men can.

Viewing the Art

Nevelson's World by Lipman (see References) is excellent for viewing the artist's works. It has huge reproductions as well as interesting photographs of Nevelson herself. Mention that we do not have many examples of her early pieces because she often destroyed them, creating enormous "barn fires." For her, it was the act of creation that was important, not preservation.

Begin by showing some freestanding works. Some choices might be *Self-Portrait, 1940*; the *Moving-Static-Moving Figures* (tell the children the viewer can actually move these figures into different positions by swiveling them on the center dowel); *Ancient City*; *The Circus Clown*; *The Open Place*; *Undermarine Scape*; *Indian Chief*; and *First Personage*. Nevelson admired African and Native American art. Can the children see any evidence of this in these pieces? Since the art activity that follows uses them as models, spend considerable time on Nevelson's *Black, White, and Gold Environments*. Discuss the meaning of environment with the children and how they should be viewed as a whole. Be sure to include such works as *Sky Cathedral* and its variants, *Sky Columns*; *Homage to the World*; *Dawn's Wedding Feast*; *Chapel of the Good Shepherd*; *An American Tribute to the English People*; and *Dawn, 1962*. Nevelson, who was Jewish, created another variant, *Homage to 6,000,000 II*, in memory of the Jews who were killed during World War II. What do the children see in this structure that relates to its subject matter?

As the children view these environments, ask whether they see any relationships among the different niches. Are there patterns? Are there particular formations that especially express the title theme? If you wish, conclude with some transparent and metal pieces, especially her celebrations of New York, a city she loved and which she felt gave her a place in its art community.

Journal Writing

Invite the children to choose one environment they particularly like and write about it at length. What does it say to them? How did Nevelson tell a story in the way she arranged her shapes? This writing is an important preparation for the art activity to follow.

Art/Drama Activity: Shoebox Sculptures

Materials

- Shoeboxes
- Wood scraps. (If the school has a woodworking room, or if there is one in the district from which you may take surplus pieces, this would be ideal. When we did this activity, we were also able to use an almost harmless tiny electric saw apparatus so that the children could shape their pieces as they wished. Second graders were able to use the machine with no difficulty or danger.)
- Found objects
- Wood glue
- Cans of spray paint in black, white, and gold
- Newspapers

Have the children create a sculpture in their shoebox using the wood scraps and other objects. They should spend some time beforehand thinking about what they wish to say, and then about what objects and arrangements they can put together that will "write" their story. In this way, they will realize that Nevelson's work is not just a random placing of "junk" which reveals very little talent. The artist often said that each piece has a relationship to the other pieces in a work. Try to encourage that same thoughtful consideration in the students. When they have arranged pieces to their satisfaction and glued them down, place the boxes on newspapers and spray paint them black, white, or gold. The color decision should have been made beforehand, since it is intrinsic to the message.

Another, more difficult, option for older children is to have the class decide on a theme together and have each shoebox sculpture work with the others to create that theme (in which case you would need spray paint of only one color). When the boxes are completed, glue them together and spray paint the whole environment. Decide on a prominent place in the school for its installation.

LESSON 5: Jackson Pollock (1912–1956)

(Unless you have an art room in which splatters do not matter, it is wise to save this lesson for pleasant weather so that the children can do the art activity outdoors if at all possible. It is quite messy and can wreak havoc on classroom floors and materials.)

❑ The Story

Dear Jackson,

I hear you're having trouble at school. Forget about that place. Why don't you join me here in New York? If you're serious about becoming an artist, this is the place to be anyway. You can study at the Art Students League. I know you don't have much money, so move in with me until you're able to support yourself.

Jackson's excitement grew as he read his older brother Charles's letter, and he made up his mind to leave Los Angeles that very week. But when he arrived in New York a few days later and tried to get settled, he discovered that life in the big city wasn't quite as wonderful as he had dreamed back home. There were poor people on every street corner. Men in tattered clothes held out their hands for money. Others sold pencils or apples on the corner. The year was 1931. The country was in the middle of a depression, which meant that there were no jobs and people could no longer afford to pay their rent and other bills. Thousands were homeless. Of course, since money was so scarce, not many people had extra to buy artworks, so artists suffered, too.

Jackson studied at the Art Students League, but he hated living with Charles. Even though Charles was very kind to him, Jackson felt he was always watching him work. "I can't paint with Charles looking over my shoulder in the same room," he said to himself. "He's such a good artist, I'm afraid he'll make fun of my work." So he moved out to a much smaller and shabbier apartment not far away. But he was having trouble getting enough money for food and rent. He got a job as a janitor, but that didn't pay very well. Finally one day, he found out that the president of the United States was starting a special job program to put people to work. Some men were building roads, others were working on bridges. And artists were hired to paint pictures to decorate government buildings. Jackson was told he could have a job if he was willing to follow all the rules. He had to work at home to paint a picture every month. And he had to go to the central office every morning and evening to punch a time clock to prove he was working. Well, Jackson hated to get up early, and it was hard for him to get to the central office by eight o'clock every day. Some days, people would see him running down the block in his pajamas to get there in time! But he kept that job for a few years.

This doesn't sound like a very good beginning for an artist's career, but Jackson Pollock did become a great and famous artist. He was only a teenager when he first went to New York, and it took many years of hard work before people began to recognize that his art was special. At first, Jackson painted pictures that people could recognize. But little by little, his paintings began to get more and more abstract. He believed a painting should tell the story of what was going on in the artist's head, not what the artist could see in front of him. As he worked on his paintings, he discovered that he couldn't get the paint on them the way he wanted just by using paints and a brush in front of an easel. So he took huge pieces of canvas and tacked them down to his studio floor. Then, instead of a palette and small brushes, he used big paint cans and sticks and big brushes to drip and pour paint onto the canvas.

At first people couldn't believe their eyes. Some asked whether this was really art. Others said that any baby could pour paint all over the place! But Jackson didn't just pour paint any old way. His paintings had a plan and a pattern. A film crew came to make a movie of him working. Reporters wanted interviews. At last, Jackson Pollock became so well known that he began to influence other artists. Some people say he was the leader of a new abstract art movement in the United States. But he did not live to continue working for long. On the way home one evening, he drove his car too fast around a curve, hit a tree, and was killed instantly. His wife, who was also an artist, took very good care of the hundreds of pictures that Jackson had painted and sold them slowly so that they would be rare and bring in high prices. His pictures began to sell for more and more money, so that today they are almost priceless. Jackson Pollock, who hardly sold any pictures while he was alive, had finally become famous!

Viewing the Art

If the children have not had any of the other lessons in this chapter, it will be important to review with them the concept of abstract art: that it is not a representation of something we can see but is the expression of a feeling or idea through the use of line, color, shape. Begin by showing some of Pollock's early more-representational work so that the children can see his development. Tell them that he grew up in Wyoming and liked people to consider him a wild cowboy. He also had a teacher in New York who painted western scenes, so some of Pollock's first works had western themes as well. Show *Camp with Oil Rig* and *Going West. Moon Woman Cuts the Circle* has a Native American art influence. *Mural, 1943* is a painting Pollock did for the art patron Peggy Guggenheim, to decorate a building. Her support was a big help to him when he was starting out. What patterns do the children see in this painting? Why do the children think Pollock used "eyes" as a motif in *Eyes in the Heat*? Show *Lavender Mist* and compare its calm and lyrical lines and colors to the more energetic and vigorous *Autumn Rhythm, No. 30*. What has Pollock done to create these differences? Examine some dribble paintings in which areas of color are filled in such as *Out of the Web, No. 7* and *Convergence: No. 10*. How are they different from the paintings that are mostly swirls? Show *Blue Poles: No. 11*. What do the children see in this picture? What is Pollock trying to say? What is the children's overall impression of his painting? End by showing some photographs of Pollock at work on his canvases.

Journal Writing

Pollock said he painted huge canvases because it enabled him and his viewers to get "into" the painting. He took his cues from the great Mexican muralists—recall Diego Rivera if the children have studied him—who were gaining importance at the time. Invite the children to focus on a painting they particularly like. Were they able to get "inside" it? What happens to THEM as viewers when they look at this picture?

Art/Drama Activity: Drip Painting

Materials

- Huge pieces of paper
- Paints (these should be of rather thin consistency)
- Paintbrushes
- Sticks (such as paint stirrers)

Invite the children to create a large painting in imitation of Pollock's dripping and pouring style. Before they begin, ask them to spend some moments in silence getting in touch with a particular feeling they wish to express. Perhaps they can think of an event in their lives and how it makes them feel—their birthday, for example. What colors will best express this feeling? What patterns will best express it? The goal is to help the children realize that while there is a certain amount of serendipity in this process, there is planning as well. Once they have done some thinking and planning, give the children time to create their paintings, dripping paint from sticks or brushes in patterns and swirls onto their papers. Just don't allow pouring from buckets or flying paint, unless you have an unusually tolerant administrator!

Note: Curriculum Connections and References follow chapter 20.

20 Computer Art

Computers shape the way we think, imagine, and remember.
They expand our imagination, allow us to create
amazing new art forms, and to dream of scientific problems
not possible before the computer age.
—CLIFFORD A. PICKOVER, in *Visions of the Future*

Background Information

One of the most exciting developments of twentieth-century art has been the possibility of making pictures using the computer as a tool. To create such work, the artist uses the computer screen or monitor as the working space much as other artists use canvas, paper, or a block of wood or marble. This screen is divided into tiny areas called pixels. The more pixels there are on a computer screen, the higher its resolution and the smoother the lines of a computer drawing will be. The computer turns each pixel on or off to make shapes and colors depending upon the commands it receives. It is possible now to have computers with a much higher degree of resolution than when computer art first came on the scene. In fact, it is often difficult to tell whether a picture or design has been created with the aid of a computer or in a traditional manner.

There are several ways an artist can put a picture into a computer. Illustration and paint or photo manipulation software programs are coming on the market at an ever-increasing rate, enabling artists to draw complete images on the screen, to retouch or embellish photos, experiment with different gradations in color and textures, provide filters, and achieve a host of other special effects. The tools at the artist's disposal when using such programs are those that replicate the equipment we associate with artists in general: pencils, pens, brushes, etc. At this writing, Adobe Photo Shop, Adobe PageMaker, Adobe Illustrator, and Quark XPress are among the most popular and useful programs.

Often artists combine processes to create their work. For example, they may use the computer to provide a background for a photograph taken in the conventional manner. They may use a scanning device to scan a picture into the

277

computer and then manipulate it to interact with computer-generated images already on the screen. Digital cameras, that is, cameras that capture images on photo-sensitive electronic chips instead of silver-based film, are also playing an increasing role in computer art.

The computer makes it possible for the artist to see many different possibilities before a work is completed. It relieves him or her of the tiresome burden of scraping paint off a canvas, mixing a new palette of colors, and trying again. With the computer, a new beginning is as simple as the press of a button. In fact, special education teachers agree that the computer has enabled many of their learning and physically challenged students to become successful artists, a feat that had hitherto been impossible for them.

Because computer art is generated by a machine, some might be tempted to consider it inferior or not "real" art. However, it is now accepted that photographers, although they use a camera instead of brushes to create their pictures, are true artists. They need to consider the composition of their pictures, the effect they wish to achieve, and the best ways to achieve that effect. It is this "eye for the creative" that separates the amateur photographer from the artist. So, too, the computer artist needs to have a sense of design, a feel for the way colors work together, a knowledge of how to make the parts work together to form a perfect whole. In a word, the computer artist must transcend the tools he or she uses to create art.

The artist discussed here, April Greiman, began her career as "class artist" in her elementary and high school years, going on to become one of the foremost graphic designers of our day. She obtained her degree at the Kansas City Art Institute, where she majored in graphic design and ceramics; studied in Switzerland; and returned to the United States, where she taught at the Philadelphia College of Art; consulted for the Museum of Modern Art; and freelanced in New York. Eventually she opened her own studio in Los Angeles; where she continues to accept commissions from companies both in the United States and abroad.

The landscape of the American Southwest, its subtle desert colors contrasted with the vibrant pinks, turquoises, and yellows favored by its large Latino population, greatly influences her work. An early pioneer of computer art and one of the first graphic designers to use the Macintosh, April now uses the computer in almost 90 percent of her work. She has received numerous awards and was hailed in 1993 by *How* magazine as one of the ten most influential designers of today.

Computer technology changes almost monthly, and artists like Greiman can do far more intricate work of better quality now than when the field first opened up in the late 1970s and early 80s. We can only imagine what wonders these men and women will create as the technology continues to evolve into the twenty-first century.

LESSON 1: April Greiman (1948–   )

❑ The Story

The head of the U.S. Postal Service walked into his head designer's office. "Well, Carl, how are we coming along in designing a new stamp for the seventy-fifth anniversary of the Nineteenth Amendment? After all, we need something really special to celebrate the day women were given the right to vote. I'm sure people will be anxious to see what we come up with."

"Well, sir, I've hired several artists, and their ideas are starting to come in. I have an appointment with a member of Congress at the end of the week. She wants to see what choices we have before we go ahead and print a stamp."

"Fine. It looks like you're on top of things, so I'll leave you to it. Let me know what happens."

Later that same week, Carl went to the congresswoman's office with his designs. "Here are the samples we have for our new stamp," he said. "What do you think?" He laid the pictures out on her desk, and the congresswoman looked at each one slowly and carefully.

"These are nice, but they're not what I had in mind at all, Carl," she finally said. "Look—they just show portraits of dead people, like Elizabeth Cady Stanton and Susan B. Anthony. Of course, they were very important people. They did so much to help women gain the right to vote. They sacrificed their time and even their lives when people threatened to harm them. But if we put their pictures on this new stamp, then the stamp will just be like all the others—celebrating the life of a famous dead person. I want this stamp to celebrate all women! I want it to stand for their struggle to gain equal rights. I want it to say somehow that the struggle is still going on. I just don't think a picture of a dead woman will give the message we want."

"I can see your point, but what do you suggest we do? Ask the artists to start all over again?"

"No, I'd like you to hire a woman to do the design. I think a woman would have a better idea of what we would like the stamp to represent."

"A woman? But we never have women design stamps. I think that has happened only once before in the entire history of the U.S. Postal Service!"

"Well, then it's about time it happened again—especially for a stamp that's about women in the first place. Don't you agree, Carl?"

"Okay, okay, but I don't even know anyone to ask."

"A graphic designer named April Greiman spoke at the Smithsonian Institution a few weeks ago. She was very impressive. Let's track her down and ask if she's interested."

And so that very afternoon Carl called April, and she agreed to design the stamp. But instead of using paint and brushes, April used the computer. The computer enabled her to layer pictures over one another to make a stamp that would capture people's attention and help them remember that we still need to make sure that all people are treated equally and fairly. It has images of the women who struggled seventy-five years ago for the right to vote alongside men and images of women today struggling for equal rights. When April's stamp came out, it was so different from any other stamp people had ever seen that it certainly did get their attention. Many people loved it. But some thought it was very strange. We've seen before that as soon as artists try something new, people who aren't used to it complain. When I show the stamp to you, you will have to make up your own minds about what you think it is trying to say and whether you like it.

April Greiman was the second woman to design a United States stamp. But she has done other things as well. Many companies ask her to create designs for them, too. Let's look at her work now and see the magical wonders she creates with her computer.

Viewing the Art

When viewing April Greiman's work, it is important to keep in mind that for the artist, space and scale are all-important. Whether she's designing a business card, the interior of a restaurant, a magazine cover, or a poster, April considers how the various components of her design relate to the allotted space. In addition, a facet of her work that will appeal especially to children is that it is rooted in a medium dear to their hearts—collage. She layers images on one another, fusing different technologies such as photography, photocopying, video, and computer, to achieve the effect she wants. It is up to the viewer to look carefully and then decide what April is trying to say and how her message affects him or her.

Color is another important aspect of April's art. In her book, *It's notwhatyouthinkitis* (see References), she discusses the interpretations some people give to the various colors:

> red—energy, creativity
> orange—receptivity, wholeness
> yellow—mental/emotional activity

green—growth, balance of yellow and blue
blue—creative expression, sincerity, patience, wisdom
purple—royalty, vision, tranquility
white—expansion, purity, divinity

As you view April Greiman's art with the children, be certain to discuss her use of space and color and her layering of images. It may be more difficult to find samples of her work than that of the other artists in this book, but it is well worth the effort. Her two books (see References) are, of course, the best sources. Her designs also appear in numerous magazines. Some of the magazines are listed in the References at the end of this chapter. A few pieces you should make certain to enjoy with the students are:

- *The Nineteenth Amendment stamp,* which is the subject of the story. There is a beautiful double-page ad featuring this stamp in the May/June 1996 issue of *Communication Arts* magazine (see References) as well as a brief article about its origin. Talk about the different images on the stamp, the contrast between the two groups of marchers, the buildings, colors, textures.

- *Graphic Design in America* (in *It's notwhatyouthinkitis,* pp. 26–27). Here Greiman uses four technologies to convey her message, and each technology produces its own texture: video creates a weave like that found in textiles; steel engraving yields fine, sharp lines; offset reveals a textured dot pattern; and the computer offers ever-higher resolution depending upon the number of little pixel squares. Try to discover the different textures in this piece. Note how the flag seems to stand out and wave over the other layers of images. What role do the different colors play?

- Follow the steps in the creation of the *Modern Poster* (*Hybrid Imagery,* pp. 122–31). Discuss the shapes, the layers, the textures, the colors.

- The children may enjoy the creatures that appear in *It's notwhatyouthinkitis* (pp. 38–39; 56–57). What do they think the creatures are? Why?

Journal Writing

How is April Greiman's work different from the work of the other modern artists discussed in this chapter? How does it affect the children? Why?

Art/Drama Activity: Computer Pictures

Several activities are appropriate follow-ups to a study of Greiman's work:

- If the children have access to computers and to art software packages, they should create their own art and designs on the computer. Young children may especially enjoy two pieces of software designed especially for them. Kid Pix II enables children to create their own pictures, combining sound, graphics and special effects. They can even add narration. Kid Pix Studio enables them to add movement to their pictures. Both are available from Broderbund Software (see References) and can be used with Windows or Macintosh.

- Visit a computer art studio in a local high school or college and watch computer artists at work.
- Work with textures.

Materials

- Materials of different textures such as silk, wool, velvet, corrugated cardboard, string, etc.
- Glue
- Paper

Have children decide on a design they wish to create. Then, invite them to choose from among the different textured objects you provide, layer their choices in a way that achieves the effect they desire, and glue them onto their papers. They should pay special attention to the way in which they arrange the objects in the allotted space. They can include pencil designs on their papers as well.

Additional Activities

Drama. Children have enjoyed acting out the following scenes:

- Matisse and Picasso meet before the invasion of Paris.
- Matisse is too ill to continue painting at an easel.
- Picasso gets into art school.
- Paris disputes the merits of Matisse and Picasso (See *Bonjour, Mr. Satie* by de Paola).
- Georgia O'Keeffe decides all her paintings are no good and starts over.
- Georgia O'Keeffe argues with Stieglitz when he exhibits her work without permission.
- Louise Nevelson demands an exhibit in Nierendorf's gallery.
- Louise Nevelson, dressed in one of her outlandish outfits, is interviewed at the opening of one of her environments at the Museum of Modern Art.

- Jackson Pollock moves in with his brother Charles.
- Jackson Pollock sees the poverty and despair of New Yorkers during the Depression.
- Jackson Pollock is filmed making one of his dripping paintings and tries to explain his art in front of the camera.
- Head of design for the U.S. Postal Service and congresswoman confer about an artist for the Nineteenth Amendment stamp.

Visit a museum of modern art that contains some of the work of the artists in this chapter.

Publish a newspaper that reviews the work of the artists in this chapter.

Have a TV talk show and interview some of the artists studied in this chapter. Plan questions which will get them to explain their work.

In imitation of *Matisse from A to Z* by Sellier, create an alphabet book about a favorite artist (or artists) from this chapter.

The illustrations in more and more children's picture books are now being generated by computer. Two such books are *The Ring* by Maizlish and *Just One Flick of a Finger* by Lorbiecki (see References). Have children study the illustrations in both books and discuss how they were done. They may wish to write to the illustrators to obtain more information or to give their opinions of the works.

Curriculum Connections
Social Studies

- Do some research about World War I and World War II. What caused these wars? Who fought in them? Who won? Find out about the Holocaust.
- Locate on a world map the countries of origin of the artists studied. For the Americans, locate the states in which they were born or worked.
- Read about the Great Depression. What caused it? What were the results? How did the government help?
- What changes in clothing styles have taken place throughout the twentieth century? Make and illustrate a timeline of male and female clothing of the twentieth century, highlighting significant styles (e.g., the Flapper clothing of the 20s). If the students can obtain clothing from relatives or other sources, stage a live fashion show.

Science

- Find out about important inventions of the twentieth century such as the car, airplane, radio, movies, television, computer. What impact has each of these inventions made on modern life? Make a mural depicting these inventions in chronological order.

- Discuss important medical advances such as vaccines, organ transplants, antibiotics, genetic research.

- Find out about some well-known scientists of the century and their contributions.

Music

- Select examples of atonal modern music and some abstract art pieces that seem to go with it.

- Plan a musical program highlighting major musical styles of the century such as Big Band music of the 40s, Rock and Roll of the 50s, etc. Learn some dances to go with the different kinds of music.

Literature

- Who are some of the great poets of the century? Find some poems to go with the pictures viewed during this study.

- Read biographies of some of the artists studied as well as some of the great figures of the century.

- Who are some of the great novelists of the century? Are any of the themes in their works echoed in modern art?

- Write a story to go with a work of abstract art studied in this section.

References

Bernstein, Saul, and Leo McGarry. *Making Art on Your Computer*. New York: Watson-Guptill, 1986. Lessons covering the various aspects of creating art on a personal computer.

Boone, Daniele. *Picasso*. Transl. by John Greaves. New York: Portland House, 1989. o.p. Discussions of major works by Picasso. Large reproductions.

Bry, Doris, and Nicholas Callaway, eds. *Georgia O'Keeffe: In the West*. New York: Random House, 1991. No text. Huge color reproductions of O'Keeffe's western paintings.

Cowart, Jack, and Juan Hamilton. *Georgia O'Keeffe: Art and Letters*. Letters selected and annotated by Sarah Greenough. Boston: Little Brown, 1989. Large color reproductions of O'Keeffe's work and a selection of her letters.

Duncan, David Douglas. *Picasso and Jacqueline*. New York: Norton, 1988 o.p. A book of marvelous photographs of the artist and his wife. Wonderful for getting the flavor of the man.

————. *Viva Picasso*. New York: Viking, 1980 o.p. A book of marvelous photographs of the artist. Wonderful!

Durozoi, Gerard. *Matisse: The Masterworks*. Transl. by John Greaves. New York: Portland House, 1989 o.p. Discussions of some of Matisse's major works.

Elderfield, John. *Henri Matisse: A Retrospective*. New York: Museum of Modern Art, 1992. Over 400 of the artist's works reproduced, over 300 in color.

Eldredge, Charles C. *Georgia O'Keeffe*. New York: Harry N. Abrams, 1991. The author traces the development of O'Keeffe's art. Color reproductions.

————. *Georgia O'Keeffe: American and Modern*. New Haven, CT: Yale University Press, 1993 o.p. Beautiful photographs of the artist fill the beginning pages. Large color reproductions.

Frank, Elizabeth. *Pollock*. New York: Abbeville Press, 1983 o.p. A thorough analysis of Pollock's paintings accompanied by biographical information. Color reproductions.

Friedman, B.H. *Jackson Pollock: Energy Made Visible*. New York: Da Capo Press, 1995. Reprint of the illustrated biography of Pollock with a new foreword by the author.

Glimcher, Arnold B. *Louise Nevelson*. New York: Praeger, 1972 o.p. Biographical information and reproductions of some of Nevelson's works.

Greiman, April. *Hybrid Imagery*. New York: Watson-Guptill, 1990. Greiman describes her design process. Filled with reproductions of her work.

————. *It's notwhatyouthinkitis*. New York: Artemis USA/Canada, 1994. Greiman discusses her more recent work. Rich source of reproductions.

Grotta, Sally Wiener, and Daniel Wiener. *Digital Imaging for Visual Artists*. New York: Windcrest/McGraw-Hill, 1994. A huge book, written for professionals in the field, that describes digital imaging and the uses of various hardware and software.

Herrera, Hayden. *Matisse: A Portrait*. New York: Harcourt Brace, 1993. Matisse's life and works. Interesting photographs.

Lambert, Rosemary. *The Twentieth Century*. Cambridge, England: Cambridge University Press, 1981. A brief introduction to the art of the twentieth century.

Landau, Ellen G. *Jackson Pollock*. New York: Harry N. Abrams, 1989. An examination of Pollock's personal life and work. Beautiful reproductions.

Lipman, Jean. *Nevelson's World*. New York: Hudson Hills Press, 1983 o.p. A big magnificent book containing huge color reproductions and discussions of Nevelson's work.

Matisse, Henri. *Jazz*. New York: George Braziller, 1983. A huge book that reproduces Matisse's original work. Wonderful for viewing.

O'Keeffe, Georgia. *Georgia O'Keeffe*. New York: Viking, 1977. O'Keeffe talks about her paintings. Large color reproductions.

Palau i Febre, Josep. *Picasso Cubism*. Transl. by Susan Branyas et al. New York: Rizzoli, 1990 o.p. Wonderful reproductions and discussions of Picasso's Cubist works.

Pickover, Clifford A. *Visions of the Future*. New York: St. Martin's Press, 1992. Various essays on the impact of the computer on human life into the twenty-first century.

Richmond, Wendy. *Design & Technology: Erasing the Boundaries*. New York: Van Nostrand Reinhold, 1990. A compilation of the author's various articles on the latest trends in graphic design and computer technology.

Ridley, Pauline. *Modern Art*. New York: Thomson Learning, 1995. A brief introduction to modern art. Color reproductions.

Robbin, Tony. *Fourfield: Computers, Art & the 4th Dimension*. Boston: Little, Brown, 1992. How the computer makes a fourth dimension possible.

Rose, Bernice. *Jackson Pollock: Works on Paper*. New York: The Museum of Modern Art, 1969. An examination of Pollock's life and work. Many reproductions, some in color.

Rubin, William, ed. *Pablo Picasso: A Retrospective*. New York: Museum of Modern Art, 1980 o.p. Picasso's works arranged in chronological order. Excellent for viewing.

———. *Picasso and Portraiture: Representation and Transformation*. New York: Museum of Modern Art, 1996. Published to accompany the museum's exhibit, this book is a comprehensive study of Picasso's experimentation with a variety of portrait styles. Contains reproductions of hundreds of the artist's portraits and self-portraits.

Selz, Jean. *Matisse*. New York: Crown, 1988. Color reproductions arranged to show the development of Matisse's talent.

Spies, Werner, ed. *Picasso's World of Children*. New York: Te Neues Publishing, 1994. Discussion of children in Picasso's art. Large color reproductions.

Solomon, Deborah. *Jackson Pollock*. New York: Simon and Schuster, 1987. A lengthy biography of Pollock.

Children's Books

Antoine, Veronique. *Picasso: A Day in His Studio*. Transl. by John Goodman. New York: Chelsea House, 1993 o.p. A child stumbles into Picasso's studio, and the artworks come to life to talk about their master's life and art.

Beardsley, John. *First Impressions: Pablo Picasso*. New York: Harry N. Abrams, 1991. Very complete biography of the artist for children. Color reproductions.

Cain, Michael. *Louise Nevelson*. New York: Chelsea House, 1990. A complete biography of Nevelson including photographs and black and white reproductions.

de Paola, Tomie. *Bonjour, Mr. Satie*. New York: G. P. Putnam's Sons, 1991. In this picture book, Mr. Satie tells his niece and nephew about a dispute that erupted in Paris over whose work was best, Matisse's or Picasso's. Great fun!

Faerna, Jose Maria, ed. *Great Modern Masters: Matisse*. Transl. by Teresa Waldes. New York: Harry N. Abrams, 1994 o.p. Gorgeous reproductions of more than sixty major works.

———. *Great Modern Masters: Picasso*. Transl. by Wayne Finke. New York: Harry N. Abrams, 1994 o.p. Gorgeous reproductions of sixty-five art works.

Gherman, Beverly. *Georgia O'Keeffe: The Wideness and Wonder of Her World*. New York: Simon & Schuster, 1994. A complete life of the artist.

Greenberg, Jan, and Sandra Jordan. *The American Eye*. New York: Delacorte, 1995. Presents the lives and some reproductions of the work of eleven twentieth-century artists, including Jackson Pollock and Georgia O'Keeffe.

———. *The Painter's Eye: Learning to Look at Contemporary American Art*. New York: Delacorte, 1991. Presents the works of twenty-one modern American artists.

———. *The Sculptor's Eye: Looking at Contemporary American Art*. New York: Delacorte, 1993. Contemporary artists comment on their work. A discussion of how sculptors use space, light, scale, and proportion in their work.

Heslewood, Juliet. *Introducing Picasso*. Boston: Little, Brown, 1993. Examines Picasso's life and art in the context of his times. Photographs and large reproductions.

Lorbiecki, Mary. *Just One Flick of a Finger*. Illus. by David Diaz. New York: Dial, 1996. A young boy takes a gun to school to ward off a bully—with tragic consequences. Background art generated by computer.

MacDonald, Patricia A., and Robin L. Sommer. *Pablo Picasso*. New York: Silver Burdett, 1990. A complete biography of the artist. Reproductions and interesting photos.

Maizlish, Lisa. *The Ring*. New York: Greenwillow, 1996. A young boy finds a magic ring that enables him to fly above the city. Pictures generated by computer.

Munthe, Nelly. *Meet Matisse*. Boston: Little, Brown, 1983. Discusses Matisse's cutouts with directions on how to make them.

Rodari, Florian. *A Weekend with Matisse*. New York: Rizzoli, 1992. The artist invites the reader to spend a weekend with him to learn about his life and work. List of museums containing Matisse's work.

———. *A Weekend with Picasso*. New York: Rizzoli, 1991. The artist invites the reader to spend a weekend with him to learn about his life and work. List of museums containing Picasso's work.

Sellier, Marie. *Matisse from A to Z*. Transl. by Claudia Zoe Bedrick. New York: Peter Bedrick Books, 1993. Matisse's life told in stories arranged using key French words in alphabetical order. An interesting and unusual presentation.

Skurzynski, Gloria. *Know the Score: Video Games in Your High-Tech World*. New York: Bradbury, 1994. Describes how electronic games and programs are created.

Turner, Robyn Montana. *Georgia O'Keeffe*. Boston: Little, Brown, 1991. Part of the Portraits of Women Artists for Children series. Color reproductions.

Woolf, Felicity. *Picture This Century: An Introduction to Twentieth-Century Art*. New York: Doubleday, 1993. Offers two or three examples of each of fourteen different contemporary art styles. Small color reproductions.

Yenawine, Philip. *How to Look at Modern Art*. New York: Harry N. Abrams, 1991. The author gives the reader tools with which to view and appreciate modern art. 137 illustrations, 62 in full color. Emphasizes seeing what can be learned from observation of different artworks.

Magazines

Since books about computers become dated quickly, magazines are listed as an up-to-date source of information.

Art Education
Box 1108
2317 Arlington Avenue
Saskatoon, Saskatchewan
S7K3N3 Canada
    An excellent magazine full of ideas for art in the classroom, including computer art.

Communication Arts
410 Sherman Avenue
Palo Alto, CA 94306-1826
(415) 326-6040
    A large reproduction of the Nineteenth Amendment stamp by April Greiman appears in an ad on pages 6–7 of Volume 38 (2), May-June 1996 issue.

How Magazine
P.O. Box 5250
Harlan, Iowa 51593
    Features work of graphic designers.

School Arts Magazine
50 Portland Street
Worcester, MA 01615–9959
    Ideas for using art in the classroom, including computer art.

Audiovisual Materials

Exploring Modern Art. Although there is quite a bit of text here that may be more suitable for older students, the visuals make this a worthwhile material. (CD-ROM for Mac and Windows. Available from Attica Cybernetics.)

Georgia O'Keeffe: Life and Work. (Videocassette. Available from Video Opera House.)

Henri Matisse: The Paper Cutouts. Evolution of Matisse's cutouts and his *Jazz* portfolio. (48 slides; 2 audiocassettes. Available from the National Gallery of Art.)

Jackson Pollock: Portrait of an Artist. Although there is some adult matter and a simulation of Pollock's car crash, this video provides a valuable view of the artist at work, his own words, and excellent views of his paintings. (Videocassette; 52 mins. Available from Video Opera House.)

Kid Pix 2. A computer software program that enables children to combine sound, graphics, and special effects. They can add their own voice narration. (Available from Broderbund Software.)

Kid Pix Studio. A computer software program that enables children to add movement to their drawings. (Available from Broderbund Software.)

Louise Nevelson, in Process. (Videocassette. Available from Video Opera House.)

Matisse in Morocco. Color reproductions of eight of the artist's works. (Slides. Available from the National Gallery of Art.)

Matisse in Nice. Shows the artist's response to the light and color of the Mediterranean. (Videocassette; 30 mins. Available from the National Gallery of Art.)

The Mind's Eye. Over 300 computer artists depict a journey through time from the dawn of creation into the future. (Videocassette; 40 mins. Available from Library Video Company.)

Picasso. Reveals the diversity of the artist's work. (16mm film; 5 mins. Available from the National Gallery of Art.)

Picasso. (Videocassette. Available from Video Opera House.)

Picasso and the Circus. A girl strolls through the exhibition entitled *Picasso, The Saltimbanques*. (16mm film; 7 mins. Available from the National Gallery of Art.)

Picasso: The Saltimbanques. Picasso's pictures of circus people. (Videocassette; 29 mins. Available from the National Gallery of Art.)

Other Materials

Boutan, Mila. *Matisse: Art Activity Pack*. San Francisco: Chronicle Books, 1996. Provides a book on the life of the artist and an activity pack containing sheets of colored paper and cutouts for the child to do a cutout activity.

Appendix A
Using the Internet
to Study Art

No educator today can ignore the rich resources available to students through the World Wide Web. Using software packages such as Netscape it is possible to "browse the net" to find the latest information on art periods, artists, and museum exhibits and to view actual works of art. Through the Internet, students can visit museums they may never be able to travel to in person and even see works not on view to the public due to lack of space. The sites are interactive so that students can explore links to topics that interest them.

Since Web sites change daily, it is almost futile to try to give a complete listing here. By the time you read this, hundreds of additional sites will probably be available for research in the fine arts, while some now in existence will have disappeared. Therefore, I shall list some Internet directories to aid you in your search and some sites in existence at this writing to give you an idea of the goodies that await you and your class as you venture into cyberspace. If you have an LCD panel or other device to enable you to project what is on your computer monitor onto a large screen, your class can view some of the offerings together. Otherwise, post a list of sites at the computer so individual students can search on their own. They may even wish to assume the role of detective and find new sites and information to share with the class.

If you do not have specific addresses, there are a number of ways you can find out what is available in the fine arts. You can click on "Net Search" and type the words "fine arts." This should locate several sites with links to even more sites. In addition, you can also use some Internet directories to aid you in your search. Here are some, with their addresses.

Internet Directories

Alta Vista
http://altavista.digital.com

Excite
http://www.excite.com

Galaxy
http://galaxy.einet.net/galaxy.html

Internet Resources Meta-Index
http://www.ncsa.uiuc.edu/sdg/software/mosaic/metaindex.html

Lycos
http://www.lycos.com

W3 Catalog
http://cuiwww.unige.ch/w3catalog

Yahoo
http://www.yahoo.com

   With each of these search engines, you will need to type in key words to get the search started. For instance, you might ask for art museums if that is your area of interest.

Source Finders

Since thousands of new sites appear each week, you might want to investigate some sources that put you in touch with the latest and the best. One of the most selective sources of those listed below is NCSA's (National Computer Security Association) What's New. It chooses those sites that are content-rich and have no sexually explicit material.

NCSA What's New
http://www.ncsa.uiuc.edu/SDG/Software/Mosaic/Docs/whats-new.html

Net Happenings
http://www.midinet/NET/

Netscape What's New
http://www.netscape.com/escapes/whatnew.html

New and/or Exciting Items on the Internet
http://www.Isu.edu/~poli/newexcit.html

SavvySearch
http://cage.cs.colostate.edu:1969
   This allows you to send a single request to five databases at once!

Starting Point
http://www.stpt.com/new.html

What's New on Yahoo
http://www.yahoo.com/new/

What's New Too
http://newtoo.manifest.com

References

Selected Art Sites

African Art—Aesthetics and Meaning
http://www.lib.virginia.edu/dic/exhib/93.ray.aa/African.html
> Online sculpture exhibition of art from Africa.

All Souls School/British Museum: Ancient Greeks Virtual Tour
http://www.rmplc.co.uk/eduweb/sites/allsouls/bm/ag1.html
> School-museum partnership: tour includes floor maps, artifacts of ancient daily life, and more.

April Greiman
http://www.greimanski.com/design/
> Provides access to the latest regarding artist April Greiman.

Art on the Net
http://www.art.net/
> Quotes or music from artists, listings of current events in the art world, and links to other art and music reference Web sites.

ArtsEdge
http://www.kennedy-center.org/
> From the Kennedy Center, Washington, D.C. Features "Learning through the Arts," "Teaching through and about the Arts," events for students and more.

Artsource
http://www.uky.edu/Artsource/general.html
> Art history sites and bibliographies, plus lots of links.

Asian Art Archive
http://solar.rtd.utk.edu/artwww/art.html
> Examples of the art of Indian Asia, China, Korea, and Japan.

Chinese Culture
http://bronze,ucs.indiana.edu/~hyuan/culture/html
> An informative site for the study of Chinese culture.

Christus Rex (Art from the Vatican)
http://www.christusrex.org/www1icons/index.html
> Images of and information regarding the Vatican City collection.

Diego Rivera Web Museum
http://www.diegorivera.com:80/diego_home_eng.html

Includes information about Rivera, a selection of paintings and murals, and articles written by the artist.

Egypt Educational Site
http://pharos.bu.edu/Egypt/Cairo
Egyptian history and culture both ancient and modern.

Eyes on Art
http://www.kn.pacbell.com/wired/art/art.html
This site provides seven activities which can be enjoyed even by young children. They enable students to create their own art museum; study the elements of art such as line, color, and texture; engage in collaborative projects with their peers; and explore artistic styles across the centuries.

Folktales
http://www.folkart.com/~latitude/folktale/folktale.htm
Different Mayan folktales by Don Pedro Miguel Say, printed in their entirety each month with permission to reproduce.

Fractal Images and Fractal Software
http://www.uncg.edu:80/~amralph/fractals/
Fractals are patterns that repeat their own shape. At this site there are forty fascinating art works produced by Randy D. Ralph and generated from fractal sets.

Frida Kahlo Home Page
http://www.cascade.net/kahlo.html
Biographical information on the artist.

Leonardo da Vinci
http://www.leonardo.net/main.html
Images of some of his inventions and a historical exhibition about his life and times.

Louvre Museum
http://www.paris.org.:80/Musees/Louvre
Important works, floor plan, and history of the fabulous Louvre.

Maya
webusers.anet—dfw.com/!vinnie/
Documents on the Maya and Guatemala, complete with pictures. Many links.

The Metropolitan Museum of Art
http://www.metmuseum.org
Overview of exhibits, floor plan, listing of current exhibits and upcoming events.

Mexican Art
http://www.mexicanart.com.mx
Links to contemporary Mexican artists, museums, galleries, and much more.

Musee d'Orsay
http://meteora.ucsd.edu:80/~norman/paris/Musees/Orsay/Collections/
Paintings: Many Impressionist and Post-Impressionist paintings from the collection, including works by Monet, Manet, Degas, Seurat, Gauguin, and Cézanne.

The Museum of Modern Art
http://www.moma.org/
> Dissertations on new exhibits and images the visitor will find on the museum's walls.

National Museum of the American Indian
http://www.interport.net/~logomanc/heye.html
> Collection of Native American art works and upcoming events.

Paintings of Vermeer
http://www.ccsf.caltech.edu/~roy/vermeer
> Wealth of information on the artist including images of his paintings and links to other art sources.

PowerSource: Native American Art/Education Center
http:www.powersource.com/powersource/gallery/default.html
> Traditional Native American and modern styles; a featured artist section; galleries; biographies of Native Americans, past and present.

Rome Reborn: The Vatican Library and Renaissance Culture
gopher://gopher.lib.virginia.edu:70/11/alpha/vat
> Access to the Vatican Library and Renaissance Culture and Art Exhibit.

Smithsonian Institution Home Page
http://www.si.edu/
> Collections, calendars, and virtual visits to Museum of the American Indian, American History Museum, Air and Space Museum, National Portrait Gallery, and National Zoo.

WWW Medieval Server
http://www.georgetown.edu/labyrinth
> Mega-server includes information about distinct regions of Europe; libraries of Middle English and Latin; philosophy, runes, more.

Web Museum
http://sunsite.unc.edu/Louvre
> Links to famous paintings as well as featured artists.

Webmuseum Paris
http://watt.emf.net/wm/paint/auth/
> Biographical information on various artists as well as displays of their works.

Worldwide Arts Resources
http://www.concourse.com/wwar/default.html
> Comprehensive database of over 7,000 visual arts resources. Links provided to Metropolitan Museum of Art, previews of museums of the United States.

World Wide Web Virtual Library: Museums
http://www.comlab.ox.ac.uk/archive/other/museums.html
> Index of museums on and off the Web and links to Web sites.

Other References

Ahmad, Nyla. *Cybersurfer*. Willowdale, Ontario, Canada: Firefly Books, 1996. Presents 250 Web sites and a disk for Windows and Mac. Free software.

Classroom Connect

1866 Colonial Village Lane
P. O. Box 10488
Lancaster, PA 17605-9981
1-800-638-1639
connect@wentworth.com

> This magazine provides ideas for integrating the Internet into the classroom curriculum. Lesson plans and projects, access to libraries around the world, tips on technology funding.

Electronic Learning
Scholastic
555 Broadway
New York, NY 10012
(212)505-4900

> Articles on computers in the classroom. Funding sources, Internet sites, hard- and software reviews, etc. Free.

Internet World
Mecklermedia
20 Ketchum Street
Westport, CT 06880

> This monthly magazine is a treasure house of information about using the Internet. Discusses many subject areas that can be found on the Net, provides "how to" information, and much more.

Appendix B
Sources for Audiovisual Materials

A & F Video
Genesco NY
(716) 243-3122

Angel Records
c/o Angel/EMI Records
810 Seventh Avenue
New York NY 10019
(212) 603-8600

Art Image Publications
61 Main Street
Champlain NY 12919
(516) 298-5432

Attica Cybernetics Ltd
Chatsworth CA
(818) 992-8484

Broderbund Software
500 Redwood Blvd.
P.O. Box 6121
Novato CA 94948-6121
1-800-521-6263

CBS Records/Sony Music
51 W. 52nd Street
New York NY 10019
(212) 833-8000

Chronicle Books
275 Fifth Street
San Francisco, CA 94103

Clearvue/EAV, Inc.
6465 N. Avondale Ave.
Chicago IL 60631
1-800-CLEARVU

Crown Video
225 Park Ave. S.
New York NY 10003

EMI Records Group North America
1290 Avenue of the Americas, 42nd fl.
New York NY 10104
(212)603-8600

Educational Resources
1550 Executive Drive
P.O. Box 1900
Elgin IL 60121-1900
1-800-624-2926

Entertainment Video
433 East 51st Street
New York NY 10022

Films for the Humanities and Sciences
P.O. Box 2053
Princeton, NJ 08543-2053
1-800-257-5126

Forest Technologies
514 Market Loop, Suite 103
West Dundee, IL 60118
1-800-544-3356

Future Vision Multi Media Inc.
300 Airport Executive Park
Nanuet NY 10954
(914) 426-0400

HarperCollins
10 East 53rd Street
New York NY 10022
1-800-424-6234

HarperCollins Interactive
See HarperCollins.

Home Vision/Public Media Inc.
5547 North Ravenswood Avenue
Chicago IL 60640
(312)878-2600
1-800-323-4222

Kartes Video Communications
10 East 106th Street
Indianapolis, IN 46280
1-800-234-7878

LCSI
Highgate Springs VT
1-800-321-5646

Library Video Co.
P.O. Box 1110
Bala Cynwyd PA 19004
1-800-843-3620

Metropolitan Museum of Art
1000 Fifth Avenue
New York NY 10028–0918
(212)570-3756
1-800-468-7386

Microsoft
Redmond WA
1-800-376-51125

National Gallery of Art
Department of Education Resources
4th and Constitution Avenue, NW
Washington D.C. 20565
(202)737-4125

PBS Video
1330 Craddock Place
Alexandria, VA 22313
1-800-328-7271

Public Media Video
See Home Vision.

The Putnam & Grosset Group
200 Madison Avenue
New York NY 10016
1-800-847-5515

Questar Video
P.O. Box 11345
Chicago IL 60611
(312) 266-9400
1-800-544-8422

Scholastic Publishers
555 Broadway
New York NY 10012–3999
(212) 505-3316
1-800-325-6149

Triloka Records
306 Catron Street
Santa Fe NM 87501
(505) 820-2833

Video Opera House
Box 800
Concord MA 01742
(508) 263-8200

Voyager, Inc.
524 West 57th St.
New York NY 10019
1-800-446-2001

WGBH Boston
125 Western Avenue
Boston MA 02134
(617) 492-2777

Wombat Productions, Inc.
250 W. 57th Street, #2421
New York, NY 10017
(212) 315-2502

Zane Publishing
1950 Stemmons, Suite 4044
Dallas TX 75207
1-800-460-2323

Zenger Media
a division of Social Studies School Service
10200 Jefferson Boulevard, Room N411
P.O. Box 802
Culver City CA 90232-0802
1-800-421-4246

General Bibliography

The following art books are useful but address the subjects of more than one chapter.

General Books

Newton, Douglas. *Masterpieces of Primitive Art.* Photos by Lee Boltin. New York: Alfred Knopf, 1978. o.p. Describes the artworks in the Nelson A. Rockefeller primitive art collection in the Metropolitan Museum of Art in New York City.

Romei, Francesca. *The Story of Sculpture: From Prehistory to the Present.* New York: Peter Bedrick Books, 1995. Some step-by-step presentations of different sculpture techniques. Many full color and black-and-white photos.

Turner, Jane, ed. *The Dictionary of Art.* New York: Grove's Dictionaries, 1996. Although it is frightfully expensive, some teachers may be fortunate enough to have nearby a library that owns this exciting 34-volume set. Some 6,700 authors have contributed articles on individual artists and art periods, art conservation, and the social and political background of great art movements.

Children's Books

Auch, Mary Jane. *Eggs Mark the Spot.* New York: Holiday House, 1996. Pauline, the hen who is famous for laying eggs bearing the image of whatever is before her, goes to the museum to make egg reproductions of famous paintings and foils an art thief. Shows paintings of several artists studied in this book.

Blizzard, Gladys S. *Come Look with Me: Animals in Art.* Charlottesville, VA: Thomasson-Grant, 1992. Twelve color reproductions of pictures of animals done by different artists. Discussion questions and background information on the artists.

———. *Come Look with Me: Enjoying Art with Children.* Charlottesville, VA: Thomasson-Grant, 1990. Twelve color reproductions of paintings by different artists, some of whom are in this book. Discussion questions and background information on the artists.

———. *Come Look with Me: World of Play.* Charlottesville, VA: Thomasson-Grant, 1993. Twelve works of art showing people at play. Different art styles are represented.

Brown, Laurence Krasney. *Visiting the Art Museum*. Illus. by Marc Brown. New York: E.P. Dutton, 1986. In a visit to a museum, a family enjoys various art periods from primitive through twentieth-century.

Chermayeff, Ivan, and Jane Clark. *First Words*. New York: Harry N. Abrams, 1990. Paintings gathered from five museums in Paris depict words in five different languages.

Davidson, Rosemary. *Take a Look: An Introduction to the Experience of Art*. New York: Viking, 1994. Introduces the history, techniques, and functions of art through a discussion of different artworks.

Delafosse, Claude, and Gallimard Jeunesse. *Paintings*. Illus. by Tony Ross. New York: Scholastic, 1993. A very small book which invites children to look closely at some of the paintings discussed in this book.

Fisher, Leonard Everett. *Number Art*. New York: Simon & Schuster, 1984. Number systems used by different cultures throughout the world including Chinese, Egyptian, Greek, and Roman.

Florian, Douglas. *A Painter*. New York: Greenwillow, 1993. Describes the work a fine arts painter does, his tools, and what he tries to achieve in his paintings. For the very young child.

Glubok, Shirley. *Painting: Great Lives*. New York: Scribners, 1994. Brief lives of European and American painters. Contains many included in this book: O'Keeffe, Rivera, Velazquez, Vermeer.

Hill, Emily, ed. *The Visual Dictionary of Ancient Civilizations*. New York: Dorling Kindersley, 1994. The story of major ancient world civilizations, including Rome, Greece, Egypt, China, the Maya, and the Aztecs.

Hurd, Thacher. *Art Dog*. New York: HarperCollins, 1996. When a painting is stolen from the Dogopolis Museum of Art, the mysterious Art Dog finds the culprits. Children will love trying to recognize the take-offs in this humorous picture book on paintings they have studied.

Isaacson, Philip M. *A Short Walk around the Pyramids and through the World of Art*. New York: Knopf, 1993. In presenting works from various times and places, the author discusses both the tangible and abstract aspects of art.

Janson, Anthony F. *History of Art for Young People*. 4 ed. New York: Harry N. Abrams, 1991. A comprehensive coverage of the art of various regions of the world. Numerous reproductions.

Jessop, Joanne. *The Xray Book of Big Buildings of the Ancient World*. Created and designed by David Salariya. New York: Franklin Watts, 1994. Describes how such famous buildings as the Great Pyramid, the Parthenon, the Colosseum, the Taj Mahal were built.

Jeunesse, Gallimard. *Paint and Painting*. New York: Scholastic, 1994. A wonderful book which uses overlays to discuss different painting techniques across the centuries.

——. *What the Painter Sees*. New York: Scholastic, 1994. A marvelous book which uses overlays, mirrors, and other devices to discuss art through the centuries including perspective, portraits, abstract art, etc.

Kidd, Richard. *Almost Famous Daisy!* New York: Simon & Schuster, 1996. In this picturebook, Daisy travels the world to find her favorite thing to paint. On her journey she sees paintings by Van Gogh, Monet, Chagall, Gauguin, and Jackson Pollock.

Knox, Bob. *The Great Art Adventure*. New York: Rizzoli, 1993. Two children take an imaginative trip through time in a wacky museum. They visit many famous paintings which come to life.

Krull, Kathleen. *Lives of the Artists: Masterpieces, Messes (and What the Neighbors Thought)*. Illus. by Kathryn Hewitt. San Diego: Harcourt Brace & Co., 1995. Brief humorous lives of different artists, including some interesting facts. Da Vinci, Michelangelo, Rembrandt, Cassatt and others are included.

Levy, Virginia K. *Let's Go to the Art Museum*. New York: Harry N. Abrams, 1988. An introduction to museums and art which includes some suggestions for activities.

Liddiard, Nicola, art ed., and Roger Tritton, project ed. *The Visual Dictionary of Buildings*. New York: Dorling Kindersley, 1992. Labeled drawings and explanations for some of the most important buildings in the world.

Micklethwait, Lucy, sel. *A Child's Book of Art*. New York: Dorling Kindersley, 1993. Family words, garden words, pet words, etc. are depicted in famous paintings. Beautiful.

———. *I Spy: An Alphabet in Art*. New York: Greenwillow, 1992. Objects beginning with each letter of the alphabet are spied in various art works.

———. *I Spy Two Eyes: Numbers in Art*. New York: Greenwillow, 1993. Numbers of objects are spied in nineteen fine paintings by artists such as Botticelli and Robert Indiana.

———. *Spot a Cat*. New York: Dorling Kindersley, 1995. Young readers are asked to find the cat in each of thirteen famous paintings. Includes list of paintings and locations.

———. *Spot a Dog*. New York: Dorling Kindersley, 1995. Young readers are asked to find the dog in each of thirteen famous paintings, a few of which were done by artists discussed in this book. Includes list of paintings and locations.

National Gallery of Art. *An Illustrated Treasury of Songs*. New York: Rizzoli, 1991. Contains 55 traditional songs, ballads, folk songs, and nursery rhymes with lyrics and musical notation. Paintings by many artists discussed in this book, including American primitives, are used throughout. A treasure indeed!

Panzer, Nora, ed. *Celebrate America in Poetry and Art*. New York: Hyperion, 1994. A book of poetry accompanied by art prints that celebrates the 200 years of America's history. Gorgeous!

Powell, Jillian. *Ancient Art*. New York: Thomson Learning, 1994. Features the art and artists of many ancient peoples, including Egypt, Greece, Rome, and the Stone Age.

Roalf, Peggy. *Looking at Painting* series. New York: Hyperion. Various dates. A series of fine books which cover such topics in art as children, the circus, dogs, cats, horses, landscapes, seascapes, flowers, musicians, self-portraits, dancers, and families. In addition to discussing what is in the artist's eye when he/she paints, the author provides dates, locations and sizes of the works presented.

Voss, Gisela. *Museum Colors*. Boston: Museum of Fine Arts, 1994. Board book of colors in famous paintings by such artists as Degas.

———. *Museum Numbers*. Boston: Museum of Fine Arts, 1993. A counting book that asks children to count objects in famous works of art.

Wilkinson, Philip, and Michael Pollard. *The Master Builders*. Illus. by Robert Ingpen. New York: Chelsea House, 1994. The story of some of the marvelous buildings of the world, including Stonehenge, Chichén Itzá in Mexico, Tenochtitlán in Mexico, and Pueblo Bonito in New Mexico.

Woolf, Felicity. *Picture This: A First Introduction to Paintings*. New York: Doubleday, 1990. Twenty-four pictures and commentary geared to help children understand art. Small reproductions.

Yenawine, Philip. *Colors*. New York: Delacorte, 1991. The author explores the function of color in various works of art.

————. *Lines*. New York: Delacorte, 1991. The author explores the function of line in various works of art.

————. *Shapes*. New York: Delacorte, 1991. The author explores the function of shape in various works of art.

————. *Stories*. New York: Delacorte, 1991. Readers are asked to uncover the stories told by various works of art.

Audiovisual Materials

Ancient Lands. Views the wonders of the ancient civilizations from the dawn of Egypt to the fall of Rome. (CD-ROM, 1994. Available from Microsoft).

Great Artists. Using artworks from the National Gallery of London, this explores the lives and times of some important artists. (Available from Attica Cybernetics).

History through Art. A series of nine CD-ROMs featuring different art periods from the ancient world to the twentieth century. (CD-ROM. Available from Zane Publishing).

Look What I See! Created for young children, this CD-ROM encompasses some of the art workshops conducted at the Metropolitan Museum of Art over the years. The program explores some of the key elements of art such as color and shape and enables children to manipulate these elements on screen. (CD-ROM for Mac and Windows. Available from the Metropolitan Museum of Art).

Masterpiece Mansion. Presents various artists' works in a game format. Viewers enter different rooms in a mansion and must answer questions about the paintings displayed there. Background music from periods in which the artists lived. (CD-ROM, 1996. Available from Library Video Co.)

Stars of the Louvre. Presents a history of art from 2650 B.C. to 1880 A.D. showing over 200 masterpieces. Sculptures can be viewed from 360 degrees. (CD-ROM, 1996. Available from Zenger Media).

With Open Eyes. A program geared to young children, this is a tour through the collections of the Art Institute of Chicago. Students can also play a variety of games with the art such as assembling a painting puzzle. (CD-ROM for Mac or Windows. Available from Voyager).

Other Materials

Art Image Preschool. An art-based curriculum for preschool children. Consists of five packets organized around themes: shapes, colors, and stories; pets; portraits; animals; and children.

Each packet contains color reproductions, a teacher's guide, and activities incorporating various aspects of the curriculum. (Available from Art Image Publications).

Temples. A discovery box containing a book about temples, especially those of the Greeks, Romans, Egyptians, Mayans, and Japanese, and a model to help students assemble the facade of a Greek temple. (Available from Scholastic Publishers).

Title Index to Art

Due to the number of artworks cited in the text, only those discussed in some depth are indexed here.

Subject Index

FRANKLIN PIERCE COLLEGE LIBRARY

00106006